MW01275489

The Feinberg Edition

A Shot of Torah

Short, fun, deep, and inspiring divrei Torah
for your Shabbos and *Yom Tov* table

Rabbi Aba Wagensberg

L'dor V'dor
Ramot Press

First Printing: 2015

ISBN: 978-0-9965158-4-9

Ramot Press

Jerusalem, Israel

www.RamotPress.com

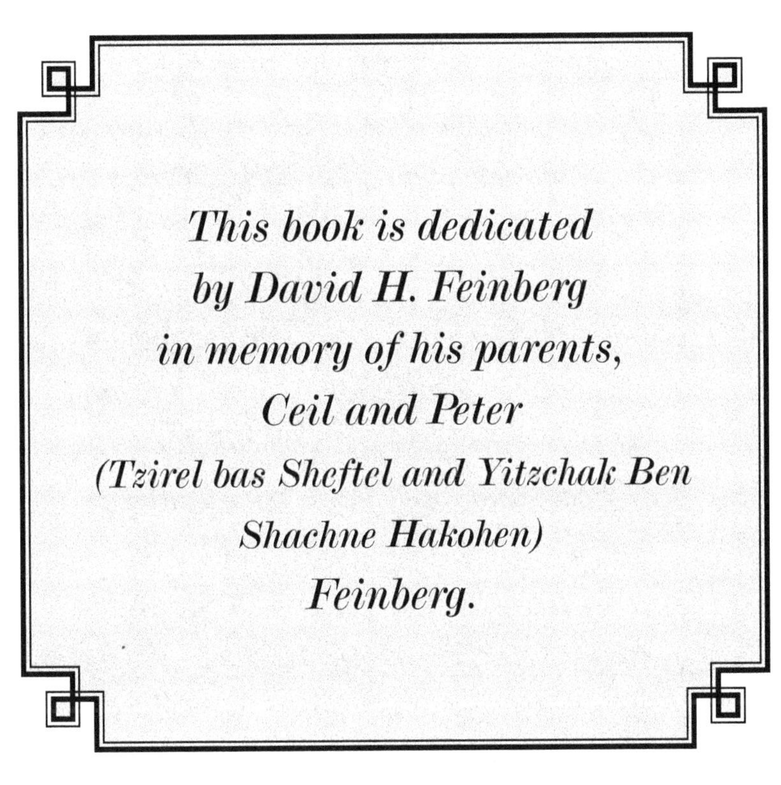

This book is dedicated
by David H. Feinberg
in memory of his parents,
Ceil and Peter
(Tzirel bas Sheftel and Yitzchak Ben
Shachne Hakohen)
Feinberg.

This book is dedicated in loving memory of my aunt Helen (Chaya Sarah) Katz who passed away at the age of ninety years old. She was a very special person, filled with optimism even in trying times. She treated everybody with respect and sweetness. We all miss the matriarch of our family. Her passing marks the end of an era. Aunt Helen, may you receive unlimited Nachas from your entire family. We love you and miss you.

B"H

ישיבה פרימרי
Yeshiva Primary
80-11 210 St / Jamaica, NY 11427
(718) 217-4700
Fax: (718) 217-8739

Rabbi Aba Wagensberg, Shlit"a

In a way, you are my Rebbe. As the Rambam writes,

הילכות תלמוד תורה פרק ה הלכה י"ב
כשם שהתלמידים חיבין בכבוד הרב כך הרב צריך לכבד את תלמידיו ולקרבן
כך אמרו חכמים (משנה אבות ד-יב) 'יהי כבוד תלמידך חביב עליך כשלך'
The Rambam continues, הלכה י"ג: התלמידים מוסיפין חכמת הרב ומרחיבין לבו.

Aba, you did this as a youngster of 9 years old and continue to do so as an adult through your shiurim, tapes, radio addresses and now with your sefarim.
אמרו חכמים: הרבה חכמה למדתי מרבותי, ויותר מהם מחברי, ומתלמידי יותר מכולם
וכשם שעץ קטן מדליק את העץ הגדול, כך תלמיד קטן מחדד את הרב, עד שיוציא ממנו בשאלותיו חכמה מפוארה
Knowing this Rambam, how can I write an approbation?!?

The Chassam Sofer in Parshas Behar, perek gimmel, pesukim 1-2 asks why the Torah chose to teach us the lesson "שכל המלמד בן חבירו תורה כאלו ילדו" by the children of Aharon HaKohen in respect to Moshe Rabeinu? The answer is that Moshe himself attested "עכשיו רואה אני שהם גדולים ממני וממך". Nadav and Avihu were greater than their Rebbe Moshe, yet once one taught a talmid Torah, even upon the talmid's rise to greatness - as you have done Reb Aba - a rebbe who nurtured a talmid remains his rebbe forever.

You attended Yeshiva High School at the Talmudical Academy of Adelphia under the Roshei HaYeshiva Rabbi Yeruchem Shain and the Menahel, Rav Dovid Trenk shlit"a. A mesivta that produced hundreds upon hundreds of bnei Torah and yirei HaShem, literally hanefesh asher asu b'Adelphia.

Upon graduation, you were presented with a fabulous business proposition where they guaranteed fabulous salaries and bonuses, yet after considering the opportunities, you turned it down and you went to Eretz Yisroel to learn under HaRav HaGaon HaRav Chaim Pinchas Sheinberg zt"l at Yeshivas Torah Ohr in Yerushalayim, where you spent many years in Kollel.

In your first sefer published several years ago "Inspiring Change", you elucidate and explain esoteric kabbalistic concepts in a down-to-earth inspirational way.
This new sefer is a parsha/holiday book meant to be user-friendly at the Shabbos/Yom Tov table. There are four divrei Torah for each parsha and for each holiday so that one dvar Torah can be shared at each meal, including melaveh malka.

As usual, you do not miss any detail and included 4 divrei Torah for each Yom Tov for bnei chutz l'aretz who will have 4 Yom Tov meals over their 2 day Yom Tov, thus ensuring that the Shabbos and Yom Tov table be "zeh hashulchan asher lifnei HaShem."

You have z'chus Avos. Your parents from day one have - countless times - emotionally articulated to me their hope that you grow up to be a ben Torah, yirei shamayim and a Rav. Their yearning and tefillos have been answered fully and their son, you Rev Aba, truly personify a ben Torah, yirei shamayim and a marbitz Torah far and wide.

It is with humility that I offer a birkat Kohen; that you be zoche to continue in avodas hakodesh, and that you have nachos from your children, your spiritual children, your talmidim and from yourself as well.

זלמן דוב הכהן דויטשר
Zalman Dov HaCohen Deutscher
Zalman Deutscher
Dean

בס"ד

Rabbi Zev Leff

הרב זאב לף

Rabbi of Moshav Matityahu
Rosh HaYeshiva—Yeshiva Gedola Matityahu

מרא דאתרא מושב מתתיהו
ראש הישיבה—ישיבה גדולה מתתיהו

D.N. Modiin 71917 Tel: 08-976-1138 טל' Fax: 08-976-5326 פקס' ד.נ. מודיעין 71917

Dear Friends,

I have read portions of the manuscript "A Shot Of Torah" by my esteemed and illustrious colleague and friend, Rabbi Aba Wagensberg.

The author presents short Divrei Torah on the Parshiyos HaTorah and on the various holidays. As in his previous works the essays are steeped in Torah wisdom and presented in a lucid manner. I found them to be informative, inspiring, and entertaining.

I recommend this work as a source of Torah knowledge and inspiration, as well as an effective tool to enhance one's Shabbos and Yom Tov table with fine Divrei Torah that will be a true Oneg Shabbos (Shabbos delight) and simchas Yom Tov (holiday pleasure).

I commend the author for producing another quality work, and pray that Hashem Yisborach bless his whole family with life, health and the wherewithal to continue to benefit the community in his many and varied ways.

Sincerely,
With Torah blessings

Zev Leff

Rabbi Zev Leff

817 Central Avenue • Lakewood, NJ 08701 • (732) 370-5043 • Fax (732) 370-5044

כד' ניסן תשע"ה

לתלמידי, ידידי אהובי ר' אבא וואגענסברג עמו"ש

שמך הולך לפניך - Your name precedes you, as does your voice!

Tuning in on Thursday nights here in Lakewood, 107.9, to the Rav Aba Wagensberg Experience, The Parsha, is a treat — ten questions, then the joy of simchas HaTorah as the answers pour forth, one by one.

The chevra is treated to... "And that is the answer to question one,"... two, etc. Rav Wagensberg, using as his sources Divrei Chazal - Midrashim, Rishonim, Achronim, Maharal, Reb Tzadok, Zohar, and a sprinkling of Kabalah - leads us, his listeners, on this exhilarating journey.

Enriched, we look forward to Shabbos and the seudos — to delve into, talk about, and give over to family and friends that which we have heard and internalized.

With this sefer we are zocheh to have at hand (and not have to wait till next Thursday) Reb Aba's Divrei Torah in sefer form.

Now every "Aba" (Daddy/Totty) has a chance to prepare a "vort" to say over at the three seudos on Shabbos... and never one to miss a beat, there's a fourth, for Melave Malka!

Plus two for seudos Yom Tov. And two more for us chutz l'aretzniks for Yom Tov sheini!

It is truly a zechus for me to share in your heilige work, by writing these words.

"אשריך ואשרי חלקך"

Sincerely,

Dovid Trenk

Table of Contents

Volume 1

Volume 2

Acknowledgements

It is with my deepest gratitude to **Hashem** that I present you with my newest publication, "A Shot of Torah." When it comes to thanking Hashem, I do not even know where to begin. However, if I were to begin, I would not know how to stop. Whether it's my family, my friends, my mentors, my students that God has given me, or the circumstances that He created which brought me to this very moment, I cannot even find the words to express my appreciation. So all I will say is: thank you, Hashem, I love you.

I have been incredibly blessed to have been surrounded by numerous good people in my life. My appreciation to these people is unending. In this section I would like to mention those who had a direct hand in this publication.

Spending hours each week to type up these teachings is a challenging undertaking. There are always matters that demand my attention. There is one thing, however, that motivates me to spend the time necessary to make this a reality, and that is you, my dear readers. Many of you were students of mine from seminary, yeshiva or study groups. Others discovered my classes online, and joined. Either way, your loyalty and support have been immeasurable, helpful and appreciated. Your e-mails with positive feedback have served as a tremendous source of *chizuk* for me. Often when typing up the next teaching, I envision your faces and your Shabbos tables, and I then picture these ideas being shared with family and friends. That alone provides me with a desire and fortitude to keep on going. With a heart full of *nachas*, I humbly thank you all.

Although I will discuss my relationship with **Mr. David Feinberg** later on in the Preface, I felt that it was absolutely necessary to mention David again over here. David, thank you for being my *chavrusa*; thank you for supporting this project; and thank you for being my friend. Laura and I are blessed to have you, your wife Carol, your son Daniel and his wife Lauren as our family friends. May you see much *nachas* from this book, and from your entire family.

Researching, collecting, organizing and printing these teachings that spanned many years was a daunting undertaking. There was one person who literally spent hours on this phase of the project. His name is **Yosef Sokol** ("Joey"), my cousin. No matter what glitch got in our way, Joey creatively found a solution ("Sokol Solutions"), and carried it out with efficiency, professionalism and alacrity. Thank you, Joey; I think we make a great team!

It's not often that an author gets the privilege of having his wife edit, proofread and do some of the type setting of his book. I did have that honor. Memories of **Laura** spending countless hours at the table with papers, pens and computers makes my heart swell with appreciation. Thank you Laura for investing so much of your time and energy into this project. Laura, I am forever grateful for your sacrifice and support.

We had a vision for the illustration, and **Mrs. Esther Gnat** delivered. "A picture is worth a thousand words," and that is the amount of words I have to express my gratitude to her for a fantastic job. Thank you, Mrs. Gnat.

Bringing this project across the finish line was done by my precious daughter, **Esther Rochel**, who stepped up to the plate, took initiative, and used her knowledge to complete this process. All I can say is Baruch Hashem, I am filled with so much nachas. Thank you Esther Rochel, I love you.

Thank God, I have been blessed to have Rebbeim in my life who are legends in their own time. I mention some of them here.

When I was a little boy in Hebrew Day School, I was failing terribly. There was one person who changed my direction in a drastically positive way. That person is **Rabbi Zalman Deutscher** *shlit"a*. Rabbi Deutscher's vast knowledge of Torah is matched by his remarkable talent as an educator par excellence. Those two qualities are complemented by his caring heart and kindness. I do not know where I would be today if not for Rabbi Deutscher. I am unaware of other Rebbeim who teach in elementary schools and then keep tabs on their students when they go on to high school, post high school, and even continue to stay in touch with them to be of service for the rest of their lives. Rabbi Deutscher does exactly that. I fondly remember the visits he made to us in Yeshiva High School (always bringing cakes and a little extra cash just in case we needed it). It was you, Rabbi Deutscher, who suggested which path I take in Eretz Yisrael; it has, Baruch Hashem, been successfully continuing until this very day. Moreover you have taken a special interest in my family as well, helping in any way that you can. Rabbi Deutscher, Thank you, Thank you, Thank you. Thank you for all you have done, and thank you for agreeing to pen a beautiful approbation for this publication, my second book. I remain your humble student.

Another legend in his time was my ninth grade Rebbi in Yeshivas Adelphia New Jersey. His name is **Rabbi Dovid Trenk** *shlit"a*. His fire for Torah and love of every Jew made an everlasting impression on me. He not only taught us *gemara*, but he taught us how to be a *mentch*, not just by what he said, but by acting as a role model. Rabbi Trenk is a mechanech par excellence. I will share just one brief story which reveals this. Before inspecting the dormitories for items that the yeshiva forbade, Rabbi Trenk would send one of the boys to the dorm to give us advance warning that he was coming. Anybody who was involved with these forbidden items had a chance to hide them before he came. By the time he arrived, we all looked like nice little boys laying in our beds and reading sifrei kodesh like little angels. What was the point of doing this? He wanted to catch us doing the right thing! This motivated us to do more and more of the right thing, so that we would make Rabbi Trenk proud. Thank you, Rabbi Trenk, for your beautiful approbation to my second book. I remain your humble student.

Another legend in his time that I have been blessed with is **Harav Zev Leff** *shlit"a*. Rav Leff has been an invaluable source of support and sage advice over the years. I am so blessed to have such a *Talmid Chacham* and *Gadol B'Yisrael* as a family friend. Thank you, Rav Leff, for all the time and guidance you have given me over the years, and I also thank you for such a beautiful approbation for my second book. I remain your humble student.

My in-laws **Mr. and Mrs. Roman and Elaine Frayman** have been so instrumental in helping me in general, and specifically with regard to this project. Not only are they avid readers of my weekly articles, but their advice on how to improve them is priceless. Thank you for your constant love, care and kindness, and thank you for taking such an interest in my project. Mom and Dad, I love you.

I cannot thank my parents **Mr. Morris (Moishe) and Mrs. Elaine Wagensberg** enough for all they have done for me throughout the years. They have constantly sacrificed and supported me on my journey through life, during the pleasant times and during the difficult times. Thank you for your love, care and kindness shown in every step I have taken. Thank you for your advice and thank you for always being there for me. Mom and Dad, I love you.

I am so proud of my children; they have all grown up into such fine human beings who are sensitive to others. They have all been excited about this book, and they have all encouraged me along the way. So, to **Esther Rochel, Nachi, Shiffy, Rivky, Shirel, and Aharon Chaim** I say Thank you. I love you all dearly and forever.

Although I have already mentioned her above, before concluding this section of acknowledgements, I must add the feelings that I have for my dear and precious wife **Laura**. Regarding this publication, Laura has spent many hours collecting, organizing and editing these teachings. It was Laura who suggested that I conclude each essay with a practical application that people can walk away with. This idea has been very well-received, to say the least. But Laura's input goes far beyond all of that. Laura has been, and continues to be, my constant source of encouragement and support. The overabundant love that I feel from Laura makes me feel as though I am walking around in Paradise. It is because of Laura that I cherish each and every day that I am blessed to spend with her. There are no words other than thank you. Thank you, Laura, I love you.

Preface

The History

Over the years I have had the privilege of staying in touch with many of my students through the *parshah*/holiday emails that I send out weekly. It is distributed to thousands. Hundreds of people print them out to share at the Shabbos table. Dozens of letters and emails have been sent to me, thanking me for them and describing how greatly these Torah thoughts enhance their Shabbos experience, while also encouraging discussion at the table.

The Idea

Thus, an idea was born. What if we were to collect these weekly publications, modify them, revise them, and add practical applications, and present them as a book? This would give our subscribers easy access to some of their favorite essays, with many new additions. It would also enable us to reach a much wider audience of people who are not yet on our email list.

It Differs

This book, *A Shot of Torah*, differs from my first publication *Inspiring Change* in the following way: *Inspiring Change* is a collection of eight chapters that are a longer and more in-depth analysis of self-improvement going in order from inner-self to outer-self. However, *A Shot of Torah* is a collection of shorter essays, hence the name, *A "Shot" of Torah.*

Each essay has been condensed from the audio/video lecture series that I have given over the years. Each class ranges between an hour to an hour and a half. In an attempt to grab onto the essence of each talk, in shorter form, these articles were created. The chapters are arranged in order of *parshiyos* and holidays. It is designed to be user-friendly for the Shabbos table, or any other time for that matter. I chose to include four pieces per *parshah*. The reason for this is so that you can share one piece at each meal on Shabbos, including *Melaveh Malkah*. There are four pieces for each holiday as well.

Although in *Eretz Yisrael* there is only one day of *Yom Tov* (excluding *Rosh HaShanah*) and only two pieces would be necessary for the two meals; we have, nevertheless, included four pieces for the four meals since in *Chutz La'Aretz* there are two days of *Yom Tov*.

Title – Illustration

The idea for the cover illustration came from the title and from the concept of this book. As we mentioned, these pieces are shorter versions of longer lectures. These *divrei Torah* are also intended to be shared as the Shabbos/*Yom Tov* table. At those tables we customarily drink a *l'chaim* between the fish and the meat. Therefore, the name my wife suggested, *"A Shot of Torah,"* is very fitting since it alludes to the small shot-glass of alcohol that is drunk at the Shabbos/*Yom Tov* table.

The idea for the illustration of wine being poured from the bottle into the Kiddush cup in the shape of Hebrew letters came from my mother. When she suggested it, the following thought came to my mind. The Gemara says "*nichnas yayin yetzei sod* - when wine enters, secrets come out" (*Rebbi Chiya Eruvin, chapter 6, "Hadar" page 65a*). One interpretation of this passage could be that wine is connected to the secrets of the Torah. Both Hebrew words *yayin* and *sod* share the same numerical value of seventy, which refers to the seventy interpretations of the Torah. Moreover wine is actually found hidden within the grapes, hinting to the secrets of Torah that are hidden beneath the surface. This idea is very connected to the *divrei Torah* found within this *sefer* because the teachings tend to cover the four levels of Torah understanding, *pshat, remez, drush* and *sod* (simplistic, code, expounding, and secrets). How fitting it would be then to drink a shot of Torah together with the shot of wine at the festive Shabbos and *Yom Tov* meals.

The Practical

As I mentioned, we have added a practical exercise at the end of each essay in order to be able to actually implement these lessons into our daily living. The motivation behind this came from my wife, Laura. Laura has been editing my *parshah* emails for some time now. She mentioned to me that there seemed to be something missing - a gap between the end of the teaching and the blessing. Laura suggested that we need to find a way of making these teachings concrete in people's lives and not just leave them without a take away message. These practical applications would be the necessary ingredient that would serve as the bridge from the Torah to the blessing.

I was thinking that this fits into the *Ramban* in his letter when he says that whenever we get up from studying a *sefer*, we should think about how we can apply what we have learned. Hopefully, we have satisfied this suggestion to some extent.

I cannot begin to tell you how much positive feedback I received from my students when I began suggesting these exercises in my lectures and emails. It has made these lessons so relevant to people's lives. Laura, I am eternally grateful for you! It is my hope that this book will help to further enhance your Shabbos and *Yom Tov* meals, generating holy Torah discussions.

David Feinberg

This book is the Feinberg Edition on account of my dear friend, Mr. David Feinberg. Many years ago, when David's son, Daniel, studied at Darchei Noam Shappells, he suggested that I begin learning with his father. Daniel, I can't thank you enough because this resulted in a close friendship and my longest standing *chavrusah* ever! David and I have studied many things together including *Chumash*, *Halachah*, holidays, prayer and philosophy, but mostly it's been Talmud.

I am very impressed with Mr. Feinberg. He is level-headed, balanced, and filled with a beautiful set of values that he lives by. To David, the study of Torah is not just learning, but rather it is an experience to explore. David savors every word and enjoys breaking the Talmudic code himself. He considers the time spent learning Torah as the highlight of his day. Good people like Mr. Feinberg are hard to come by, and I am proud and thankful to have him as a study partner; but more importantly, I am blessed to have him as a friend. These qualities of David are matched by his generosity, which enabled me the privilege of bringing this publication to fruition.

Thank you, David, for your help; thank you, David, for your support; thank you, David, for your caring; thank you, David, for your warmth; thank you, David, for your listening ear; thank you, David, for your advice. And thank you, David, for being my friend. Thank You, G-d, for bringing David into my life; thank you, Daniel, for making the *shidduch*; and thank you, Carol, for sharing David with me.

May I take out a moment to also thank my students and readers for sharing these thoughts and teachings with your families and friends. In a way, it is as if you have invited me into your homes for Shabbos. For that, I am forever grateful.

Warmest wishes,

Aba Wagensberg

Introduction

In a very complicated and technological world, the Shabbos table may be the only setting for real quality family time. There are no appointments or meetings to attend, and no gadgets beeping and ringing to distract us. The time we spend with our families and friends around the Shabbos table may be the only "shot" we have left to impart our values to them, and create an everlasting bond.

The Shabbos table conversations are the memories that our children will savor, and carry with them throughout their lives. If they have positive feelings when they reflect on those moments, they will want to have Shabbos tables of their own and pass on the message to the next generation.

Shabbos meal time is limited. Typically, people spend just an hour or two on Friday night and Shabbos day meals. The third meal and *Melaveh Malkah* are considerably shorter. Besides catching up with each other, what better way to spend that time together than Torah conversation. Since the Torah is eternal, the conversation will build an everlasting relationship. This is my hope with this publication - namely, that it generates Torah discussion, bringing us closer to each other and closer to G-d.

In addition, when Torah is shared at a meal, the table is transformed into the Altar, the food we eat is transformed into Offerings, and we are transformed into *Kohanim* (see *Avos* 3:4). Moreover, when Torah is spoken during the meal, then an angel comes down and creates a spiritual image of our table, and brings it up as a present to G-d; as it says, "This is the table that is before G-d" (see *Me'am Lo'ez*, Lv. 2:13; Eze. 41:22).

Sefer Bereishis

Bereishis

Three's Company

When the news first hits, people are shocked. The death of a famous personality, such as a president, actor, comedian or athlete brings with it a level of sadness. People wonder how we are going to move on without them; yet, we always manage. The same holds true in the religious Jewish world. When one of the Torah Giants leaves us, people feel lost and orphaned. How can we go on? But the truth is that we can, because the answer lies within us.

As we begin a new cycle of the Torah, we must first ask ourselves about the juxtaposition between the end of *Devarim* and the beginning of *Bereishis*. Rabbi Moshe Wolfson, in his *Emunas Itecha*, writes that he was once at the grave of Shimon HaTzaddik when the following idea occurred to him.

In *Avos* (1:2) it says that "Shimon HaTzaddik was one of those remaining from the Men of the Great Assembly. He used to say that the world is supported by three pillars: Torah, and *avodah* (prayer), and *chessed* (acts of kindness)." One could question the need for the Mishnah to stress that Shimon HaTzaddik was of the last of the men of the Great Assembly. How is that piece of information connected to the end of the Mishnah which lists the three pillars upon which the world stands?

Rabbi Moshe Wolfson explains that during the Temple era, the Jews were living in their land, the Divine presence was palpable, and they had access to the altars and sacrifices. As a result, it was much easier for the Jews to serve Hashem.

However, after the Jews were exiled, they no longer had the Temple with its altars and sacrificial service, and it became harder for the Jews to serve

Hashem. So how did God assist the Jewish people? God established an institution called the *Anshei K'nesses HaGedolah* (the Men of the Great Assembly) which was comprised of 120 *tzaddikim*, many of whom were prophets, such as Ezra, Mordechai, Chaggai, Zechariah, and Malachi. They established the prayers that we have today which are substituted in the absence of the sacrifices. They thereby created a situation in which it became easier, once again, for the Jewish people to serve God.

But then, with time, the people of the *Anshei K'nesses HaGedolah* aged, and one by one, they began to die. The Jewish people were concerned; how would they survive without the *Anshei K'nesses HaGedolah*? When all the people of this institution passed away except for the last one, Shimon HaTzaddik, the Jews became frightened regarding the future of Judaism upon Shimon HaTzaddik's death. They knew he wouldn't live forever. This is why the Mishnah stresses that Shimon HaTzaddik was of the last.

According to the *Emunas Itecha*, he wasn't only one of the last; he was the very last one. Shimon HaTzaddik saw the concern in the eyes of his followers, and therefore told his people, "Do not think that the world stands on the *Anshei K'nesses HaGedolah* alone. Do not think that without us the world will not survive. This is not so because the world is supported by three things: Torah, *avodah*, and *chessed*. These three things will remain with the Jewish people forever."

Now we understand why the Mishnah stresses that Shimon HaTzaddik was the last, and how that piece of information is connected to the three pillars upon which the world stands. It is precisely because Shimon HaTzaddik was the last and saw the people's concern, that he was motivated to tell them: do not fear, because the three things that keep the world going will be at your fingertips for all time. This approach explains the juxtaposition between the end of *Devarim* and the beginning of *Bereishis*.

At the end of *Devarim* it says that Moshe died (34:5), and if the Jews were concerned about the survival of Judaism when Shimon HaTzaddik was about to die, imagine their terror upon the death of their leader Moshe Rabbeinu. We have to understand that Moshe was everything to them. He was the prophet, the king, the priest, the *Rebbe*, the *Levi*, etc. The Jews questioned their growth or even survival without Moshe Rabbeinu. The book of *Devarim* concludes with this concern. This is precisely where *Bereishis* picks right up, to comfort us with the knowledge that the world does not stand on the merits of even Moshe Rabbeinu alone. Rather, the world stands on the pillars of Torah, *avodah*, and *chessed*. This is hinted to in the first word of the Torah, *Bereishis,* which doesn't merely mean "in the beginning."

The word *Bereishis* is really two words in one. The letter *Beis* stands for the word *bishvil,* which means "because of," or "on account of." The next part of the word hints at something which is called *reishis.* In other words, because of *reishis,* God created the Heavens and the Earth. We just have to find out what is defined as *reishis.*

The Torah is called *reishis.* As it says (*Mishlei* 8:22), "*reishis darcho,*" which means that the Torah is "the beginning of His way." So far, we see that the word *Bereishis* hints at the Torah.

The word *Bereishis* also hints at *avodah.* In *Tikunnei Zohar* (*Tikkun Beis),* it says that the word *Bereishis* can be divided into two words. The first half of the word is spelled *bara* which means "created" and the second half of the word read backward spells *tayash* which means "a lamb" as an allusion to the ram that was used for *Akeidas Yitzchak.*The story of the *Akeidah* is one about sacrifices, for which prayer serves as a substitute. Now we see that the word *Bereishis* also hints at *avodah.*

The word *Bereishis* also alludes to *chessed* because all the gifts that are given to the poor are called *reishis,* as it says in the Midrash in *Bereishis Rabbah* (1:4), the world was created in the merit of three things and they are: *challah*, tithes, and the first fruit. *Challah* is called *reishis* (*Bamidbar* 15:20), the tithes are called *reishis* (see *Devarim* 18:4), and the first fruits (*bikkurim*) are called *reishis* (*Shemos* 23:19).

So once again we see that the juxtaposition of the end of *Devarim* and the beginning of *Bereishis* comes to teach us that although Moshe Rabbeinu passed away, we must realize that the world does not stand on the merits of Moshe alone; rather, the world stands on the three pillars of Torah, *avodah*, and *chessed.*

At this time of year it would be a good idea to invest a little extra effort in these three areas. We could set aside one extra minute a day to learn Torah; we could add one small prayer to our standard daily *tefillos*, and we could do one more act of *chessed* each day. These resolutions will be the legs which will support us in this world and the next.

So, as we leave the month of *Tishrei*, with all of its incredible *mitzvos*, such as *shofar, sukkah, lulav, esrog*, etc., and we enter the darkness of the winter, let us not be concerned about our survival and growth, because there is a tomorrow, as long as we strengthen ourselves in Torah, prayer, and acts of kindness. May these three pillars remain with us for the rest of the year, so that we deserve the coming of our *Moshiach* and with him, the ultimate redemption to *Eretz Yisrael*, our *Gan Eden* on Earth.

Bereishis

The Transformers

If we want our possessions and furniture to be in good condition, we are going to have to take good care of them. The same holds true with all of our vessels. The implication of this statement is far-reaching.

Many connections between the Torah's conclusion and its beginning have been skillfully crafted by various commentaries. One approach by the *Admo"r* Reb Meir Yechiel Molgenitzer (cited in the *Iturei Torah*) is as follows.

The Torah concludes with the words, "*Moshe l'einei kol Yisrael* - Moshe [performed] before the eyes of all Israel" (*Devarim* 34:12). When you unscramble the acronym of those four Hebrew words (*mem, lamed, kaf, yud*), it spells the word *keilim*, vessels.

Interestingly enough, towards the beginning of the Torah it says, "*V'choshech al p'nei tehom* - With darkness upon the surface of the deep." (*Bereishis* 1:2). When you take the last letter of each of those four words (*kaf, lamed, yud, mem*), they spell, in order, the word *keilim*, vessels.

The coded word "*keilim*" found at the start and end of the Torah hints at a Mishnah at the end of tractate *Keilim* which says, "Fortunate are you *keilim* that you entered in impurity, and you have exited in purity" (Ch. 30, *Klei zechuchis,* Mishnah 4, the opinion of *Rebbi Yosi*).

The simplistic understanding of this Mishnah is that *Rebbi Yosi* was addressing the tractate of *Keilim* itself. *Rebbi Yosi* said to it: you are fortunate because although you began by discussing matters of impurity (*Avos Hatumos* - the highest levels of impurity, such as insects, semen, corpses, a *metzora,* etc... Ch. 1 Mishnah 1), you have, nevertheless, concluded by discussing matters of purity (i.e. glass vessels that are pure).

This pattern is found in the Torah itself. Although the Torah commences with matters of impurity (darkness), it concludes with matters of purity (Moshe and Israel). Therefore, the word *keilim* is coded into the beginning and end of the Torah, to demonstrate that the Torah and the Mishnah share this commonality.

Perhaps we could add to the Molgenitzer Rebbe's explanation by suggesting that the word *keilim* refers to the Jewish people. The Jews are meant to be the *klei shareis*, ministering vessels, that are dedicated to the service of God. There is even a hint in the word *keilim* itself, suggesting that the Jews are indeed considered to be the vessels under discussion.

The singular word for *keilim* is *kli* (vessel). This word is spelled with three Hebrew letters - *kaf, lamed, yud*. These three letters stand for three other Hebrew words. The *kaf* stands for *Kohanim* (priests), the *lamed* stands for *Leviim* (Levites), and the *yud* stands for *Yisraelim* (Israelites). These are the three classes that formulate the constitution of the Jewish people. Since the Torah begins with the word *keilim* in connection with darkness and impurity, it teaches us that we enter the world from a place of darkness, surrounded by impurity. We are formed by a putrid drop and we are born surrounded in blood.

However, since the Torah closes with the word *keilim* in connection with Moshe and Israel, it teaches us that by the time we leave this world we can become completely transformed into something pure and holy.

Which ingredient is necessary in order for us to make this transformation? Between the first coded *keilim* and the last coded *keilim* is the Torah itself! This shows us that the study of Torah itself can convert something tainted into something pure.

Torah study accomplishes this in two ways. Firstly, it teaches us how to behave in a dignified fashion. Secondly, Torah study itself has a magical power that simply alters the person involved in learning it.

This message is very fitting for this time of year. Over the last month and a half we have been involved in so many different types of *mitzvos* and *minhagim;* for example, *Selichos, shofar, simanim, tashlich, kaparos*, fasting, *vidui, teshuvah, tzeddakah, sukkah, lulav, esrog, ushpizin, Simchas Beis HaSho'eivah*, and *aravos*. When the holiday season ends, one may begin to feel saddened and alone, wondering how we will be able to grow spiritually and stay connected to God.

To alleviate this concern, we have *Simchas Torah* and *Shabbos Bereishis* where we conclude one cycle of Torah, and begin a new round. This adjacency draws our attention to the end of *V'zos Haberachah* and to the beginning of *Bereishis*, where Hashem teaches us that we *keilim* can make a huge spiritual transformation just by engaging in the study of Torah.

This would be a timely opportunity for securing a solid slot in our busy schedules to learn Torah. This could be accomplished by attending a regular class, or by establishing set times to study with a partner. However, during these learning sessions, one should make sure to include the study of one topic relating to a personally challenging area where one knows that one needs to improve. Not only will the Torah serve as a guide in how to deal with these issues, but the mere study itself will empower us with the strength to persevere.

So, may we *keilim* all be blessed to learn, to grow, and to be transformed into the purest vessels that will overflow with blessings for us and our entire families.

Bereishis

From the "Bashes"

As drivers, we have to ask ourselves, what would be better: to sit in traffic on the road that is most direct to our destination, or to avoid traffic by taking an alternate route that is much more indirect to where we are headed. Many a driver would opt for the latter, and rightfully so, because in life, sometimes going in the opposite direction can get us to our destination faster.

In this week's portion, *Bereishis*, the first topic of discussion is that of Creation. The Torah tells us that in the beginning the Earth was "*tohu va'vohu* - null and void" (*Bereishis* 1:2).

The *Aron Eidus* points out that this chaotic state of *tohu va'vohu* was also a stage of Creation. Eventually, in the process of Creation, the *tohu va'vohu* was formed and shaped into the Heavens and Earth.

This development begs us to ask why God felt it was necessary to create this confused stage of *tohu va'vohu*. Why didn't Hashem just create the Heavens and Earth in the way that they were meant to be, without going through the stage of *tohu va'vohu*?

The *Aron Eidus* teaches that in the world of spirituality it is impossible to remain on one level. Not only that, but sometimes it is even necessary for a person to experience a drawback, a spiritual low, so that he can then ascend to an even greater and stronger spiritual high.

We all know that this is true in the physical domain. For example, if a person wants to look at the sun, he must first don a very sophisticated pair of dark glasses. Initially, it appears that he is living in darkness; however, in reality it is only then that he will be able to see the light.

Similarly, in regard to spiritual pursuits, sometimes we have to feel distance in order to become even closer.

The *Aron Eidus* explains that this was the necessity of creating a stage of *tohu va'vohu*. *Rashi*, on the spot, explains *tohu va'vohu* to mean that a person witnessing that state would be *tohu* (astonished), at the *bohu* (concealment), of the matter. An onlooker would wonder what all this chaos and darkness was about.

The answer to this question is found in the very next verse. There it says, "Let there be light" (*Bereishis* 1:3). Meaning, only through darkness can a person behold the light. The purpose of darkness is that it enables one to witness light.

The example of the sun and dark glasses is now very apt. Whether the issue is physical light or spiritual light, the message is that sometimes we need to go through dark periods in our lives in order to appreciate and even withstand the light.

We all have darkness in our lives. We all struggle. We all have challenges. Sometimes we don't know what to do, or where to turn.

Yet here, we are being taught that there is so much light in the darkness. Going through the darkness strengthens us so that we can then receive the light.

The timing of this message is most apropos. The winter has begun and the nights are getting longer. This physical manifestation may be a reflection of our spiritual standing. But, God is right next to us; He is telling us not to worry. God says, "I am with you."

The words "*na'aseh adam* - let us make man" (*Bereishis* 1:26), are as relevant today as they were when Hashem first uttered them. Why did God speak in the plural form, "let us…"? It would seem that God should have said "*e'eseh adam* - I will make man" in the singular.

One answer is that God was speaking to man. Hashem's message was, "Let you and I make you into who you can become." Hashem says that He will provide us with the tools. All we have to do is utilize them.

Even when we experience the difficulties of life, Hashem is with us, holding our hand every step of the way. How comforting is the knowledge that the Source of Light accompanies us in the deepest darkness, assisting us to such a degree that we will encounter that light and even become a beacon of light for others to follow.

In order to acclimate ourselves to this mindset, perhaps we could train ourselves to say, "*tohu va'vohu, vayehi ohr*" every time we experience challenging situations. This will remind us that it may be bitter now, but we will soon taste the light.

May we all be blessed with the courage and strength to meet the challenges of life with a smile on our faces and with a song in our hearts, feeling God's presence in our lives, and thus merit to witness the light to the degree that we will become one with it.

Bereishis

Body and Soul

As the sculptor put his finishing touches on his creation, he felt a surge of pride in his work, a muscular statue of a man. True, it was a work of art, but the man chiseled out of stone could never hope to breathe the breath of life, nor choose to accomplish anything. He is stuck in the position that his creator molded him into. By contrast, The Sculptor of Sculptors crafted man into a creature that could breathe, make choices and ultimately connect with the Higher Power in the deepest of ways.

This *Shabbos Bereishis* we anticipate recommencing a new cycle of Torah which, God willing, will begin a year of much Torah study, allowing us to reach greater depths of understanding and inspiration to carry into our lives.

We are told, "*Vayitzer Hashem Elokim es ha'adam* - And the Lord, God formed Man" (*Bereishis* 2:7). The word *Vayitzer* (and He formed) here is written with two letter *yuds* when normally one would have sufficed (see verse 19). We may ask why *Vayitzer* is written with a seemingly superfluous letter *yud*? An observation by the *Zohar* provides us with an insight with which we can address this question.

The *Zohar* observes that in the story of the six days of Creation, only the name of God (***Elokim***) is used. Only later, during discussion of the creation of Heaven and Earth (2:4), does the Tetragrammaton name of God (***Shem Havayah***) appear for the first time in the text. The *Zohar* explains the reasoning behind this by imparting the following principle.

God employs the *Shem Havayah*, which is the loftiest name, only in association with things that are eternal, and not with objects or entities that are temporary. In the verses leading up to *Bereishis* 2:4, God describes the six days of Creation, during which the animals and plants were created. Since these creations are temporary as they eventually wither and expire, God employs His name *Elokim,* and **not** the *Shem Havayah,* when referring to them. The Heavens and Earth, however, are everlasting, and God therefore allows His highest Divine name to appear in association with these creations.

We find proof in the *Shulchan Aruch* that the *Shem Havayah* represents eternity, as it stands for the words "*Hayah Hoveh V'Yiheyeh* - He was, He is and He will be" (see *Orach Chaim* 5:1). God's eternality is represented in His Tetragrammaton name which is why it is used in association with creations that have perpetual existence.

In response to the *Zohar*, the *Gan Raveh* asks the following questions. If the *Shem Havayah* is used only in connection with eternal creations or creatures, why then does it appear in the text in relation to God's formation of Man (see *Bereishis* 2:7), who is a mortal being and not eternal? (One may argue that at this point in the text, Man had not sinned and therefore **was** destined to live forever. Nevertheless, God knew that Man would sin and that he would have the status of a mortal, temporary being; so the question still remains).

We will understand, with the help of the following *Rashi*, why it is indeed fitting that God's *Shem Havayah* is employed in connection with the creation of Man. *Rashi*, on the word *Vayitzer* (*Bereishis* 2:7), offers an explanation as to why the word is spelled with a double *yud*. The two *yuds*, explains *Rashi*, indicate the two formations involved in the creation of Man. Firstly, there is what he calls, "*yetzirah l'olam hazeh* - a forming for this world," referring to the formation of the mortal body. Secondly there is "*yetzirah l'tchiyas hameisim* - a forming for the resurrection of the dead," referring to the creation of the spiritual part of Man.

While providing an explanation for the apparent superfluous *yud* in the word *Vayitzer*, *Rashi* simultaneously answers the query of the *Gan Raveh* as to why the Tetragrammaton Name of God is utilized when discussing the creation of Man. Although, as the *Gan Raveh* argues, Man is a mortal being and should therefore not be associated with the eternal name of God, *Rashi* points out that Man possesses a soul, a piece of God, which is eternal, besides a body which is temporary and mortal, thereby justifying the use of God's loftiest name in connection with Man. It is highly appropriate for God to associate His highest name, which symbolizes eternity, with Adam (Man) who possesses a Godly element which is also everlasting.

It is interesting to note that many *sefarim* print God's name (the *Shem Havayah*) as two *yuds*. Although a double *yud* is not in itself one of God's names, we could suggest that one of the sources for representing God's name in this way is *Bereishis* (2:7) where the word *Vayitzer* with its double *yud* represents both the mortal and immortal components of Man. By referring to God with two *yuds*, it serves as a constant reminder to man that his creation was achieved with two *yuds*, representing the fact that a spark of God exists within every single Yid (Jew).

Furthermore, we are told in *Ha'azinu* (32:9), "*Ki cheilek Hashem amo*," which is commonly translated, "God's portion is His Nation." However, if we translate this more literally, we can say that, *Cheilek Hashem* (a piece of God), i.e. the *neshamah*, is present in every single individual within the Jewish nation. Each time we see God's name written in this form, it reminds us to serve God with both aspects of our being.

Once we appreciate the fact that we possess a Divine soul, a "piece of God" which is everlasting, all our decisions regarding the way we conduct ourselves and our lives take on a new perspective. As we begin the Torah once again with the portion of *Bereishis*, and read about the creation of Man, we should take the opportunity to contemplate the foundation of our existence and rebuild ourselves, cultivating the eternal, Divine part of our being.

No matter how we fared over the High Holidays, we can take a message from this week's Torah Reading to begin anew and develop ever further, cultivating both sides of ourselves to serve God in totality. After all, *Krias HaTorah* does not only translate as the "reading of the Torah," but can also be translated as the "**calling** of the Torah." The Torah is calling out to us to utilize both components (body and soul) to maximize our potential.

We should invest at least as much time, energy and effort in our eternal, spiritual *neshamah*, as we devote to our mortal, temporary body, because, as it says in *Koheles* (12:13), "*Ki zeh kol ha'adam* - this is what humanity is all about."

Every time we do something meaningful with our bodies or physical possessions, we infuse them with spirituality and transform them into something eternal. We are surrounded with so many opportunities to achieve this goal.

For example, once a day, during a meal, we could say out loud, "Wow! This tastes so good, thank you Hashem for this pleasure."

In this way, we can generate appreciation for God. We can then use the strength from the food to do more good in the world. This transforms a base activity into something meaningful, spiritual and eternal.

May we all be blessed to strike a healthy balance between body and soul and, thus, merit living the life of eternity.

Noach

Practicing What We Teach

Mike struggled over whether to make the call or not, but finally mustered up the courage, so he picked up the phone and dialed. "Hello, is this Mr. Klepper? I was a student of yours a number of years ago when I was studying law. Well, I thought of you today. The cashier at the grocery store gave me too much change; I was tempted to keep it. But then, I remembered that I once watched the man in the post office give you too much change, and as you walked away counting your money and realized the mistake, you went back to return it. That made such a positive impression on me, that I did the same thing today. I just wanted you to know. Thank you!"

We are all teachers, people are always watching. Let's try to set the best example possible.

This week's portion, *Noach*, begins with the famous words, "*Eileh toldos Noach; Noach ish tzaddik tamim hayah b'dorosav* - These are the offspring of Noach; Noach was a righteous man, perfect in his generation" (*Bereishis* 6:9). The repetition of Noach's name in this verse, *Noach Noach*, teaches us a number of things. (The following ideas are based on the *Aron Eidus*).

1) One definition of "*Noach*" is "pleasant." Therefore, the repetition "*Noach Noach*" tells us that Noach was pleasant to the upper world, and he was pleasant to the lower world (see *Bereishis Rabbah* 30:5). This in itself is an important lesson. Sometimes our religious fervor in serving God can lead to neglecting the needs of people. At other times, our desire to help people can cause us to disregard our responsibilities to God.

However, Noach succeeded at striking the essential healthy balance in paying attention to both, without focusing on the needs of one at the expense of the other. Thus, Noach was pleasant to God above and to the people below.

2) The verse "*Eileh toldos Noach Noach,*" with its repetition, teaches us that perhaps the greatest offspring (*toldos*) that one can produce is by making oneself into a *tzaddik* (righteous person). This is the meaning of "*Eileh toldos Noach Noach* - These are the offspring of Noach, Noach." This was Noach's greatest child, *toldos*. Who was that? It was Noach himself! With the right choices, we create who we become.

Furthermore, we all know that Hashem has a vision of just how great each and every one of us can become. By repeating the words "*Noach Noach*" we are being told that the "Noach" below lived up to God's expectation of the "Noach" above.

3) The repetition of "*Noach Noach*" shares another idea. A true *tzaddik* leaves behind in this world people (*toldos*) who have learned from his ways and emulate them. These people can either be biological children or students who are considered as children (see *Rashi*, on *Bamidbar* 3:1 citing *Sanhedrin*, Ch. 2, *Kohen Gadol*, pg. 19b, where the opinion of *Rabbi Yonasan* is mentioned, concerning one's students being considered as one's children).

We are all teachers since we never know who is watching us and learning from our ways. When we behave as positive role models for others, then we live through them even after we die.

Noach was such a role model. Therefore, the words "*Eileh toldos Noach Noach*" teach us that through the *toldos* (children or students of Noach), Noach lives on.

How can we ensure that our children or our students will indeed lead their lives in accordance with the values that we represent? One idea is hinted to in our verse. It says, "*Noach ish tzaddik* - Noach was a righteous man." The last letters of these three Hebrew words are *ches*, *shin*, *kuf*. Together they spell the word *cheishek* (desire).

This teaches us that if we approach the commandments with desire and enthusiasm, then our children and students will want to follow.

Excitement is contagious! When passion is applied to serving God, others will also want to join in. Everybody wants to have fun. If that is the way Torah comes across, then people will beg for the opportunity to participate.

It is not arbitrary that the letters which spell the word "*cheishek*" appear at the **end** of each word. This positioning itself teaches us that in the **end**, through this eagerness and fervor, our children and students that come **after** us, will walk in our path.

There are two more points which require mentioning with regard to impacting the next generation positively.

> 1) Our own Torah study must be done in the right way as enumerated in *Avos*, (6:6), and known as "The Forty-Eight Ways."
>
> 2) We must pray for our children's success from the bottom of our hearts. This means that our prayers should be done with much feeling and emotion.

These two ideas are hinted to in the very names that Noach gave to his children. The names of Noach's three children are *Shem*, *Cham* and *Yefes* (*Bereishis* 6:10). The name *Cham* is spelled with two Hebrew letters *ches* and *mem*. Numerically, these two letters add up to forty-eight, representing "the *Mem Ches* - the Forty-Eight Ways" through which a person can really acquire the Torah properly.

The names *Shem* and *Yefes* are spelled with five letters - *shin*, *mem, yud, phey, saf*. When unscrambled, these five letters spell *sefasayim* (lips), representing the lips which pray to God. However, prayer cannot just be "lip service." Rather, prayer must be done with heated passion, represented by the name *Cham* which means "heat."

Whether involved in Torah or in *tefillah* (prayer), Noach really applied himself by using his lips properly. This is hinted at when it says that Noach was a "*tzaddik tamim hayah bedorosav* - a completely righteous person in his generation." The letters of the word *bedorosav* (generation) can be rearranged to spell *diberosav* (his words). By offering heartfelt "words," Noach impacted his "generation."

We can implement these lessons on a practical level. First of all, at the end of the *Amidah*, let's stop, close our eyes and say to God, in our own words and language: "Please God, I beg of you, help me have children that bring You, me, and all the Jewish people, incredible *nachas*."

Additionally, we should be sure to include a topic that really interests us during the times that we have set aside for Torah study, so that we get naturally excited by it. That enthusiasm will be felt by the members of our family. It won't be long before they will want to participate.

May we all be blessed to make the right choices, shaping ourselves into the *tzaddikim* that God knows we can become, by approaching Torah and *tefillah* with such zeal that it infects the people in our lives in a most positive way.

Noach

Noach Flipped Out

As a young boy, Reb Menachem Mendel of Kotsk studied the story about our exodus from Egypt. Little Menachem Mendel commented that he was extremely enamored with Pharaoh. The *cheder Rebbe*, concerned that young Menachem Mendel was demonstrating a bad streak by idolizing the villains of the story, tried to prevent Menachem Mendel from going off the *derech*. The Rebbe asked, "Why are you so impressed with Pharaoh?" Menachem Mendel responded, "Because he shows us how one should hold on tenaciously to his belief. If this is true when the belief is false, how much more important is this holy stubbornness when your belief is true." The bottom line is, we can learn from everybody.

This week's Torah portion opens with the following statement: "Noach was an ***ish*** (man) ***tzaddik*** (righteous) ***tamim*** (perfect)" (*Bereishis* 6:9). The word ***ish*** is a compliment in its own right and the additional descriptions heap honor upon honor on Noach. No other personality is described with so many consecutive praises in one verse!

The first verse in *Sefer Tehillim* teaches: "Fortunate is the man (***ish***) who has not gone in the counsel of the wicked, and has not stood in the path of sinners, and has not sat in the company of scoffers." The *Midrash Shocher Tov*, in the name of Rabbi Yehudah, comments that the phrase "Fortunate is the man (***ish***)," refers to Noach, since Noach is called ***ish***, as in our *parshah*.

Why is Noach described as "fortunate"? According to the Midrash, Noach was fortunate in that he did not follow the evil ways of the three categories of people (wicked, sinners, scoffers) cited in *Tehillim*. These three negative categories correspond to the three generations that arose in the world over the course of Noach's lifetime: the generation of Enosh (Adam's grandson, who initiated the practice of idolatry); the generation of the Flood (immersed in immoral behavior); and the generation of the dispersion (who built the Tower of Babel in order to wage war against God). Noach was praiseworthy for not following the paths of any of these three generations.

The Midrash teaches us that Noach spent his entire life surrounded by evil and wickedness, yet he managed to become one of the most righteous people who ever lived. This is a remarkable feat. How is it possible for a person to maintain such a high level of spirituality while surrounded by an environment of depravity and corruption?

A passage from the Talmud will help us resolve this question. *Ben Zomah* says, "Who is a wise person? One who learns from everyone" (*Avos* 4:1). This is a strange statement. It seems reasonable for us to emulate righteous people - but where is the wisdom in learning from the wicked?

The *Berditchever Rebbe* remarks that righteous people are able to perceive positive qualities in even the most negative situations. From everything they encounter, they learn how to serve God better.

For example, if a righteous person were to witness someone passionately engaging in sin, he would recognize and appreciate the tremendous motivating power of passion. However, instead of taking that power and using it to accomplish negative goals, the righteous person would redirect it for a meaningful purpose. The correct channeling of passion has the potential to transform rote, sterile performance of God's *mitzvos* into *mitzvah* observance driven by enthusiasm and fire! (*Kedushas Levi*, end of *Parshas Bereishis.*)

Noach epitomized the ability to channel negative forces toward a higher purpose. A hint to this is found in his name. The Torah tells us (*Bereishis* 6:8) that Noach found *chen* (favor) in the eyes of God. The name Noach (*nun - ches*), when reversed, spells ***chen***, (*ches - nun*)! Noach found favor in the eyes of God by mastering the art of reversal. Noach had the ability to redirect energy from a negative goal to a positive one, making it into *chen*, something beautiful.

This is why a wise person learns from everyone. Instead of being corrupted by his evil generation, Noach used it as an opportunity for spiritual growth. He had the "best" teachers available! All Noach had to do was learn to take their ingenuity, arrogance, passion, jealousy and zeal, and use them in a productive, constructive way to get closer to God.

Let's make it a practice to learn from everybody by studying and analyzing people. From some of them we'll learn what to do; from others we'll learn what not to do; and yet from others we'll learn how to do it better.

May we all learn how to transform the power of every energy and drive into positive action in order to become the best we can possibly be.

Noach

Noach "Meats" God

If someone were to ask you to define the connection between a stone, a tree, an animal and a person, what would you say? They are not all intelligent, not all of them grow, and they are not all alive. The secret thread bonding these four items is found in the paragraphs below.

In this week's *parshah*, Hashem informs Noach of the imminent destruction of the world, and instructs him to build an ark in which to assemble all the types of animals on Earth. Hashem then continues, "Take from the food that you will eat and gather it, and it will be for you and for [the animals] for food" (*Bereishis* 6:21). In this verse about food, Noach is mentioned before the animals. We can, therefore, infer that Noach was allowed to eat before feeding the animals in his care.

This is problematic, however, since the Talmud (*Gittin* 62a) explicitly states that it is forbidden for a person to eat before feeding his animals! This prohibition is derived from the order of the words in the verse where Hashem says, "I have placed grass in the field for your **animals**, and **you** shall eat and be satisfied" (*Devarim* 11:15). If animals must be fed before those caring for them, how can Hashem permit Noach to eat before feeding the animals in the ark?

The *Sh'vus Yaakov* (responsa 3:13) states that the prohibition of eating before feeding one's animals is Rabbinically instituted. We could resolve the difficulty by proposing that Noach was not obligated to keep Rabbinic law. However, the *Magen Avraham* (271:22, citing response of the *Maharan*) and the *Taz* (*Orach Chaim* 167:7) both maintain that this is a Torah prohibition. If we propose that Noach was not bound by Torah law, since he lived before the Torah was given, we must still argue that according to the Rambam

(*Hilchos Avadim*, 9:5), Noach was still expected to be humane by being compassionate and taking pity on one's animals.

As a last resort, we could claim that when Hashem told Noach he could eat before feeding the animals in his care, He was referring to the non-kosher species, whereas the Talmud's prohibition is referring to kosher animals. Yet the *Sh'vus Yaakov* explains that the law of priority in eating makes no distinctions among domesticated animals, wild beasts of the field, fowl, and the resulting differences between kosher and non-kosher species. So, our question remains. Why was Noach permitted to eat before feeding his animals?

The *Gan Raveh* (based on the *Alshich* in *Parshas Acharei Mos*) explains that animals must be fed before people in order to elevate all four levels of creation and bring them to completion. The four levels, in ascending order, are ***Domem*** (inanimate objects, such as rocks), ***Tzome'ach*** (things that grow, such as plants), ***Chai*** (living things, such as animals), and ***Medaber*** (things that speak, namely people).

Each level of existence gives sustenance to the level above it. The inanimate earth sustains the plant life that grows on it; plant life sustains the animals that feed on it; and animals sustain people, who eat them. Therefore, the purpose of feeding animals before people is to progressively elevate the four levels of creation. The level of ***Tzome'ach*** (plants) must be elevated to ***Chai*** (animals) before ***Chai*** (animal life) can be elevated to ***Medaber*** (people).

This idea will finally answer our question. Before the Flood, people did not eat meat. Hashem permitted the consumption of meat only after the floodwaters receded (*Bereishis* 9:3; see also *Sanhedrin* 59b). Since the sustaining connection between the levels of ***Chai*** (animal life) and ***Medaber*** (people) did not exist pre-Flood, there was no need for Noach to feed the animals first. The four levels of Creation could not be elevated in order, so Noach was permitted to eat before the animals.

We can learn from here the vital importance of channeling all levels of Creation toward purposeful, meaningful, spiritual goals. *Parshas Bereishis* states that humanity was created "*b'tzelem Elokim*" as a reflection of Godliness (*Bereishis* 1:27). If we elevate and refine ourselves to express Divine qualities, we can harness and channel the energy within the lower levels of Creation toward the service of Hashem.

We can understand the story of Noach through this lens. Once Hashem permitted the consumption of meat after the Flood, the four levels of Creation could be elevated in order. Then, Noach could direct all levels of Creation toward spiritual ends.

Practically speaking, each day when reciting the morning blessing "*She'asah li kol tzarki* - God has made for me all my needs," which is a blessing instituted on wearing leather shoes, let us think about how all three levels of Creation are meant to serve man. The Earth nourished the plants, who in turn sustained the animals, which now serve men in the form of a pair of shoes. Man, however, is meant to serve God, bringing all levels to Hashem. By reciting this blessing slowly with concentration, we can then go about our day in the right direction, utilizing all of Creation in the service of God.

May we all be blessed to reflect Divine qualities, so that we can participate in elevating all levels of Creation to an eternal, spiritual purpose. May we witness our success, which will be evident when *Moshiach* comes and we sit down to eat a meat meal consisting of the offerings we bring God in our rebuilt Temple in Jerusalem.

Noach

A Towering Temptation

Has technology really made our lives any easier? Arguably it has made life more complicated. We thought we would save time, but every new device used to speed up the process brings higher expectations, and that put us right back where we started. Society also struggled with this issue thousands of years ago.

Towards the end of this week's portion (*Bereishis* 11:1-9), the Torah discusses the incident of the Tower of Babel. The episode is recorded as follows.

"The whole Earth was of one language and one speech. It was when they traveled from the east that they found a valley in the land of Shinar and settled there. And one man said to his friend, 'Let us make bricks and burn them thoroughly.' They had bricks for stone and bitumen as mortar. And they said, 'Let us build a city and tower whose head reaches the Heavens, and we'll make for ourselves a name, lest we be scattered across the face of the Earth.' God descended [as it were] to see the city and tower that man had built, and God said, 'Behold they are one nation with one common language, and this is what they do? Now nothing will be withheld from all that they propose to do. Let us descend and confound their language in order that a man will not understand the language of his friend.' And God dispersed them over the face of the Earth; and they stopped building the city. That is why it was called Babel; because it was there that God confused the language of the entire Earth, and from there God scattered them across the face of the Earth."

The Midrash (*Bereishis Rabbah* 38:6) comments that the crime of the *Dor HaMabul* (Generation of the Flood) is mentioned explicitly in Scriptural verse, as it says (*Bereishis* 6:13), "*...malah ha'aretz chamas* - ...the Earth is filled with robbery." However, it is not clear from the text what offense the *Dor Haflagah* (Generation of the Dispersed) committed, as the text just informs us that the people built a city and a tower. What could be wrong with that?

There are many opinions regarding the transgression of the *Dor Haflagah*. The *Abarbanel* suggests the following approach. When God created the world, He envisioned man as living a life of simplicity, as close to nature as possible. This would enable each individual to devote the majority of his time and energy to the service of God. The problem with the *Dor Haflagah* was that their focus involved seeking power and pursuing passions. This particular generation desired to build a city and tower in order to increase their might and control.

As technology develops, so does the intensity of power and passionate desires. This can lead one to a more complicated life, which is the antithesis of what God anticipated for man. Although one has the ability to cease leading such a complex life, it is more difficult and challenging as the development of technology increases. Technological advancement can encourage one to continue pursuing these physical desires. The tower and city represented this corrupt lifestyle and mindset, and it was for this that they were punished.

Building a city and tower for the purpose of increased control and self-glorification provided the people with a feeling of permanence in the physical world. This is why it was necessary for God to punish the *Dor Haflagah* by scattering them across the Earth, as this generated a sense of transience. This would lead them to recognize their misconceived approach to life. Then, they could understand that the true aim of life, as God anticipated, is to lead a simple existence in order to focus on the more meaningful, eternal, and spiritual goals.

This message is especially poignant at this time of year since *Parshas Noach* is always read soon after the holiday of *Sukkos*. Moving into a *sukkah* teaches us about how unstable we really are in this world (*Drashos Chasam Sofer* #53 and the *Yehi Ratzon* prayer said upon entering the *sukkah*). Noach's Ark is similar to the *sukkah*, in that it also represents transience. (How interesting it is that a *sukkah* on a boat is *kosher* (Mishnah *Sukkah* 2:3); and by Noach, the ark itself contained the spiritual essence of a *sukkah*.)

The tower, however, was meant to be the symbol of permanence in this world. We should ask ourselves if we possess "Towers of Permanence" in our own lives. Could it be that our homes or professional positions we consider to be "Towers of Permanence"?

There is a good exercise that we could implement in order to maintain our sense of what is temporary and what is eternal. Whenever we make a mortgage payment on our house, or every time we receive our paycheck, we should write down on a piece of paper what it would take for our homes or jobs to be taken away from us.

The realization of how easy it is to lose that which we cherish so much, will not only increase our appreciation for it, but it will establish clearly for us the difference between that which is fleeting and that which is constant. Once this has been firmly planted in our minds, we will lead our lives accordingly.

May we all be blessed to wage war successfully against lustful passions in our complicated lives that seem to tower over us, saving ourselves from the floods of power and desire, and directing us toward simplistic behavior and the ability to dedicate our lives to the service of God.

Lech Lecha

Down to Earth

Were you one of those sent away to study at a *yeshiva* or a seminary? Did you change your entire life around? Are you like a completely new person? If so, you should try to never forget who you were, and where you came from. At times, it may even be imperative that we go back to those early places in order to fulfill a unique mission.

Although we have already been introduced to Avraham and Sarah at the end of last week's portion (*Bereishis* 12:26, 29), we begin to get a broader glimpse of their personalities in this week's portion, *Lech Lecha*. Let us explore their lifestyle so that we can glean a lesson as to how we can further improve our own lives.

The opening statement of this week's portion contains the words, "*Vayomer Hashem el Avram, lech lecha mei'artzecha umimoladetichah umibeis avicha el ha'aretz asher areka* - Hashem said to Avram, 'Go for yourself from your land, from your relatives, and from your father's house to the land that I will show you'" (*Bereishis* 12:1).

The *Aron Eidus*, shares a deeper understanding of God's command "*lech lecha mei'artzecha* - Go from your land." He suggests that the word *mei'artzecha* (from your land) does not simply mean that Avraham was supposed to leave his country. Rather, *mei'artzecha* hints at leaving a lifestyle that emphasizes a quest for materialism.

This is indicated by the root of the word *mei'artzecha* which is *eretz* (earth or earthliness). In other words, God was commanding Avraham to abandon a society whose aspiration was the pursuit of *artziyus* (physicality).

Avraham was surrounded by a culture whose value system was about self-gratification. There was a concern that Avraham could have been drawn after the lusts of his hometown. It was precisely due to this concern that God commanded Avraham to leave his *eretz* (land) that was steeped in earthliness, physicality, and materialism.

However, the *Aron Eidus* says that it is not God's desire that we completely shed ourselves of *artziyus* (physicality) during our journey towards spirituality. On the contrary, God's wish is for us to constantly contend with our physical urges and overcome them. In this manner, we are always involved in serving Him.

This means to say, that as much as God's aspiration for us is to abandon *artziyus*, we must not throw it away completely. Rather, we must always return to it in order to battle against it.

This is hinted at in the words "*lech lecha* - go to you," meaning, that Hashem commanded Avraham to always go "back to himself" and to his origins. No matter how high Avraham would climb up the spiritual ladder of success, he was expected to persistently return to his roots, a place of lustful passions, and overcome those proclivities. Thus, Avraham would be in perpetual service of God.

The *Aron Eidus* says that this concept explains the tradition in Jewish law which tells us to take three steps back after concluding the *Shemoneh Esrei* (the eighteen or nineteen benedictions of the silent prayer, otherwise known as the *Amidah*). (See *Shulchan Aruch, Orach Chaim*, 123:1, based on *Yoma*, chap. 5, *Hotziu Lo,* pg. 53b, the opinion of *Rebbi Alexandary* in the name of *Rebbi Yehoshua Ben Levi.*) Prayer ought to be a very powerful experience. During communication with God, one can become so connected to the Divine that he can shed himself of any trace of physicality.

However, this is not what Hashem wants, because then this person discontinues serving God. So, in order to refrain from being completely absorbed into the spiritual, Hashem commands us to take three steps back.

This indicates our return to the physical world where we must strengthen ourselves, once again, by overcoming temptations.

This is the ultimate way of serving Hashem. The battle is more precious to God than the victory! It's more about the journey than the destination!

We could add that this is all hinted to in our national name. We are called "*Bnei Yisrael*" (The Children of Israel). The name *Yisrael* was given to Yaakov Avinu (Jacob, our father) after he wrestled with an angel. The verse there says, "No longer will it be said that your name is Jacob, but Israel, for you have struggled (*sarisa*) with the Divine and with man and have overcome" (*Bereishis* 32:29). *Sarisa* (struggle) is the root of the name *Yisrael,* pointing at our mission - to constantly contend with our challenges.

We see from here that the life of a Jew is more about the struggle than the triumph! This is true not only because it's through the fight that we are shaped, but because in this way we are continuously involved in serving Hashem.

This is why the Torah stresses that Lot went with Avraham (*Bereishis* 12:4). Lot was the personification of the *yetzer hara* (evil inclination) (see *Zohar* vol.1 pg. 78-79). This teaches us that although Avraham set out on a path of service to God to improve his spiritual standing; he did not dispose of the evil inclination altogether. Rather, Avraham traveled with Satan (Lot), combating him at every junction, just like a warrior.

We are meant to follow in the footsteps of our father Avraham. This is coded in the first paragraph of the "*Shema.*" There it says that we are commanded to love Hashem our God "*B'chol l'vavecha uv'chol nafshecha uv'chol m'odecha* - with all your heart, with all your soul, and with all your resources" (*Devarim* 6:5).

The words *B'chol l'vavecha* (with all your heart) teach us to serve God not just with the *yetzer hatov* (the good inclination), but even with the *yetzer hara* (the evil inclination). (See Mishnah *Berachos*, Ch. 9, *Haro'eh*, pg. 54a.)

In order to accomplish this, we have to fulfill the command: *lech lecha*. This means that even when we fly spiritually high through the Torah and the *mitzvos*, we must "*lech* - go back" "*lecha* - to our origins and roots," i.e. to the evil urges that we may have been exposed to when we were younger, and overcome them.

Therefore, the verse about loving God with both inclinations concludes with the words, "*uv'chol nafshecha uv'chol m'odecha* - with all your soul and with all your resources." The last letters of each of these four Hebrew words are *lamed, chaf, lamed, chaf*. Together they spell the words "*lech lecha*"!

This teaches us about the purpose of life where, as we move forward towards God, we must also "*lech lecha* - go back" to our core impulses that can create a distance between ourselves and Hashem, and overcome them.

This was the lifestyle of Avraham and Sarah. It was one of constant *milchemes hayetzer* - a battle with the evil inclination. Following in the footsteps of Father Avraham and Mother Sarah would involve embracing challenge and accepting obstacles with a deep resolve to fight until our last breath.

From now on, when we step back, out of the *Amidah*, let us pause before saying the *Oseh Shalom* section of the prayer, to ponder the meaning of stepping back into the physical domain. This will determine that the entire day ahead will be set on the right path.

May we be blessed to emulate our Patriarchs and Matriarchs by espousing the determination to champion evil with all our hearts, souls, and strength, which means that we must be willing to step back in order to leap forward.

Lech Lecha

Lead the Way

When we go through challenging times, we always turn to a professional for help. If we are having eye trouble, we run to an ophthalmologist; if we feel pain in our chest, we run to a cardiologist; if our income is being threatened, we turn to a lawyer. It should not be any different when experiencing a spiritual crisis. We must turn to a spiritual professional; a leader, such as a competent Rabbi, Rebbetzin or mentor. Let's get the help we need, and move on, because we cannot do everything by ourselves.

At the beginning of *Parshas Lech Lecha,* Avraham and Sarah set off for the land of Israel, together with "the souls they made in Charan" (*Bereishis* 12:5). *Rashi* explains that these souls were converts to monotheism; Avraham used to convert the men, while Sarah converted the women. Strangely enough, we don't hear anything further about these converts after the deaths of Avraham and Sarah. What happened to them?

The Alexander Rebbe suggests that, after the deaths of Avraham and Sarah, these new followers of monotheism declined to accept Yitzchak as their leader. They felt that his greatness was not equal in stature to that of Avraham, their "real" Rebbe. As a result, they were left leaderless. Since they had no direction, over the course of time, they became dispersed and this is why we hear nothing further about them in the Torah.

We can learn from here the vital importance of having a leader to preserve our connection with Hashem. The Mishnah (*Avos* 1:6 and 4:16) teaches, "Make a Rabbi for yourself." Being connected to a Rabbi ensures connection with a representative of Godliness in this world. Furthermore, we must accept that the righteous leaders of each generation are appropriate and fitting for the people of that time. Rather than wringing our hands over the lack of Torah greats such as we had in the past, we must recognize that each generation is given the leaders it needs and deserves.

In order to get through the tough situations of life, it is vital to seek out a Rebbe for guidance. Here are some of the qualities we are looking for:

1) A person who is filled with Torah.

2) A person with life experience.

3) A person who knows you personally.

A person with these characteristics can apply his Torah knowledge and life experiences to your unique situation. Let's start building relationships with competent leaders, get their advice and thus stay on the path of life.

May we all be blessed with righteous leaders, and may we learn to accept their leadership in order to stay connected to Hashem forever.

Lech Lecha

Keep it in Mind

Billy was in class, but his thoughts were far away, thinking about the upcoming football game in which he was to star. As the teacher drew ideas together and connected the point, Billy drew up the scrimmage and connected the various plays they would use against the other team. What do you think? Did Billy really attend that class or not?

In this week's portion God commands Avraham to go to the Promised Land, *Eretz Yisrael.* When he arrives there, Avraham finds that there is a very heavy famine in the land. On account of the food shortage, Avraham leaves Israel and goes down to Egypt (see *Bereishis* 12:1-11).

The *Ramban* criticizes Avraham for leaving the place that he was Divinely commanded to go to because he should have trusted in God who has the power to save people, even during a famine. Because Avraham failed this test there was a heavenly decree on his descendants that they too would have to descend to Egypt and become Pharaoh's slaves. However, there is a general rule of thumb from the students of the *Ba'al Shem Tov* that we have the responsibility to justify Avraham's actions, since he was a righteous person. Moreover, the *Ramban* himself hints at this when he says that Avraham sinned "accidentally." Obviously, Avraham didn't do anything intentionally wrong, and therefore it behooves us to understand the depth of Avraham's actions.

There is a famous principle from the *Ba'al Shem Tov* that a person is found where his thoughts are. This concept explains the ancient Jewish custom on *Yom Kippur* to say aloud the sentence after *Shema Yisrael:* "*Baruch shem kevod malchuso l'olam va'ed* - May the name of His glorious kingdom be blessed forever and ever." This is unlike the rest of the year, when we recite it in an undertone.

This particular sentence is a prayer which the angels say to God. Therefore, during the year we say it quietly because we don't want the angels to prosecute us, claiming that we have no right to utter such holy words since we are not angels. However, when *Yom Kippur* arrives, we behave like angels; for example, we do not eat or drink, nor do we wash or anoint ourselves. In other words, since we disengage from the materialistic world, we can say this sentence out loud and not be concerned about any angelic prosecution. This is because the angels will regard us as "fellow angels" uttering these holy words (see the *Tur* in *Orach Chaim* chapter 619).

However, there is a question regarding this custom. Why on *Motzei Yom Kippur* (the night right after *Yom Kippur*) do we no longer say that sentence aloud? It seems strange, because on the eve of *Yom Kippur* not only are we stuffing ourselves with food in preparation for the fast, it is even a *mitzvah* to do so! When we walk into the synagogues on the night of *Yom Kippur* we are so full we can hardly move! And this is when we say the angelic verse out loud? Whereas after *Yom Kippur* - a day filled with confession, tearful repentance, and fasting - we whisper "*Baruch Shem...*"? Shouldn't it be the other way around?

One would think that we are more like angels post-*Yom Kippur* than at its outset. However, based on the aforementioned teaching of the *Ba'al Shem Tov*, we will gain clarity into this ancient Jewish custom. On the night of *Yom Kippur*, although our stomachs are filled with food, our minds and thoughts are focused on the holiness of the day, and therefore we are considered to be living in *Yom Kippur* - thus, we are compared to angels. However, once *Yom Kippur* ends, although our stomachs are empty and we have purified ourselves, our thoughts are then occupied with the food and drink that will be served after the evening service. Since our thoughts are on eating and drinking, we lose our angelic status and are considered humans once again.

Based on this concept, the *Emunas Itecha* explains Avraham's decision to leave Israel, even though God commanded him to go there. First of all,

Avraham found himself in a dilemma because he felt that his unique personal calling in life was to perform the *mitzvah* of hospitality, which is impossible in a land where there is no food! Therefore, he felt compelled to leave the land and go to another place (i.e. Egypt) which was not affected by the famine, so that he could perform the *mitzvah* of hospitality.

Nevertheless, Avraham was aware of the Divine command to go to Israel so although he physically left Eretz Israel he made sure to keep his mind, heart and thoughts on the Land at all times. Therefore, based on the above-mentioned teachings from the *Ba'al Shem Tov* (that one is found where his thoughts are), he never really left the land. This was the compromise to which Avraham arrived.

A lesson we can learn from all this is to always keep our minds on holy matters - regardless of the circumstances and situations in which we find ourselves - since our thoughts determine where we truly are.

This week, let us try an exercise. No matter where we find ourselves, (in the office, in the street, on a business trip) let's close our eyes for just a few moments and focus on a holy place, perhaps a *yeshiva,* seminary, or *beis midrash* (study hall). Imagine sitting there learning Torah or doing a *mitzvah.* When we do so, we will be magically transported there, and then we benefit by rejuvenating our spiritual batteries. This can make a big difference in how we go about our day.

May we be blessed to maintain holy thoughts, so that we are clothed by their spiritual energy, and thereby benefit by being enclosed in a bubble of holiness no matter where we find ourselves.

Lech Lecha

Please Sign Below

In order for the Declaration of Independence to be meaningful, it had to have a "John Hancock," meaning the signatures of those who created it. On the same note, God's declaration that there be an independent creation who can choose his destiny, had to have a Divine seal on it. This is where our teaching begins.

Towards the end of this week's portion, *Lech Lecha*, God commands Avraham to circumcise himself and his entire household (*Bereishis* 17:1). The *Emunas Itecha* proposes that there are two aspects of a *bris milah* (literally, covenant of circumcision):

- *Bris HaNeshamah* - covenant of the soul
- *Bris HaGuf* - covenant of the body

He explains that the former, spiritual type of *bris* is referred to in *Lech Lecha* (17:1) where God appears to Avraham and says, "Walk before Me and be perfect." The latter, physical covenant is mentioned a few verses later (17:11) where God commands Avraham, "Every male among you shall be circumcised."

The *Emunas Itecha* points out that the act of circumcision forms a Divine seal, or signature, on the individual who is circumcised. We allude to this in the blessing that is recited following the *bris:* "*V'Tze'etza'av* ***chasam*** *b'os bris kodesh* - And He **sealed** his offspring with the sign of the Holy Covenant." While the *milah* is performed, God simultaneously signs and seals His name, so to speak, onto the person's body and soul.

The following examples show how an observable manifestation of God's name is evident on our bodies:

- The nasal septum that divides the nasal cavity into two nostrils forms the shape of the letter *shin*.
- Our arms produce the shape of a *daled* when bent at a ninety-degree angle.
- A *yud* shape becomes apparent once the skin of the *milah* is removed.

When we combine these letters, the word "*Shakai*" (spelled *shin*, *daled*, *yud*), one of God's Holy Names, is produced. (As we mentioned earlier, Hashem places His seal on our souls also, but this is clearly un-observable.)

A signature is authentic only if it is written by the signature holder himself. Thus God does **not** appoint an agent to seal His name at a *bris*, but rather, He does it Himself.

We find this concept in *Rashi* (*Bereishis* 17:24) who explains that the verb "*B'himolo* - when he was circumcised" is passive, suggesting that someone other than Avraham was involved in the *bris*. According to the Midrash (*Bereishis Rabbah* 49:2), when Avraham took hold of the knife to perform the circumcision, God placed His hand on Avraham and guided him through the procedure.

This idea is derived from the book of *Nechemiah* (9:8) where it says, "*V'charos* ***imo*** *habris* - He cut **with him** the covenant," implying that God carried out the *bris* **together with Avraham**, guiding and directing every single movement.

The *Emunas Itecha* illustrates God's involvement in circumcisions by comparing the role of the *mohel* (one who performs the *bris*) to the function of the quill in the hand of the scribe. Hashem is compared to the scribe who directs the process and is responsible for the action, while the *mohel* resembles the quill, which has no active role as it merely follows the movements of the scribe.

It is understood that a newborn male is named after his *bris milah*. One of the underlying reasons is that we want to remove the *pesoles* (spiritual waste) before attaching the name - the essence of the soul - to the person.

Why, then, was Avraham named before his circumcision? (See 17:5 where God changes his name from Avram to Avraham prior to his *milah*, which is discussed in 17:24-26.)

The *Emunas Itecha* resolves this apparent anomaly by pointing out that although Avraham was named before his *Bris HaGuf* (physical circumcision), the *Bris HaNeshamah* occurred prior to this (in 17:1).

We learn from here that the *Bris HaNeshamah* is, in fact, superior to the *Bris HaGuf*. Even if we stumble by defiling our bodies, we must not lose hope because our primary, spiritual connection to God through the *Bris HaNeshamah* is constant and indestructible.

We can make it our business to share this idea with at least one person a week. By doing so, we just might be saving a person from despair. Simultaneously, we will drive this point home within ourselves and have a better chance to be on a positive note.

Additionally, let us remember, at least once a day, that God's name is sealed upon our bodies and souls. This can help us behave appropriately throughout the day.

May we be blessed to make an everlasting covenant with God by realizing that our souls are always connected to Him, regardless of our behavior and physical actions. May this awareness provide us with the strength to never despair, so that we always return to God, come what may.

Vayeira

Delayed Reaction

When looking for an allergy pill, we don't just want immediate relief, but we also want the effect to be long-lasting. Our kindness towards others should be measured by the allergy pill, providing them with quick relief coupled with long-lasting benefit.

In this week's portion, *Vayeira*, God visits Avraham on the third day after his circumcision, and Avraham asks God to wait for him while he runs to tend to the needs of the three guests who passed by his home (see *Bereishis* 18:1-3, and *Rashi* citing *Bereishis Rabbah* 48:9). Rav Yehudah said in the name of Rav that we learn from here that the *mitzvah* of hospitality is greater than receiving the Divine presence itself (see *Shabbos* 127a).

We all know that Avraham's "pet project" in life was kindness. Let us explore an added dimension to this great *mitzvah*. *Parshas Vayeira* has something in common with *Rosh HaShanah,* because at the end of the portion it discusses the Binding of Yitzchak (*Bereishis* 22:1-19) - which is the very section that we read on the second day of *Rosh HaShanah* (see *Shulchan Aruch, Orach Chaim* 584:2).

The *Emunas Itecha* says that Avraham shares the same essence as *Rosh HaShanah* because just like *Rosh HaShanah* is the head of the year, so Avraham is the head of the Jewish people. Furthermore, just like *Rosh HaShanah* impacts the rest of the year, so Avraham's influence reaches until the end of all generations. (See *Horiyos* 12a and *Krisus* 6a. See also *Shulchan Aruch, Orach Chaim* 583:1-2 where it says that signs are meaningful and that the way we behave on *Rosh HaShanah* has an effect on the rest of the year.)

This is perhaps seen most vividly when Avraham prayed on behalf of Sedom (*Bereishis* 18:23-32). Although Sedom was ultimately destroyed (*Bereishis* 19:24-25), the *Emunas Itecha* says that we should not assume that Avraham's prayers went unanswered. Even though Avraham's prayers did not have a visible effect in that generation, they may have an impact on the generation living at the end of days.

This is based on a teaching of *Rabbeinu Bachya* that the inhabitants of Sedom were reincarnations of the people who built the Tower of Babel. When Sedom was destroyed, the souls were again reincarnated into those people who followed Korach in his rebellion against Moshe. (See *Rabbeinu Bachya* in *Bereishis* 19:4 and in *Bamidbar* 16:29, and all the verses he cites in support of this.) The *Emunas Itecha* takes this teaching one step further and says that when Korach and his followers perished, those souls were recycled one more time and placed into the people living in today's generation, at the end of days. (This is also based on *Rabbeinu Bachya*, *Bamidbar* 16:29.)

The point is that even though Avraham's prayers on behalf of the Sodomites may not have saved them in that generation, they did not go to waste. His prayers were stored for our generation, to help us rectify that which needs to be fixed. In other words, Avraham, back then, was praying for us today.

This teaching offers us a deeper understanding of the definition of kindness. Kindness is not only about touching another person's life, but it also includes causing constructive, long-lasting effects from one generation to the next. Everything that Avraham did was with the intention of producing an everlasting, positive effect.

We, too, can become disciples of Avraham Avinu. Pick one person to daven for, and pray not just for him, but for that person's family until the end of time. Ask Hashem to grant them health, *shidduchim*, children, and *parnassah*, and that will perpetuate spiritual growth from generation to generation.

May we all be blessed in the era called "The Footsteps of the Messiah" to follow in Avraham's footsteps by always searching for new ways to do kind deeds for each other, in order to make a perpetual impact on future generations. In that merit, we will deserve to receive the Divine presence with the building of our final and eternal Temple.

Vayeira

For the Greater Good

It was hard for the Brothfeld's (name is fictitious) when their daughter chose a more observant lifestyle. Did that mean that their child had rejected them? Quite the contrary, as we will now see.

In this week's portion, *Vayeira* (18:1), God appears to Avraham in the plains of Mamre. *Rashi*, citing a Midrash (*Bereishis Rabbah* 42:8), comments that Hashem revealed His presence to Avraham in Mamre's property specifically, because Mamre advised Avraham in circumcision, and encouraged him to go through with the procedure.

The *Sfas Emes* elaborates on this Midrash and explains that all of Avraham's friends understood that by entering a covenant with God through circumcision, Avraham and his descendents would become spiritually elevated and separate from the nations of the world. That is why Mamre's brothers - Aner and Eshkol - discouraged Avraham from circumcising himself (see *Rashi* on *Bereishis* 17:23); they benefited from their connection to Avraham and did not want to lose it!

Mamre, on the other hand, was willing to forego his desires for the sake of the greater good. Although he was aware that by undergoing circumcision, Avraham and his offspring would become somewhat removed from the rest of the world (including Mamre himself), he was able to appreciate the broader picture and support Avraham in carrying out God's Will. That is why God honored Mamre by appearing to Avraham on his land.

We learn from here the importance of conceding and nullifying our own wishes and desires in order to carry out the will of God. Once we become aware of His Will, we must learn to let go of our ideas and opinions (even those that we perceive to be based on spiritual grounds), and execute God's wishes with a full heart.

One area where this can hit home is when a child begins to observe the Torah and *mitzvos* in a more stringent fashion than his parents. This can often lead to resentment. Parents feel that they aren't good enough and that they are being rejected by their own child. It is the child's responsibility to explain himself clearly to his parents that a stricter observance of the law in no way implies less love or respect for his parents. On the contrary, it was the very values that they instilled into their child which prompted a more intensified level of observance.

At the same time, it is the parents' responsibility to encourage their child in his choice to be even more intensely observant. Parents must be ready to sacrifice for the greater good, even though it may feel like there is a distance and awkwardness at first. Eventually, with proper communication and lots of TLC, everybody will see that in actual fact, no distance has been created at all.

May we be blessed with the humility to nullify our thoughts for the sake of God - even when those thoughts are well-meaning - so that Hashem responds by annulling the evil decrees against us, and returning us to *Eretz Yisrael* in its entirety.

Vayeira

It's No Laughing Matter

We may have witnessed people passing quick and critical judgment on others and especially on Torah Greats. It would behoove us to take it easy and slow down, because we often find out that we have jumped to grossly mistaken accusations.

In *Parshas Vayeira*, Sarah hears that she will have a child the following year, and this news causes her to laugh. Hashem appears to Avraham and wants to know why Sarah laughed. Sarah denies that she reacted in this way, but Avraham insists, "No, you did laugh" (*Bereishis* 18:10-15).

This incident is troubling for a number of reasons. First, why does Hashem address the problem of Sarah's laughter behind her back? This seems almost like *lashon hara* (improper speech). Why would Hashem tell Avraham that Sarah laughed, instead of speaking directly to Sarah? We could suggest that Sarah's inappropriate laughter caused her exalted spiritual level to drop so that she no longer deserved prophecy. Because of this, Hashem had to speak to Avraham about Sarah, because Sarah herself was temporarily unable to receive Divine communication.

We are faced with other difficulties in understanding this incident however. In last week's *parshah*, when Avraham is informed that he will have a son, he also laughs (*Bereishis* 17:17). *Onkelos* defines Avraham's response as joyful laughter. Yet when Sarah laughs in this week's *parshah*, *Onkelos* defines it as mocking laughter. In such a situation, mocking laughter is practically heretical! How could Sarah, our first Matriarch, possibly doubt Hashem's ability to perform a miracle and enable a ninety-year-old woman to give birth?

Furthermore, when Avraham confronts Sarah about her inappropriate laughter, she is frightened, so she denies having laughed altogether (*Bereishis* 18:15). Sarah's moral standing appears to be rapidly deteriorating. How are we to understand Sarah's behavior? After all, she was one of the holiest people who ever lived.

We can gain a deeper insight into this incident by comparing the contexts in which Avraham and Sarah are informed that they will become parents. Hashem Himself tells Avraham that he will have a child the following year, whereupon Avraham laughs out of joy. (Avraham did not share this news with Sarah, because prophets are forbidden from sharing the contents of their prophecies unless Hashem gives them explicit permission to do so. The Talmud (*Yoma* 4) derives this from the word ***leimor*** (saying) which is an abbreviation for the two words ***lech emor*** (go and say). When Avraham learns that he is to have a child, the Torah does not use the word ***leimor***. Thus, Avraham keeps the information to himself.)

We can assume that, had Sarah heard this news from Hashem, she would have responded with joyful laughter as well. Instead, Sarah hears the news from three unexpected guests. Although these guests are actually angels, they appear in the form of wandering, idolatrous Arabs. Imagine for a moment how you would react if a group of disheveled, tattooed thugs, reeking of alcohol and hungrily devouring a meal, were to inform you, a senior citizen, "Next year at this time you'll have a son!" Sarah laughs mockingly because the bearers of this news are so disreputable. Why would she possibly think that such vagabonds were actually messengers from God?

Sarah's laughter seems like a natural response, yet apparently something was wrong with it. Why was Hashem upset?

The Torah teaches that our behavior and our actions make an inner impression on us, whether or not we are aware of it. Although Sarah laughed because the news provided by her guests was so incongruous, this same laughter subconsciously caused some part of her to believe that it was impossible for her to have a child.

Sarah was not even aware of the inner impression her laughter had created. Nevertheless, on some level, she closed herself off to the possibility of a ninety-year-old woman giving birth. Due to this infinitesimal loss of belief, her power of prophecy was temporarily taken away. We see from here how exacting Hashem is with the personalities in the Torah. Although Sarah wasn't even aware of the change that had taken place within her, she was still held accountable for the minute spiritual blemish it created.

When Avraham confronts Sarah and asks why she laughed, Sarah understands that he means, "Why did you laugh heretically?" This is why she replies, "I didn't laugh" - because, consciously, she didn't laugh **like that**. She merely laughed because the guests' news was so improbable.

The verse (*Bereishis* 18:15) continues with the words ***ki yare'ah***, which we previously translated as "because she was afraid." Now, however, we could understand these words to mean "because she was [God]-fearing" (hinted to in the word ***yare'ah*** itself, which can also spell ***yireh*** **H**[ashem]). When read in this way, the Torah is defending Sarah. As a God-fearing woman, Sarah would never intend to mock Hashem's ability to perform miracles.

Nevertheless, Avraham's final words to Sarah in this passage are, "No, you did laugh" (*Bereishis* 18:15). Even though Sarah did not intend to express doubt about Hashem's abilities and was unaware of the inner effect of her laughter, Hashem noticed the impression it made. For someone on the spiritual level of Sarah Imeinu, even the tiniest flaw matters. We can learn from this story how wrong we can be when we pass quick, critical judgments against the great personalities in the Torah.

May we all be blessed with the humility to recognize that the deficiency could be in our understanding, and not with the individuals themselves.

May we also be blessed to rub shoulders with the Torah Greats in our generation in order to be privy to a world that would otherwise be closed to us. Unless we witness greatness in our own generation, we will be unable to appreciate the greats of previous generations.

Vayeira

Keeping the Faith

There have been events in recent history that have really shaken us up. In light of these atrocities, some of us struggle with the question of God's existence; and if He does exist, some people do not have a very good impression of Him. Although we may not have all the answers, this much we can say: we are not alone, because the first Jew struggled with these questions as well. Apparently this is a process that each and every one of us needs to go through.

In *Avos* (5:4), it says that our Patriarch Avraham was tested with ten tests and stood up to them all. The commentaries agree (see *Rambam, Bartenura, Vilna Gaon*, and the *Tiferes Yisrael* in *Avos*) that the tenth and final of these tests was *Akeidas Yitzchak* (the Binding of Issac) found in this week's *parshah, Vayeira* (22:1-19). This means that this portion concludes the tests of Avraham Avinu.

One could ask what the nature of this test was. Avraham had already gone through the test of *Ur Kasdim*, where he preferred to be thrown into a fiery furnace rather than bow to idols. (See *Bereishis* 11:28 and *Bereishis Rabbah* 38:13, the opinion of Rabbi Chaiya Bar Brei D'Rav Ada of Yaffo.) Avraham had already clearly demonstrated his willingness to sacrifice himself for God. Therefore, it is obvious that Avraham was prepared to do whatever it would take to serve Hashem, even if that would require bringing his son as an offering.

Moreover, one could argue that *Ur Kasdim* was in fact a harder test for Avraham than the Binding of Yitzchak, as Hashem had not yet revealed himself to Avraham Avinu at that point. The whole world mocked him and his only recognition of God came through his own intellectual exploration.

By the Binding of Yitzchak, however, Hashem had already appeared to him, allowing Avraham to recognize Him personally. Therefore, once again we must ask, what was added with the test of *Akeidas Yitzchak*?

When Avraham was on his way to the *Akeidah*, the Torah says, "*Vayar es hamakom merachok* - And [Avraham] saw the place from a distance" (*Bereishis* 22:4). The *Emunas Itecha*, based on the *Zohar*, teaches us that what this really means to say, on a deeper level, is that Avraham saw that Hashem, who is called *Makom*, the Place (see *Bereishis Rabbah* 16:9 where it says the world is not God's place, but rather, God is the place of the world) was distant from him. Human sacrifice went against everything Avraham believed in, and was the antithesis of his whole understanding of God and the Torah.

This was in addition to the fact that God was apparently contradicting Himself. He had promised Avraham that he would have his son, Yitzchak, who would have a son, Yaakov, who would develop into the Jewish people (see *Bereishis* 21:12 and the Talmud in *Nedarim* 31). But now Hashem said, take that very Yitzchak, the seed of the Jewish people, and sacrifice him. This was before Yitzchak got married, and before he had a Yaakov.

Yet, Avraham had faith in Hashem and went to do His Will anyway. Meaning, the test of *Akeidas Yitzchak* was not to see whether he was prepared to sacrifice everything for Hashem, for that had already been proven back in *Ur Kasdim*. Rather, the test of *Akeidas Yitzchak* was to see whether or not Avraham had the stuff that it takes to follow Hashem, with questions on God, with doubt's about Hashem, and even with seeming contradictions within Hashem Himself.

In this aspect, *Akeidas Yitzchak* was harder than *Ur Kasdim*. Back at *Ur Kasdim*, it was clear what to do; as *halachah* states, if there is a choice between idolatry and death, one must choose death (*Sanhedrin* pg. 74a the opinion of Rebbi Shimon Ben Yehotzadak citing the consensus of the Sages in the *Nitzeh's* attic in Lod). At least Avraham had clarity. By the *Akeidah,* however, Avraham was confused, in the dark, and God's presence was concealed from him. And yet, Avraham marched forward anyway.

All too often we are faced with very difficult challenges. Sometimes they can make us bitter. When these situations arise, maybe a good idea would be to read this section of *Akeidas Yitzchak,* and remind ourselves that Avraham was capable of moving on anyway. Therefore, we too, have that power because we are descendants of his and, as such, inherited his spiritual DNA.

So, as we go through our tests in life, may we be able to walk in the footsteps of Avraham Avinu and keep the faith, even in the darkest of times when we don't understand.

Chayei Sarah

One Foot in Heaven

The dying man said to his inquisitor, "What difference does it make, I've already got one foot in the grave." You know, it doesn't have to take a deathbed or terminal illness for us to feel like one foot is on the other side. Each and every one of us can live each day of our lives with this outlook.

One of the most remarkable people in all of *Tanach* is Sarah *Imeinu*, (Sarah, our mother). Although Sarah dies in this week's portion, it behooves us to discuss her life and accomplishments. After all, the name of this week's portion is "*Chayei Sarah* - the Life of Sarah."

Sarah was the first of the Matriarchs. She supported her husband completely, following him wherever he had to go (*Bereishis* 11:31). She held onto her faith in God, even though she struggled with being barren for many years (*Bereishis* 11:30).

Not only was Sarah strong in silence, but she also knew when to be vocal and take a stand. For example, she knew how to deal with Yishmael (*Bereishis* 21:10). She was extremely active in outreach (*Bereishis* 12:5 and *Rashi* there citing *Bereishis Rabbah* 39:14, the opinion of Rav Hunah), and was considered an even greater prophet than Avraham (*Bereishis* 21:12 and *Rashi* there, citing *Shemos Rabbah* 1:1).

So great was Sarah that she is even compared to none other than Moshe Rabbeinu (Moses, our Teacher) himself! According to the *Aron Eidus*, Sarah, like Moshe, died by a Divine kiss (For further exploration on this subject, see Tractate *Bava Basra*, Ch. 1, *Hashutfin*, pg. 17a).

A hint to this is found in the words "*Vatamas Sarah* - And Sarah died" (*Bereishis* 23:2). These two words are spelled with seven letters - *vav*, *taf*, *mem, saf, shin, reish, hey.* When unscrambled, these seven letters spell the words "*Toras Moshe* - The law (or way) of Moshe." This teaches us that Sarah left the world in the same "way" that Moshe did; namely, by a Divine kiss.

Additionally, Sarah's body did not wither as she aged. We see this from the verse that says, "Sarah's lifetime was one hundred years, twenty years, and seven years" (*Bereishis* 23:1). The Torah could have just said, "Sarah's lifetime was one hundred and twenty-seven years." Why did God choose to express Himself by adding the word "years" after each group of numbers?

One answer to this is so that we can learn something by comparing one group of numbers to the other. For example, when she was twenty, she was as youthful as a seven-year-old girl (*Rashi* citing the *Bereishis Rabbah* 58:1; also see *Bereishis* 21:7 where it says that Sarah nursed many children in her old age).

This youthfulness is also mentioned with regard to Moshe, as the verse says, "His eye did not dim and his vigor did not diminish" (*Devarim* 34:7). Why didn't their bodies decline in old age? Furthermore, why would the Torah stress that Sarah was so youthful? Is it the Torah's practice to praise women's beauty?

Says the *Aron Eidus*, the weakening of the body comes to those who live a life based on materialism. This is because the nature of physicality is that it wanes and deteriorates. However, one who leads a life based on spirituality, in spite of being found in a materialistic world, will benefit even in a physical way. This is because the nature of the spiritual is that it is eternal. It never fades.

Herein lies the secret to Sarah's success. Although she was a full participant in this physical world, Sarah had an acute awareness of the spiritual realm. Sarah understood that every person has two components, a body and a soul.

Sarah's message was that whatever we do for our bodies in the physical world has ramifications on the soul and the spiritual realm. Therefore, Sarah taught that the body must serve the soul, and the physical world must be directed at assisting the spiritual domain.

It's as though Sarah lived in both the physical and spiritual spheres simultaneously. Sarah was able to walk on Earth and fly in Heaven at the same time. This assured that everything Sarah did was for a higher purpose. The Torah, in its eulogy for Sarah, hints at this dual citizenship. The verse says, "Sarah's lifetime was one hundred years, twenty years, and seven years, *Shnei Chayei Sarah* - [these were] the years of Sarah's life" (*Bereishis* 23:1).

Why was it necessary for the Torah to repeat at the end of the sentence, "*Shnei Chayei Sarah* - These were the years of Sarah's life?" Once the verse begins with "Sarah's lifetime was...," apparently that should be sufficient. For what purpose was this reiterated at the end of the verse?

The *Aron Eidus* suggests an alternative translation to the words "*Shnei Chayei Sarah.*" The Hebrew word "*Shnei*" can either mean "These are the years of" or it could mean "two." So, instead of translating the end of this verse to mean "These are the years of Sarah's life," it can be read as, "These were the two lives of Sarah."

This communicates to us that Sarah lived two lives. These two lives were not contradictory to one another; rather, they complimented each other. The dual life that Sarah lived was one in which she fully participated in the physical world, while concurrently living up to God's spiritual expectations of her.

In order to strike this balance, one must dedicate his physical experiences toward spiritual goals. Such was Sarah's greatness. She lived life with one foot on Earth, and the other in Heaven.

With this insight, we can understand that Sarah did not die. She just continued living in heaven. In light of this, the name of our portion takes on new meaning. Although Sarah "died" in this *parshah*, it is called "*Chayei Sarah* - the Life of Sarah." This teaches us that although Sarah died on Earth, she still kept on living in the spiritual domain that she had been operating in until now.

The life of Sarah serves as a huge lesson for us all. We can all obtain this level. All we need to do is remind ourselves that we function in two dimensions simultaneously. This awareness will help us make the right choices.

After *Shacharis*, prior to going off to work, let's say the words "*Shnei Chayei Sarah*" in order to set the course for the day on the right path.

May we all be blessed to live the life of Sarah, transforming the body into a soul by channeling physical activities into spiritual achievements, and thus being connected, always, to the fiftieth level of holiness. This is hinted to in the name "*Chevron*," the city in which Sarah was buried (*Bereishis* 23:19), which is formed with the letters "*Chibur Nun* - connected to the fifty." (The letter *nun* is numerically fifty.)

Chayei Sarah

From the Peaks to the Depths

Who today has not visited the *Kosel*, and the Machpelah Cave? For many of us, there is a definite similarity between the energy in these two places, yet they stand apart. What is the commonality and difference between the two?

This week's portion, *Chayei Sarah*, discusses the death and burial of our Matriarch Sarah.

What is the significance of the juxtaposition of Sarah's burial (mentioned at the beginning of this week's portion), with *Akeidas Yitzchak* (the Binding of Yitzchak, recounted at the end of last week's portion, *Vayeira*)?

The *Emunas Itecha* provides an insightful answer to this question. He explains that there are two holy places that are beloved to the Jewish people, and are antithetical to each other:

1) Mt. Moriah in Jerusalem

2) The Cave of Machpelah in Chevron

Mt. Moriah represents revelation, a place where the Divine presence is palpable and obvious to all. We learn this from the Mishnah in *Avos* (5:7) which lists the ten miracles that occurred on a daily basis in the Temple (i.e. on Mt. Moriah). Furthermore, Mt. Moriah - the site of *Akeidas Yitzchak* - was named "*Hashem Yireh*" (see *Bereishis* 22:14) because, as *Rashi* explains, this mountain is the location where God appears to His people throughout the generations.

The Cave of Machpelah, on the other hand, symbolizes concealment and the hidden aspect to God's presence. Although there is an actual place called Chevron, there is no real, defined shape to the cave. The Talmud in *Eruvin* (53:1) says that the Patriarchs and Matriarchs are buried in a cave beneath a cave, very deep under the ground.

Thus, Chevron - whose holy site is deep down under the Earth and hidden from our eyes - lies in direct contrast to Jerusalem, whose most sacred location is on a mountaintop, clearly visible to all.

The *Emunas Itecha* continues, "Essentially, destruction (*churban*) entails *bitul makom* (nullification of place) and *hester panim*" (concealment of [God's] presence). Thus, *churban* can occur only to defined entities where God's presence is noticeably apparent. After all, if there is no distinct location in the first place, how can it be destroyed? If God's presence is not exposed in the first place, how can it be concealed?

Hence we find that on account of our sins, the Temple on Mt. Moriah was destroyed, concealing the Divine presence, but never was the Cave of Machpelah affected in this way.

There are two sources in *Bereishis* that point to the concrete, defined nature of Mt. Moriah. In verse 22:4, Avraham notices the mountain from afar, indicating its outstanding and obvious appearance; and in verse 28:11, Yaakov encounters "the place" which, according to *Rashi*, was Mt. Moriah. (In both instances the word "*HaMakom* - **The** place" is used in reference to Mt. Moriah. The use of the definite article in itself suggests an explicit and obvious location.)

To summarize the ideas discussed thus far:

1) Mt. Moriah in Jerusalem represents the revealed presence of God, while the Cave of Machpelah in Chevron symbolizes His existence in a hidden form.

2) Since destruction entails the removal of a certain place and the concealment of God's presence, it follows that *churban* may be

> applicable to Mt. Moriah because it is a defined location where the Divine presence is revealed; but **never** to the Machpelah Cave, which is undefined in form and location, and where God's presence is already hidden.

The *Emunas Itecha* then develops this idea further as he applies this concept to our lives. Just as there is a revealed and hidden aspect to the dimension of place, so there is an overt and covert aspect to the dimension of self. Every individual is composed of an external body which is visible and which can be clearly defined, and an invisible, internal soul which cannot be delineated.

As we have already learned, *churban* can only affect places that are defined and revealed. Conversely, areas that are concealed and undefined in location will never experience *churban*. Similarly, our bodies may become ruined through the transgressions we commit, but our souls can never be destroyed. No matter what wrongdoings we carry out externally, the piece of God within ourselves remains untouched. All penitents who wish to return to God can do so from this point of inner, concealed holiness which is everlasting.

Now we can answer our original question regarding the significance of the juxtaposed topics of *Akeidas Yitzchak* and the burial of Sarah. The connection between *Akeidas Yitzchak* (which occurred on Mt. Moriah) and Sarah's burial (which took place in the Cave of Machpelah) is, in fact, what these locations represent. Mt. Moriah symbolizes the revealed aspect of holiness while the Machpelah Cave represents the hidden dimension. Even when destruction occurs in the revealed dimensions of place and self, there will always remain a concealed holiness which is eternal and indestructible.

May we be blessed to do what is right externally and tap into the internal hidden light by serving God with body and soul; so that, ultimately, we will merit leaving our places of exile and destruction, and make a public comeback to the holy city of Jerusalem.

Chayei Sarah

Smarty Pants

In a world that is so crooked, we need our heads screwed on straight. A confused society needs clarity. An upside-down generation needs to be put back on their feet. This requires a lot of wisdom.

There is a verse in this week's *parshah* that states, "And Avraham was old (***zaken***), advanced in years, and Hashem had blessed Avraham with everything" (*Bereishis* 24:1). The juxtaposition of the two parts of this verse seems odd. What is the connection between being old and being blessed with "everything"?

The *Gan Raveh* approaches this question based on the Talmud's statement (*Kiddushin* 32b) that a person is considered a ***zaken*** when he has acquired wisdom. The Talmud derives this understanding from the first two letters of the word ***zaken***, which stand for ***zeh kanah*** (this one has acquired).

The *Divrei Chanoch* explains how we are able to infer this, based on another Talmudic statement (*Nedarim* 41a): "If you are lacking wisdom, what have you acquired? If you have acquired wisdom, what are you lacking?" According to the *Divrei Chanoch*, the words ***zeh kanah*** (this one has acquired) must refer to wisdom - since the Talmud explicitly states that a person without wisdom has not acquired anything!

We could suggest another way of looking at the word ***zaken*** that hints at its connection with wisdom. In this approach, the letters of the word ***zaken*** stand for the words ***zeh kanah nun*** (this one has acquired the letter *nun*). The letter *nun* has the numerical value of fifty, hinting to the fifty levels of understanding. Therefore, a ***zaken*** is a person who has acquired the wisdom contained within all fifty levels.

This idea will help us understand the connection between the two parts of the verse, "And Avraham was old (***zaken***), advanced in years; and Hashem had blessed Avraham with everything." In order to be called a ***zaken***, a person must have acquired wisdom - all fifty levels of understanding. Once Avraham reached this level, he already had everything.

Today's world is characterized by mixed-up priorities and confusion between truth and falsehood. In such challenging times, wisdom is the key to a healthy, balanced, successful life. If we want to nip difficulties in the bud, we must begin with education.

We see an example of the value of wisdom at the beginning of King Solomon's reign (I Kings 3:5-14). Hashem appears to King Solomon in a dream and tells him, "Request what I should give to you." Instead of asking for wealth, or power, or long life, King Solomon asks for wisdom. Hashem is so pleased with this request that he even grants King Solomon the riches and honor that he didn't ask for.

The priority given to wisdom is also evident when we look closely at the *Amidah*. After the opening three blessings, in which we praise Hashem, the first request we make is for ***da'as***; wisdom and knowledge. In addition, the tallest letter in the Hebrew alphabet is ***lamed***. The letters of the word ***lamed*** also spell the word ***limud***, meaning "learning." The fact that ***lamed*** is the tallest letter indicates that ***limud*** is the highest priority, hinting once more to the extreme importance of acquiring wisdom.

There are three things we can do to acquire wisdom:

- Study.
- Pray for it.
- Seek advice from a wise person.

We should complete all three suggestions, not just for Torah knowledge itself, but also to know how to apply it in making the right choices in life - like who to marry, where to live, what schools to send the children to, and what type of livelihood to pursue. We require this wisdom when making decisions that completely alter the direction of our life.

May we be blessed to be filled with the knowledge of Torah, and blessed with the ability to apply that knowledge to our life experiences, so that we will have the clarity to decide which direction we need to take in a world that is filled with confusion and sophisticated stupidity.

Chayei Sarah

Taking the Oath

In today's society, you can hear people say in idle chatter "I swear to God," in order to make their point. The seriousness of an oath should be revisited. Any court of law would agree, and the Torah certainly does.

In this week's portion, *Chayei Sarah*, Avraham instructs his servant Eliezer to find a wife for Yitzchak (*Bereishis* 24:2-9). Not only does Avraham command Eliezer to go on this mission, but he goes so far as to swear him in (24:3).

One might wonder why it was necessary for Avraham to insist that Eliezer take an oath, when we find that Eliezer was such a trusted person. For example, it says that Eliezer ruled over all the possessions that Avraham had (24:2). This indicates that Avraham considered Eliezer trustworthy in monetary matters.

We also find that Eliezer is referred to as *Damesek* (15:2). In addition to the meaning that he came from Damascus, it also teaches us that he taught Torah to the masses. This is hinted to in the word *Damesek*, which is the acronym for *Doleh U'mashkeh* (to draw, and to give others to drink). From this we learn that Eliezer drew from his master's Torah, and gave to others so that they might also drink from those teachings (see *Yoma* 28b the opinion of Rebbi Elazar). So why didn't Avraham trust Eliezer, his faithful servant, to do this mission properly as well?

The *Beis Yisrael* says that as long as Eliezer was in Avraham's home - a place permeated with holiness, purity, and sanctity - he was affected by the spirituality and was in complete control of his evil inclinations. However, once Eliezer was no longer in that cocoon of the Divine presence, Avraham was concerned that he would lose his lofty levels and be impacted by the forces of impurity lurking in the outside world, and thereby not fulfill his mission properly.

In order to strengthen Eliezer before venturing outside, Avraham had Eliezer take an oath because the seriousness of an oath is something which encourages and empowers the person to do the right thing (see *Nedarim* 8a the opinion of *Rav Gidel* in the name of *Rav* who says that if a person takes a vow to learn a certain portion of Torah, he has made a great vow to the God of Israel). The *Emunas Itecha* says that this explains to us what the Talmud (*Niddah* 30b) says that before a soul descends from the Throne of Glory to enter into this world, they make the soul swear to be a righteous person and to not be a wicked person. This is in order to strengthen the soul so that it doesn't go astray with the drives of this world that pull us in every direction.

Not only does this apply when a person goes to a dangerous place, but it also applies when a person is about to embark on a journey to a dangerous time. Meaning, every Shabbos is an oasis of light and holiness, where the day lends itself to Torah study, prayer and *zemiros*, etc. However, right after Shabbos a person is about to fall into the darkness of the mundane, and could possibly drown in an ocean of lustful passions and heresy.

One practical lesson that we can learn from this *parshah* is that right before we make this transition (i.e. at the end of the third meal which stretches into the night representing bringing the light of Shabbos into the weekday), we should take an oath and say, "I am about to enter into the darkness; therefore, I swear to maintain spiritual activity during the course of this week, so that I don't drown in the ocean of lustful passions and heresy."

So may we all be blessed to take the oath in order that we carry out the Divine mission we've been sent to do.

Toldos

Inner and Outer

In this world, there are all types of people. This applies to righteous people as well. The important thing is how we treat our bodies and souls, because those two components are most complicated, and together they shape the human condition.

We all know that Yitzchak and Rivka were a unique and special couple. After following the events that led to their marriage in last week's portion, there really isn't much more to say other than, "The matter has come from God" (*Bereishis* 24:50). They truly were a match made in Heaven.

The *Zohar* reveals to us that, mystically speaking, Yitzchak and Rivka were indeed meant to be together. This is because on a deeper level Yitzchak represented the soul, whereas Rivka represented the body (*Midrash Ne'elam*, vol. 1, pgs. 129 & 131). I guess we could apply to them the age-old adage which dictates, "Opposites attract!"

Although they came from two completely different perspectives, they nevertheless complimented each other by working together harmoniously. This will become clarified after sharing the mechanics of how the body and soul are meant to work together as a team.

We all know that the human body has 613 parts (248 limbs and 365 sinews). Paralleling those 613 parts of the body are the 613 elements of the soul. We also know that there are 613 *mitzvos* in the Torah (*Makkos*, Ch. 3, *Eilu Hein Halokin*, 23b-24a, the opinion of *Rebbi Samlai* based on *Devarim* 33:4). It turns out that these three sets of 613 all parallel each other. The 613 *mitzvos* correspond to the 613 parts of the body, which in turn correspond to the 613 components of the soul.

Every time we perform one of the *mitzvos* with any limb of the body, we energize the component of the soul that is connected to that *mitzvah,* and to that part of the body. In turn, the limb that was used for that *mitzvah* is made holy as well by the soul that was just energized (for further analysis on this subject, see the first teaching in the *Toldos Yaakov Yoseph* by Rabbi Yaakov Yoseph Polonoye).

This illustrates the distinctive partnership that Yitzchak and Rivka shared. Together they worked at serving God by performing the *mitzvos*, thereby strengthening the soul and sanctifying the body.

This information will help us understand why Yitzchak loved Esav, their older son, while Rivka loved Yaakov, their younger son (*Bereishis* 25:28). The *Aron Eidus* teaches that there are two types of *tzaddikim* (righteous people) that come into the world.

The first type of *tzaddik* is one who is born with an evil inclination just like everybody else. However, through hard work this *tzaddik* overcomes his temptations and even transforms his evil inclination into a good inclination.

Conversely, there is a second type of *tzaddik* who is so holy that he is born with practically no evil inclination. Yaakov and Esav are examples of these two prototypes of *tzaddikim*.

From Yitzchak, who represented the soul, came Yaakov, the *tzaddik* with virtually no evil inclination. Whereas from Rivka, who represented the body, came the *tzaddik* Esav who possessed an evil inclination.

At first, both Yaakov and Esav were *tzaddikim* (see *Rashi Bereishis* 25:27 citing *Bereishis Rabbah* 63:10, the opinion of *Rebbi Levi*). Both of them served God. They just had different missions to carry out in life, appealing to different types of people.

Ironically, although Yaakov came from Yitzchak's aspect of the marriage, Yitzchak loved the Esav approach. The concept of transforming the evil inclination into a good one attracted Yitzchak. After all, that is Yitzchak's job because Yitzchak, the soul, is supposed to transform the body from a physical creation into a spiritual entity.

On the other hand, although Esav came from Rivka's aspect of the marriage, Rivka loved the Yaakov approach. This is because Rivka, the body, recognized the danger of falling prey to the evil inclination. Rivka, therefore, preferred a *tzaddik* who basically did not have an evil inclination. I guess we could say it again, "Opposites attract!"

So essential were these two models of *tzaddikim* that they were found at the heart of the Jewish nation. The holiest country on Earth, Israel, was given to the Jewish people by God (*Bamidbar* 33:53-34:15). The holiest city in Israel is Jerusalem (Mishnah *Keilim*, 1:6). The holiest place in Jerusalem is the Temple; and the holiest part of the Temple is the Holy of Holies (Mishnah *Keilim* 1:9). Inside the Holy of Holies was the Holy Ark (see *Melachim* 8:6). On top of the Ark were the two *Keruvim* (*Shemos* 25:18-22). The two *Keruvim* represented the two aforementioned types of *tzaddikim*. At the center and very core of the Jewish people, we are being shown that there is a need to have two different types of leaders with two diverse paths of service.

Although Esav himself eventually fell to temptation, in The End of Days, Esav and his descendants will, nevertheless, repent and return to the ways of holiness and purity. (See *Bereishis Rabbah* 63:12 citing *Rav Yudan* in the name of *Rav Eivu*, *Rav Pinchas* in the name of *Rav Levi* and the *Rabbanan* in the name of *Rav Simon* and *Rav*, based on *Bereishis* 25:29.)

This is hinted to when it says, "After that his brother emerged with his hand grasping on to the heel of Esav" (*Bereishis* 25:26). Esav's heel (*eikev*) which is at the "end" of the body represents the "End" of Days, the "*Ikvesa*" *D'meshicha*. Yaakov's grabbing of Esav's heel teaches us that in the "end," Yaakov will have control over Esav, bringing him back to God.

This returning of Esav is hinted to in a verse about the *Keruvim*. It says,

"*Up'neihem ish el achiv* - with their faces toward one another" (*Shemos* 25:20). The last letters of each of these four Hebrew words are *mem, shin, lamed, vav*. When unscrambled, these four letters spell *shalom* (peace).

The word *shalom* numerically equals 376 - the same exact numerical value as the name *Esav*, spelled with three letters: *ayin, sin, vav*. This shows us that in the end, Esav will be at peace. This is because Esav will be "complete," another definition of the word *shalom* or *shalem*. It is so interesting that this is all alluded to in the *Keruvim* which represent both the Yaakov and the Esav.

This, says the *Aron Eidus*, is the meaning of a difficult *Rashi* found in the very beginning of this week's portion. The first verse reads, "And these are the generations of Yitzchak" (*Bereishis* 25:19). *Rashi,* on the spot, comments, "Yaakov and Esav who are mentioned in the portion." Isn't it obvious from the text of the portion that Yaakov and Esav were Yitzchak's children? Why was it necessary for *Rashi* to tell us what is apparent to anybody who reads the continuation of the verses?

Rashi wants to teach us that ultimately both Yaakov and Esav will be considered Yitzchak's descendants, once Esav repents in The End of Days.

One way to synthesize our body and soul would be to pick one *mitzvah* a week (charity, for example), and every time we do that *mitzvah* with a part of our body, we can stop and think how we are strengthening the part of the soul connected to that *mitzvah.* We can think about how we are infusing sanctity into the limb that was utilized in fulfilling that *mitzvah.* This will help combine the body and soul into an orchestrated harmony.

May we all be blessed to synthesize our bodies and souls in a spiritually-healthy, balanced way by doing as many *mitzvos* as we can, permeating our essence with supernatural light, and may we merit to dance with our Cherubic *tzaddikim* back to our holy land, *Eretz Yisrael,* serving God in the *Beis Hamikdash.*

Toldos

The Undisputed Heavyweight Prayer Champ

The day that they create a pill or device that can change our circumstances into a more favorable situation, is the day that somebody is going to become exceedingly wealthy. We already possess such an instrument, and it is literally right under our noses.

This week's *parshah, Toldos,* begins with a description of Yitzchak and Rivka praying for children. The Torah continues by telling us that Hashem answered Yitzchak's prayer, but not Rivka's (*Bereishis* 25:21). The Talmud (*Yevamos* 64a) explains that the prayer of a righteous person whose parents were righteous (*tzaddik ben tzaddik*) is not comparable to the prayer of a righteous person whose parents were wicked (*tzaddik ben rasha*).

The implication of this statement is that it is better for a righteous person to be descended from righteous people than to have achieved righteousness on his own. Since Yitzchak had illustrious ancestors, whereas Rivka did not, the merit of Yitzchak's prayer seems to have been greater.

This idea, however, directly contradicts the Talmud's statement (*Berachos* 34b) that the place where returnees to Torah (*ba'alei teshuvah*) stand in the coming world will be inaccessible to righteous people who never strayed from the Torah path! This statement implies that *ba'alei teshuvah*, whose parents are not yet righteous, are better than righteous people with illustrious ancestry! How can we resolve this contradiction?

We could suggest that *ba'alei teshuvah* do, in fact, stand on a higher level than *tzaddikim*. We can explain this idea in a way that does not contradict the previous statement in the Talmud.

We can assume that Yitzchak and Rivka, like all parents-to-be, prayed for their children to be healthy and righteous. But Hashem had other plans. He wanted to bring the wicked nation of Esav into the world in order to keep the nation of Yaakov in check. Over the course of history, the role of Esav is to pounce on Yaakov the moment he begins to abandon his heritage, so that Yaakov will return to a righteous way of life.

Esav will never let Yaakov forget that he is different. As the saying goes, "If a Jew (Yaakov) doesn't make *kiddush*, then a non-Jew (Esav) will make *havdalah*." This seesaw of power is implied in Yitzchak's blessing to Esav, "When Yaakov goes down; you will be able to throw off his yoke from your neck" (*Bereishis* 27:40). Esav is given dominion over Yaakov during the times that Yaakov is failing in his life's mission of sanctifying Hashem's Name in the world.

Rivka, a righteous child from a wicked family, was a *ba'alas teshuvah* of the highest degree. Because of this, her prayer for righteous children was extremely powerful. Had Hashem accepted it, He would have been "compelled" to provide her with two righteous twins. There would have been no Esav in the world, and thus, no force to keep the Jewish people on the right path. As a result, the Jews would have eventually disappeared altogether, thereby destroying Hashem's vision for the world.

In order to prevent this chain of events from happening, Hashem ignored Rivka's prayer. Instead, He answered Yitzchak's prayer, which was on the slightly lower level of *tzaddik ben tzaddik*. This lower level provided Hashem with the opportunity to fulfill the request only partially; He did grant one righteous child (Yaakov), but He gave them a wicked one (Esav) as well. In this way, the world would always contain a force to keep the Jewish people on track.

We could suggest that this idea fits in exactly with the first statement that we mentioned from the Talmud. Although we initially assumed that the prayer of a *tzaddik ben tzaddik* is higher than that of a *tzaddik ben rasha*, the words of the Talmud say only that the two types of prayers **are not comparable**! And that's true, they are not comparable. You simply cannot compare the prayer of a *tzaddik ben tzaddik* to a prayer of a *tzaddik ben rasha*, because the prayer of a *tzaddik ben rasha* is by far greater. Hashem ignored Rivka's prayer not because her wicked ancestry detracted from the merit of her prayer, but only because God had a greater purpose to fulfill.

In this generation, we all have the status of *ba'alei teshuvah*, at least to some degree. As such, the power of our prayers is awesome. Let's try to improve our prayers a little bit. Here are some suggestions.

- Give charity before praying.
- Learn Torah before praying.
- Take the time to say a small section of the liturgy that you are going to say slow and loud.
- Add an additional prayer that you **want** to say besides the prayers you **have** to say.

May the Jewish nation be blessed with healthy and righteous children who will lead us back to the Holy Land, dancing on eagle's wings.

Toldos

God Bless You

Tikkun Olam is a very popular term throughout the Jewish world, crossing all lines of separation. However, what does it actually mean?

In this week's portion, *Toldos*, Yitzchak initially attempts to bless Esav but winds up blessing Yaakov instead. Yitzchak's blessing to Yaakov is, "And so God should give you from the dew of the Heaven, and of the fat of the Earth, and plenty of grain and wine" (27:28).

This episode raises at least two questions:

Firstly, why did Yitzchak originally want to bless Esav and not Yaakov? This difficulty is reminiscent of another question that many ask: Why did Yitzchak love Esav more than Yaakov? Didn't Yitzchak realize that Yaakov was a completely rightous person dwelling in the tents of Torah (25:27)?

Secondly, why are these blessings focused only on physical matters? Why doesn't Yitzchak bless his son with spiritual things? Aren't they the intention and purpose of Creation? Could someone of Yitzchak's stature not understand that? Not only doesn't he stress the spiritual blessings, he doesn't even mention them at all.

The Slonimer Rebbe explains that Yitzchak thought Yaakov and Esav were on two completely different paths of serving God. Yitzchak understood that Yaakov was likened to the Holy of Holies, completely disconnected from the physical realm, which means that Yaakov would serve Hashem with spirituality. However, Yitzchak perceived that Esav was on a different track. Esav was very much connected to the material realm and is described as "the man of the field" (25:27). This meant that Esav would serve God with physicality.

Yitzchak understood the *tikkun olam* would come about through this path of Esav, because God already has a dwelling place (so to speak) in the spiritual realm. However God's vision, desire, and aspiration for the lower world was that He should have a fitting dwelling place on the physical Earth (see *Tanchumah Bechukosai* 3). This will happen only when the mundane is lifted up, sanctified, and directed towards God. This is why Yitzchak loved Esav more than Yaakov, because Yitzchak perceived that it was Esav's approach - not Yaakov's - to serving God that would bring about the fixing of this world.

This also explains why Yitzchak wanted to bless Esav initially. Yitzchak did indeed recognize that Yaakov was a completely righteous person. It is exactly for that reason that Yitzchak never intended to bless Yaakov; not because he didn't want to, but because there was no need to. Yaakov is like an angel, and as such he does not need the assistance of a blessing to succeed in serving God because it is easy to be spiritual in a spiritual realm. However, Esav, who has the task of harnessing materialism and elevating it towards God, would be fraught with challenges in the physical realm. Elevating materialism is not an easy accomplishment.

Esav needed the assistance of a blessing to succeed at transforming this planet into an abode worthy of housing the Divine presence. This is why Yitzchak's blessings were all in physical terms. From this we should understand that one should attempt to take the physical and direct it towards the Divine.

Rivka, however, understood that Esav's involvement in the material world was not in order to bring it closer to God; rather, Esav's preoccupation with physicality was only to further satisfy his own lustful passions. Rivka understood that Yaakov would have to be the one to serve God on both paths simultaneously, and do the job his brother Esav failed to do. Eventually Yitzchak realized this as well, which led to his later blessing of Yaakov.

We should also try to elevate our physical realm into a spiritual place. One opportunity to accomplish this is on Shabbos. After a wonderful meal and a good rest, try to go to *shul* fifteen minutes earlier than usual in order to study Torah with the renewed strength we've just acquired.

Doing this will ensure that our *davening* afterwards will be especially powerful. This exercise will pave the way for repeated performances during the week. This is literally taking the physical and channeling it towards the spiritual.

May we all be blessed to elevate everything in the human world to the angelic realm, including ourselves, and thus merit witnessing the time when the universe will indeed be a spiritual place.

Toldos

Stealing From the Thieves

The Maggid of Mezritch once said that we can learn seven things from a thief.

1) Whatever he does, he does secretly.

2) Whatever he does not obtain today, he will try to obtain tomorrow.

3) He is loyal to his accomplices.

4) He is ready to sacrifice himself for the object of his desire, even if it has no value to others.

5) Once the desired object becomes his own, he loses interest in it and looks for a new one.

6) He is not afraid of hardship.

7) Nothing can make him change his trade, meaning he does not want to be anybody but himself.

Just imagine living a Torah life committed to these principals. We would really be able to go places!

No matter how many times we read about Yaakov's birth every year, it still baffles us that he was born in a very peculiar position - namely, grabbing onto his brother Esav's heel (*Bereishis* 25:26). Why do we even have to know about his unusual manner of entrance into the world?

Moreover, God gave Yaakov his name on account of grasping Esav's heel, as the root of Yaakov is *eikev*, heel (*Bereishis* 25:26, and *Rashi* there). In which way was this event so important that he had to be named after it? What was Yaakov even thinking by clutching Esav's heel?

The Midrash says that Esav is compared to the swine, because when a pig crouches it stretches out its hoofs that are split, as if to say, "Look, I am *kosher*," when in actuality it is not *kosher* because it does not chew its cud. Esav behaved in a similar fashion by trying to project himself as a righteous person when really, on the inside, he was the furthest away from righteousness (*Vayikra Rabbah* 13:5, based on *Vayikra* 11:7).

This brings us to another question. Where does the pig/Esav get a sign of *kashrus* from? God could have created a pig without a hoof, or with a hoof that is not split. Why does the pig/Esav deserve to have such a holy sign to begin with?

To make things worse, the Talmud tells us that in the future, Esav is going to wrap himself in a *tallis* (prayer-shawl) and sit amongst the righteous in *Gan Eden* (paradise). God will then come and drag him out (*Yerushalmi Nedarim*, Ch. 3, *Arba'ah Nedarim*, *halachah* 8, the opinion of *Rebbi Acha* in the name of *Rav Huna*, based on *Ovadiah* 1:4, and *Daniel* 12:3).

Why would Esav think that he deserves to sit with the *tzaddikim* in *Gan Eden*? Doesn't he know that he was a *rasha*? This is going to happen in the future when there will no longer be any falsity or concealment in the world, because the light of truth will shine so brightly. So, what does Esav think he's doing? Furthermore, if God Himself has to drag him out, it implies that nobody else could because of some claim that Esav has to be in *Gan Eden*. What legitimate claim could Esav possibly have?

There is a very fundamental lesson buried in all of this. That is that we are supposed to learn how to serve God by observing the wicked. The wicked of the world have invented many methods on how to obtain their lustful passions. For example, they are extremely motivated and zealous when they run after their evil impulses. If they don't succeed at first, they try and try again.

We must learn from their techniques, and use them in the service of God. We have to take the vehicles that they created, and drive them to a different and holy destination. (See the *Chovos Hal'vavos, Sha'ar Cheshbon Hanefesh,* Ch. 3, *V'Hashneim Asar*; *Kedushas Levi, Noach,* 6:9; *Zerah Kodesh, Ba'al Shem Tov* cited in *Tiferes Shlomo, Toldos, Vatikach Rivka.*)

This is why Rivka dressed Yaakov in Esav's clothing before sending him off to receive Yitzchak's blessings (*Bereishis* 27:15). The verse describes those clothes as being "*chamudos.*" Literally, this means "clean" or "cherished." However, there is another translation of that word, and that is "desires" (from the word "*chemdah*").

Esav's clothing represented all of his evil urges and negative proclivities. Rivka dressed Yaakov in them conveying to him the message that he must adopt all those drives and direct them into the service of Hashem.

Yaakov listened to his mother's advice. We can see this clearly when it says, "And Yaakov stole the heart of Lavan the Aramean by not telling him that he was fleeing" (*Bereishis* 31:20). When Lavan met Yaakov for the first time, he saw that Yaakov was eager to learn all of his tricks. Lavan thought that this was because Yaakov wanted to become a charlatan, just like Lavan. So Lavan, seeing Yaakov as his apprentice, taught him everything that he knew. But Lavan was mistaken. Yaakov only wanted to learn Lavan's *shtick* in order to utilize those tools in the service of God.

This explains why Esav thought that he actually deserved to sit in *Gan Eden* with the *tzaddikim*. When Esav looked around and saw all those *tzaddikim* sitting in paradise, he realized that they got there by learning from his creative methods which they applied to Divine service. Esav argued that since they all got there on his lapels, he deserved to sit amongst them.

Nobody could argue with Esav. After all, it was true. They did learn from

Esav's methodologies about how to serve God even better. Only God Himself, who knows what lurks in a man's heart, could drag Esav out of *Gan Eden*. God basically said that Esav's intentions were not to help people do *mitzvos* better. On the contrary, history has proven that Esav and his Edomite Empire have tried to prevent the Jews from performing the commandments. Through the ages they attempted to rip Jews away from Judaism. Therefore, there is no place for Esav amongst the righteous in *Gan Eden*.

Although it seems to be recommended to learn from the wicked, there are some dangers in doing so. Firstly, when we learn from the *resha'im*, they nurse from the holy sparks of the *mitzvos* that we are doing because of them. These holy sparks strengthen the wicked and their forces of evil in the world. They are then empowered to perpetrate even more criminal and malicious activities.

This is why God said that we don't need Bilaam to teach us zealousness. This is referring to the time when he saddled his own she-donkey early in the morning to go and curse the Jewish people. We don't require Bilaam's lesson because we already learned zealousness from Avraham who also saddled his own donkey early in the morning when he went to the *Akeidah* (*Sanhedrin*, Ch. 11, *Cheilek*, pg. 105b, *Bamidbar* 22:21, *Bereishis* 22:3). Learning from the wicked Bilaam would have given more strength to the dark side.

The *Yismach Moshe* (*Vayishlach*, 19 *Kislev*) adds that although, when initially learning to serve God, it's okay to learn from evil people; nevertheless, later on, when we have children or students, it's very dangerous to learn from them. This is because when our children or students see that we are looking over our shoulders to study the wicked, they will also be inclined to pay attention to the wicked. However, they may not understand why we turned to the wicked, and therefore they may not be as good at sifting as we are. They may accidentally pick up some of their bad habits and eventually go off the deep end.

The *Shevilei Pinchas* says that this is why at first, when Yaakov began his journey of serving God, he did learn from the wicked of his generation, Esav and Lavan. However, once he had his own children, he ran away from Lavan, and refused to hang around with Esav (*Bereishis* 31:17-18; *Bereishis* 33:14; *Bereishis Rabbah* 78:14). This is because he did not want his children to be influenced by their wickedness.

The *Shevilei Pinchas* adds that this could explain the difference between the names "Yaakov" and "Yisrael." "Yaakov" represents the path of learning how to serve God from the wicked. This is why God named him "Yaakov" after grabbing hold of Esav's "*eikev*" (heel). When Yaakov held onto Esav's heel, he was basically saying that I am going to follow in your footsteps. Meaning, you create the devices, and then I'll use them in Divine worship.

However, the name "Yisrael" represents an even higher level where the *tzaddik* learns from his own *kishkes* how to serve God properly. Through meditation and looking inward, he can find a reservoir of God-given talents and techniques that indicate the way to serve God even better (see *Bereishis Rabbah* 61:1). This approach is hinted to in the name "Yisrael." When this name is divided in half, it spells two words, and they are "*Yashar Kel* - straight to God." This means that we can go straight to God in our Divine service on our own, without the help of the wicked.

Once Yaakov had a family, he just wanted to be left alone, separated from the wicked. This is hinted to when it says later on in *parshas Vayishlach*, "And Yaakov was left alone" (*Bereishis* 32:25). But Esav's archangel would not leave him alone, and began wrestling with him in order to force Yaakov to continue learning from Esav (*Bereishis* 32:25). When the angel saw that Yaakov could not be swayed, he struck Yaakov's thigh (*Bereishis* 32:26). The thigh is the place from where we produce children. The angel meant to say that if I cannot convince Yaakov to study from the wicked, then at least I will be able to trap his children into doing so. This way the dark side can nurse off of their Divine service and be empowered to do more evil.

Besides, who knows, maybe we will be able to teach Yaakov's descendants how to actually be bad in the process.

But Yaakov would not let the angel go until the angel himself blessed Yaakov with the fortitude to be an even higher *tzaddik* who does not need to learn from the wicked, but rather draws from his own inner strength to get the job done properly.

So the angel, with no other choice, asks, "What is your name?" He replied, "Yaakov." The angel said that no longer will you be called Yaakov, representing the approach of learning from the wicked, but rather your name will be "Yisrael" representing the higher level of achieving perfection on your own (*Bereishis* 32:28-29).

The *Shevilei Pinchas* says that all of this explains where the pig/Esav got his holy sign of *kashrus* from. He got it from Yaakov who learned the tools of Divine service from Esav's creativity. Since Yaakov walked in Esav's footsteps, indicated by grabbing his heel, that explains why the sign of Esav's *kashrus* is in his foot or hoof, and not in the chewing of the cud.

Perhaps we could apply this lesson practically by reading up on successful people, even if they were not especially righteous, in order to learn methodologies for us to implement in our *avodas Hashem*. Who knows, if they receive merit because of us, maybe they will be motivated to live a more spiritually-based life.

We could suggest that this was precisely what Noach had in mind when he learned how to serve God from the wicked in his generation. This was his way of trying to save his generation, and even bring them around to Divine service. This was why Noach found *chein* (favor) in God's eyes (*Bereishis* 6:8). Meaning, whatever came Noach's way, from those decadent societies, he turned it around into something positive. This is hinted to in the verse that says that Noach found *chein* in God's eyes. The Hebrew letters that spell "Noach" are *nun, ches*. When spelled backwards, these letters spell the

Hebrew word *chein.*

But subsequently, let us creatively improve upon what we've learned from the wicked, drawing from our own inner strength, so that we don't constantly feed the forces of evil, and also so that our children and students aren't affected negatively.

May we all be blessed to learn from everybody what to do, how to do it, and what not to do, so that we, our children, our students, or anybody in the circle of our influence will continue waving the flag of "Yisrael" with the *tzaddikim* in *Gan Eden.*

Vayeitzei

The Dark Knight

The explorers thought that they would never make it out of the forest alive. It was so dark that they could not even see their hands right in front of their faces. Not to mention all the wild animals that threatened them as well. It was only because of that small glimmer of light, shining from a star when the clouds cleared a little, that they were able to guide themselves out of their dismal situation to safety. This is analogous to our mission on Earth: to explore a fascinating new world, and seek out the meaning of life; to live as a civilized nation; to boldly go where man has gone before. We may find ourselves in darkness, but as long as we cling to the light, we will be able to not just survive, but thrive.

As Yaakov fled from Esav his brother, who wanted to kill him, the verse says that he arrived at the place that was going to be the future site of the *Beis HaMikdash* (see *Bereishis* 28:11 and *Rashi* there based on *Bereishis* 22:4).

The story goes on to say that the sun set abruptly, and then Yaakov instituted *Ma'ariv*, the evening service. (See *Bereishis* 28:11, and *Chullin*, Ch. 7, *Gid HaNasheh*, pg. 91b, the opinion of *Rav Yitzchak*, and see the *Beraisah* in *Berachos*, Ch. 4, *Tefillas HaShachar*, pg. 26b).

Of what significance to us is the fact that Yaakov established *Ma'ariv* at night, specifically when the sun had set abruptly. How is this information relevant to our lives?

The *Lekach V'Halibuv* explains that praying *Ma'ariv* at night when it is dark comes to teach us that even in the darkest of times we can connect with God. Yaakov taught us that there is never a situation in which we are severed from Hashem. Therefore, we must never give up hope. This is because no matter how far we have drifted away, we can still attach ourselves to the Divine. Even if we have fallen to the lowest of places, we can always connect to God.

Now, there are two types of darkness. The first kind is a darkness that is anticipated. As difficult as it is to deal with darkness, we can still prepare ourselves for it. Once we know that darkness is on the way, we can organize ourselves by preparing the light and heating that will be required when the darkness actually arrives.

The second type of darkness is one that occurs suddenly. Not only do we have to struggle with the darkness, but now we are unprepared. Since the darkness took us by surprise, we are not ready, and we lack the necessary materials to withstand the gloomy blackness.

Obviously, the second type of darkness is worse than the first category. These two forms of darkness illustrate two types of tragedy that a person can experience.

The first type of calamity is one that we expect. For example, when a family has an older relative who has been ill for a while, and the doctors say that it's just a matter of time. We all know what is going to transpire inevitably. As difficult as this is, we can nonetheless brace ourselves and prepare for the eventuality by seeking therapy and making the necessary arrangements.

However, the second category of catastrophe is one that happens unexpectedly. For example, this type happens when somebody suddenly dies young. We are taken by surprise. We are not prepared, and therefore feel incredibly overwhelmed in addition to the biting pain of bitterness.

This is the significance of Yaakov introducing *Ma'ariv* specifically when it became dark suddenly. He was teaching us that not only can we connect with God in dark times, but we can even connect with Hashem during dark times that occur unexpectedly. This is the type of prayer that Yaakov created.

Moreover, Yaakov prayed the evening service when he was on his way out of the Promised Land (*Bereishis* 28:10). We all know that according to Jewish mysticism, Israel is a land of light, whereas all other countries are places of darkness.

Therefore, Yaakov's prayer takes on an added dimension. He was teaching us that we can connect with God through prayer even if we are found in the darkness of the Diaspora.

When you think about it, there were three levels of darkness when Yaakov prayed:

1) It was night.

2) It got dark suddenly.

3) Yaakov was on his way to the land of darkness.

In spite of all that, Yaakov prayed, teaching us that we can always get close to God through prayer even though we may be going through triple darkness.

When I saw this approach from the *Lekach V'halibuv*, I thought that perhaps this could answer a famous question. If I were to ask an audience of people who they thought was the greatest of the Patriarchs, I am sure that I would get all sorts of answers.

Personally, I would never be able to make such a call. Who am I to judge? However, the Midrash does take a stand on this issue.

The Midrash says that of the three Patriarchs, Yaakov was the greatest. This position is based on a verse in *Tehillim* (see *Bereishis Rabbah* 76:1 and see *Tehillim* 135:4). There are a number of reasons for this, but they are beyond the scope of this essay.

We also know that the Patriarchs founded the three services that we pray each day. Avraham composed *Shacharis* (The Morning Service), Yitzchak initiated *Minchah* (The Afternoon Service), and Yaakov established *Ma'ariv* (The Evening Service). (See *Berachos*, Ch. 4, *Tefillas HaShachar*, pg. 26b, the opinion of *Rebbi Yosi* in the name of *Rebbi Chaninah.*) Although *Shacharis* and *Minchah* are mandatory, as far as *Ma'ariv* is concerned, the Talmud says that the evening service is *reshus* (optional). (See *Berachos*, Ch. 4, *Tefillas HaShachar*, pg. 27b, the opinion of *Rebbi Yehoshua.*)

If the first two services are mandatory even though they were created by Patriarchs who are considered to be second fiddle to Yaakov, then certainly *Ma'ariv* should be mandatory because it was produced by an even greater person. How can it be that the greatest Patriarch institutes a service which is secondary to the services that lesser Patriarchs formed? It does not seem logical.

Perhaps we could suggest the following: Yes, it is true that Yaakov was the greatest Patriarch. Therefore, his service was not secondary to the others. What, then, does it mean that *Ma'ariv* is a *reshus*? Here, we could offer an alternative translation to the word *reshus*. One definition is "optional," as we mentioned earlier. However, *reshus* also has another definition - permission.

In other words, the type of prayer that Yaakov created gives us "permission" to connect with God even in the darkest of situations. Avraham only had the power to connect us with God when it was morning time, representing good times when the birds are chirping, and all is well. Yitzchak only had the strength to connect us with Hashem during the day when things are going smoothly.

They did not have the power to connect us with God in the most difficult of times and places. It is precisely because Yaakov was the greatest of the Patriarchs that he had the power to introduce a prayer that carries with it the strength to connect us with God even in the most trying of times.

Yaakov broke the ice and paved the way for us to attach ourselves with God even in the darkest chapters of our lives. Only the greatest of the Patriarchs could have accomplished such a feat.

We should make a special effort to pray the evening service. Before beginning, take a look out the window, observe the darkness, and declare that we are going to connect with God even through the pockets of darkness we are experiencing in our lives.

May we all be blessed with the knowledge that we can get close to God through prayer, and start afresh, even when the darkness springs up on us suddenly. In this merit, may Hashem rescue us speedily from darkness, by bringing us back to the promised land of light, at a time when there will be no more war, no more illness, no more poverty, and no more suffering.

Vayeitzei

Who's on First? What's on Second?

Hershel was at a crossroad. He did not know what to do. One medication would totally destroy his illness quickly, but there would be considerable pain. The other medication would work on strengthening the healthy part of his body, which would help avoid pain, but the illness would linger on inside of him for a long while before it eventually dissipated. Which pill would you take? Your answer may just define what type of person you are.

In this week's story, as Yaakov runs away from his brother Esav, to his uncle Lavan in Charan, he winds up staying overnight at the future site of the *Beis HaMikdash* (*Bereishis* 28:10-11). It is there that Yaakov takes a vow and says, "If God will be with me and guard me on this way that I am going, and give me bread to eat and clothes to wear, and I return in peace to my father's house, then Hashem will be for me a God - *V'hayah Hashem li Leilokim*" (*Bereishis* 28:20-21).

The Midrash comments on this, saying that God replied to Yaakov that since he used the word *V'hayah* (then) to accept God's sovereignty upon himself, therefore, God promises to give Yaakov's descendants a variety of blessings using the same word *V'hayah*. For example, regarding the final redemption, it says, "*V'hayah bayom hahu* (and it will be on that day) that a great *shofar* will be blown." (See *Bereishis Rabbah* 70:6, the opinion of *Rebbi Yehoshua D'sichnin* in the name of *Rebbi Levi*, citing verses in *Zechariah* 14:8; *Yeshaya* 11:11; *Yoel* 4:18; *Yeshaya* 27:13.)

This may make us wonder what benefit there is in receiving these blessings specifically through the word *V'hayah*. What difference does it make to us that God used that wordage to promise us gifts? As far as we are concerned, we just want the blessings. The manner in which they come is irrelevant and unimportant. What advantage is there in receiving the blessings by God using the specific word *V'hayah*?

Let us begin by sharing an idea found in the *Zohar*. By the Burning Bush, God said, "This is My *Shmi* (name) forever, and this is My *Zichri* (remembrance) from generation to generation" (*Shemos* 3:15). In the preface to the *Tikkunei Zohar* (pg. 4b) it says that the word *Shmi* is numerically 350. If you add the number 15 from the first half of God's *Shem Havayah* (*yud hey*) to that, then you get the number 365, which represents the 365 negative commandments.

On the other hand, the word *Zichri* is numerically 237. If you add the number 11 from the second half of God's *Shem Havayah* (*vav hey*) to that, then you get the number 248, which represents the 248 positive commandments. This teaches us that the 365 negative commandments are connected to the letters *yud hey*, whereas the 248 positive commandments are connected to the letters *vav hey*.

Based on this *Zohar*, the *Meor Einayim* (*Parshas Bereishis*, pg. 13b, *Amru Razal*) says that this explains why the Hebrew word for sin is "*aveirah*," whereas the Hebrew word for a good deed is "*mitzvah*." The word *aveirah* is spelled with five Hebrew letters: *ayin*, *veis*, *yud*, *reish*, *hey*. When you unscramble these letters and divide them into two words, you get "*Avar-Kah*" (meaning, one who transgressed "*Kah*" or "*yud hey*"). This teaches us that when a person does an *aveirah* by disobeying one of the 365 negative commandments, he is actually damaging the letters *Kah*, or *yud hey*, from God's Name.

However, when a person does a *mitzvah* from the 248 positive commandments, he strengthens the *vav hey* in God's Name. One can see this clearly in the Hebrew word *mitzvah*, which has the letters "*vav hey*" in it. When I saw this, I wondered about the significance of the first two letters of the word *mitzvah* (*mem tzadi*). I thought that maybe they serve as an acronym for "*meyached tziruf* - to unify the combination of." In other words, when we do a *mitzvah*, we are *meyached* the *tziruf* of the letters *vav hey* by strengthening them.

In any case, the Talmud teaches us that a positive commandment has the power to push away a negative commandment (*Yevamos*, Ch. 1, *Chamesh Esrei Nashim*, pg. 7a). For example, although it is forbidden to wear *SHA'ATNEZ*, a garment mixed with wool and linen; nevertheless, one can have that very mixture on a pair of *tzitzis* (fringes) because the positive *mitzvah* of *tzitzis* pushes away the negative commandment of *SHA'ATNEZ*.

The *Ramban* (*Shemos* 20:8) offers a reason for this by saying that, in general, when a person performs a positive commandment, it comes from a place of love. However, in general, when a person refrains from a negative commandment, it stems from a place of fear, because of the possible consequences. Since serving God from love is greater than serving God from fear, then a positive commandment can push away a negative one.

However, this brings us to another difficulty. Why did God choose to spell His special Name *Havayah* with the *yud hey* preceding the *vav hey*? This order implies that the 365 negative commandments (represented by the *yud hey*) are greater than the 248 positive commandments (represented by the *vav hey*). Apparently, God should have spelled His Name the other way around, with the *vav hey* before the *yud hey*, because love is greater than fear.

The *Shevilei Pinchas* cracks this case wide open by quoting a famous verse in *Tehillim* (34:15): "Turn from evil and do good." He says that one thing we learn from the order of this verse is that when it comes to serving God, we must first wash ourselves clean from the sins of the past (turn from evil), and only then proceed to engage in the performance of *mitzvos* in the future (do good). The verse reads like this; "Turn away from evil, **and**

afterwards do good."

If we do not first cleanse ourselves from the spiritual filth of the past, then how can we approach the service of God? This would constitute a lack of respect. After all, it says, "Because it is forbidden to enter into the king's gate in a garment of sackcloth" (*Esther* 4:2). Often, in *Megillas Esther*, the reference to *HaMelech* (The King) can be taken on two levels. On the one hand it refers to Achashveirosh, the earthly king at that time; but on the other hand it is a hint to The King of Kings, God. So, if it is forbidden to appear before the mortal King Achashveirosh with dirty clothing, then how much more so is it forbidden to approach The King of Kings with disgusting clothes.

The *Shevilei Pinchas* suggests that it is for this very reason that God spelled His Name *Havayah* the way that He did. Although it is true that *vav hey* (connected to the 248 positive commandments) is greater than the *yud hey* (connected to the 365 negative commandments) because love is greater than fear, God specifically spelled His Name the other way around (*yud hey* and then *vav hey*) in order to caution us that first we have to tend to *yud hey* and purify ourselves of negative sins of the past, and only then can we begin to be involved in the *vav hey*, positive *mitzvos* of the future.

Now, everything that we mentioned up until now is a great approach for those of us who happen to be *tzaddikim* (righteous people). Because, truly righteous people do not have that much sin to begin with, and even the "wrongdoings" that they do have are not actual sins but rather that which smatters of sin. For *tzaddikim* it is easy to repent on the "sins" of the past and get to work on the *mitzvos* of the future.

However, for the rest of us simple folk, who have committed many sins in our lives, some of which may be very serious ones, it is very hard to first shed the spiritual pollution of the past before getting involved with the *mitzvos* of the future. If we refrain from doing *mitzvos* until we first break all the bad habits of the past, we might never get around to ever doing *mitzvos* to begin with, and that is dangerous.

Therefore, for the regular guy, the way to approach the service of God would be to do the *mitzvos* anyway, and hope that the light of those *mitzvos* will dispel any pockets of darkness that we still harbor within our constitutions. The new reading of our verse would go like this: "Turn away from evil, **through** doing good." Actually, there was a debate between two personalities in Jewish history who argued about which of these two approaches should be espoused. Those two people were Yaakov Avinu and Yosef HaTzaddik.

Before Yaakov died, Yosef brought his two boys (Menasheh and Efraim) to be blessed by their grandfather. Yosef positioned Menasheh and Efraim in front of Yaakov in such a way that Yaakov's right hand would go on Menasheh's head, and his left hand would be placed on Efraim's head. However, Yaakov crisscrossed his hands and did just the opposite. Yosef tried to set Yaakov's hands straight, but Yaakov refused (*Bereishis* 48:17-19).

The *Sfas Emes* (*Mikeitz-Chanukah*, citing his grandfather, the *Chidushei Harim*) explains what the argument between Yaakov and Yosef was. He teaches that Menasheh and Efraim represented two different approaches in *avodas* Hashem. Menasheh represented "Turn from evil." We can see this in his name, Menasheh, which comes from the word *Nashani* (to forget) the *Amali* (hardships or sins) (see *Bereishis* 41:51; and *Tehillim* 7:17) of the past by doing *teshuvah* on them.

However, Efraim represented "do good." We can see this from his name, Efraim, which comes from the word *hifrani* (fruitful) (*Bereishis* 41:52), which refers to the fruits of fulfilling the positive commandments.

Now, Yosef was given the title "HaTzaddik," the most righteous person that ever lived. As such, Yosef was a huge fan of the approach in *avodas* Hashem which dictates to turn away from evil first and only then move on to do the positive *mitzvos*. This is why Yosef named his firstborn son Menasheh (representing removing the sins of the past) and only then called his second son Efraim (representing performing the *mitzvos* of the future). Yosef set up his family that way to teach us that this is the order in which things need to take place.

It is for this reason that Yosef insisted that Yaakov's right hand rest upon Menasheh, and his left hand rest upon Efraim. This is because, generally speaking, the right comes before the left. Therefore, placing the hands in the way Yosef wanted would be a stamp of approval that his approach in *avodas* Hashem is the one to be adhered to.

Yaakov said to Yosef that he was so proud of him because Yosef had turned out to be such a *tzaddik*. However, Yaakov argued that while this approach worked for the righteous (including Yaakov himself), it would, nevertheless, be harmful for the multitudes of regular people who are not *tzaddikim*. So, Yaakov crisscrossed his hands showing that, for most of us, we have to just start doing the positive *mitzvos* (Efraim) and then hope that their light will eradicate any spiritual contamination within our systems (Menasheh).

We could suggest that the very act of crisscrossing the hands shares with us a message, and that is, that although this may not be *glatt* (straight or ideal), it is, nonetheless, a necessity.

The *Shevilei Pinchas* continues by saying that when Yaakov was on his way to Lavan, he understood with Divine inspiration, that he was going there to begin building the Jewish family. Yaakov foresaw prophetically that not all of his children would be *tzaddikim*. Therefore, Yaakov prayed to God that He accept his children's mode of service, which most often will be by doing the positive commandment before purging themselves of the blemishes of sin. When the majority of Jewish people serve Hashem in that way, they will be putting the letters *vav hey* (positive) before the letters *yud hey* (negative). When that happens, a new combination of God's Name is formed, and that is "*V'hayah*!"

Therefore, Yaakov begins his prayer with the word *V'hayah,* implying that even when my children approach Your service in the way of "*V'hayah*-ness", placing the *vav hey* (positive) before the *yud hey* (negative), please accept it even though it is out of order. This is why *Rashi* adds that Yaakov asked, "that no defect will be found in my seed" (*Bereishis* 28:21, citing *Sifri, Devarim* 6:4). With this he meant, that even if their approach is not ideal, and even backwards, please consent to it.

Not only that, but the next word of Yaakov's prayer (right after *V'hayah*) is "*Havayah.*" (*V'hayah Havayah li Leilokim*) This juxtaposition was intended to imply that Yaakov asked of Hashem that He not only accept the people's service of *V'hayah*, but that Hashem should even transform it from *V'hayah* (whose out-of-order-ness represents harshness and strict justice) into *Havayah* (which is in order, representing mercy and compassion). In other words, Yaakov requested from God that He credit the Jewish people as if they did it the ideal way.

Yaakov argued that logically this should be the case because, deep down, every Jew wants to serve Hashem the ultimate way. It's just that we are confronted with so many issues, that we find it so hard to lift ourselves to that level. Since our intent is to be like a *tzaddik*, then we ought to be treated that way because God always considers a good intent as if it was actually completed (*Kiddushin*, Ch. 1, *Haishah Niknis*, pg. 40a).

God acquiesced, and even promised to bring the final redemption in the merit of the Jews' service that would be like the essence of *V'hayah*. That's why God said, "***V'hayah** bayom hahu yitakah b'shofar gadol* - And it will be on that day that a great *shofar* will be blown..." (*Yeshaya* 27:13).

Perhaps we could suggest a few practical applications of these ideas to implement in our daily living. First of all, take one *mitzvah* a day, and before performing it, do a quick *teshuvah* on the sins of the past by saying, "Dear

God, I am so sorry for all my wrongdoings, please forgive me, I'll try better next time." Then, do the *mitzvah*. In this way, we are connected (at least a little bit) to the ideal approach of "Turn away from evil" and then "do good."

Additionally, we should pick one *mitzvah* and say the preparatory prayer "*Hineni Muchan Um'zuman*" that precedes it, because in the text of that liturgical passage it says that we are doing this, "To unify the Name '*yud hey*' with '*vav hey*' in perfect unity." This, too, will remind us to do a quick *teshuvah* on the sins of the past (*yud hey*) before doing the *mitzvos* of the future (*vav hey*).

However, we must always remember that it is better to do the *mitzvos* anyway, even if we have not yet done *teshuvah*, rather than not doing the *mitzvos* at all. Then, after doing the *mitzvah*, say, "Dear God, please allow the light of this *mitzvah* to burn out any spiritual poisons within my personality."

By implementing both of these ideas, we are demonstrating a desire to be like a *tzaddik*. At the same time, we humbly realize that we are only human, and as such we just try our best to serve God in the best way we can.

May we all be blessed with *tzidkus* and the ability to remove any negativity from our personalities before engaging in proactive *mitzvos*, so that our *avodah* is holy and pure. But if that task is too difficult for us, then may we be blessed to just get to work with Torah study and *mitzvah* performance so that their light will dispel any pockets of darkness within our constitutions, so that we deserve to witness the name *Havayah*, in order: remember us, and come to redeem us.

Vayeitzei

How to Make an Impression

Today's modern man can access practically anything he wants at just the touch of a button. Secular influence is on the rise; so many people are exposed to so many horrifying and inappropriate behaviors. Those who want to preserve holiness are scrambling for ways of fortifying themselves. The answer may not be without, but it may be found within.

In this week's portion, Yaakov went to sleep on the future site of the *Beis HaMikdash,* and had a dream in which a ladder was set up on the Earth. The ladder reached from the ground into the Heavens and angels of God ascended and descended on it (28:12). *Yonasan Ben Uziel* and the *Da'as Zekeinim Miba'alei HaTosfos* on this verse (based on *Bereishis Rabbah* 68:12) comment that the angels who ascended the ladder were the same angels who went to destroy Sedom and save Lot (i.e. Gavriel and Raphael).

These angels had been banished from returning to the Heavens on account of two sins they committed whilst in Sedom. Firstly, they revealed to Lot the Divine secret that Sedom would be destroyed. Secondly, they credited themselves as the destroyers of Sedom and did not attribute that power to God (see *Bereishis* 19:13). They were wandering around this Earth for 138 years until this moment of Yaakov's dream, where they were accepted once again back in Heaven after accompanying Yaakov on his journey.

One might wonder how such holy angels came to sin? Additionally, why were these angels chosen specifically to escort Yaakov out of *Eretz Yisrael*? Additionally, how did they suddenly achieve atonement?

The *Emunas Itecha* says that the ladder represents a person's soul. Its legs, like our feet, stand on Earth and its top, like our head, reaches into the

Heavens - representing and teaching us, symbolically, that what a person does here on Earth can have an effect even on the Heavens themselves (see *Zohar Parshas Tzav* pg. 31). The effect can be positive or negative.

We are already familiar with the concept that a person is affected by his surroundings (see *Rambam Hilchos De'os* 6:1). Although this is true and, therefore, makes it very important to try and live in an environment that is conducive to spirituality; nevertheless, we find a degree of spiritual deterioration, even in the best of communities, resulting from secular influences infiltrating our neighborhoods. It becomes increasingly hard to rely upon a spiritual cocoon in order to grow in the holy and pure ways of our Torah.

This means that we have no choice; we must build ourselves to such a degree that not only are we resistant to outside influences, but we also make a positive impact on our surroundings. This idea is even more crucial for those people, who for whatever reason, do not live in a spiritually-inclined community or for people whose livelihood takes them around the world to places outside of Torah bubbles.

In *Shemos* (12:12) God says that He Himself will pass though Egypt to slay the firstborn. The Passover *Hagaddah* expounds on this verse that God meant to say that it is I, not an angel, who will kill the firstborn Egyptians. The Arizal explains that God had to do the job Himself, because the Egyptians were so abominable in their misbehavior. They turned Egypt into an impure place to such an extent that, even if an angel were to enter that country, it would have been affected in a negative way. Only God Himself could enter and exit the land unscathed. So it was with Sedom. The people of Sedom were wicked and sinned against God exceedingly (*Bereishis* 13:13), and it was considered the worst village of all time (see *Bereishis Rabbah* 41:9).

The two angels who entered Sedom came to sin, even though they were so holy, because they were impacted negatively by the Sodomites. This is an example of people having an effect on their surroundings, including heavenly beings, in a negative way. Having been banished from the Divine court, the angels were broken. Only a *tzaddik* could fix their predicament; and not just any *tzaddik*, but the type of *tzaddik* who was so powerful that he was not negatively affected by evil surroundings and, moreover, had a positive effect on those very places.

Yaakov was that type of righteous person. For fourteen years prior to his trip to Lavan, Yaakov hid out in the Torah Academy of Eiver, fortifying himself with sanctity (see *Bereishis Rabbah* 68:12 and *Rashi Toldos* 28:9) so that he would not be impacted by the impurities of Charan; and it worked. Even though Yaakov was with Lavan for twenty years, he never adopted Lavan's wicked ways (see *Rashi Vayishlach* 32:5). Not only that, but Yaakov even had a positive impact at that time on the souls of the people who perished during the Great Flood. These souls were reincarnated into the sheep of Lavan's flock. Because of Yaakov's influence on the souls, they were given another chance to be recycled again as Jews throughout the ages (see the *Yalkut Reuveini VaYeitzei* citing *Gali Razya*).

It was because of the angels' need to be rectified, and Yaakov's ability to affect those around him, that those same angels who went to Sedom were specifically chosen to accompany Yaakov out of *Eretz Yisrael*. Just by being in Yaakov's presence, they were positively affected and fixed, and thereby returned to their original status. This is the explanation for how they were suddenly forgiven.

We, too, can make a positive impact on our surroundings which will fortify us against negative influences. In our homes or places of work, we can create a spiritual environment by having *sefarim*, Jewish music, and pictures of *Gedolim* there.

Additionally, keep the name of God on our lips at all times with statements like "Thank God," "Please God," etc. Above all, deal honestly in business and treat people with respect and with a smile. This will impress the people around you in such a way that they will also be more inclined to lead an honest and holy life.

May we all be blessed that not only do we climb the spiritual ladder of success, but that we also make a positive impact on everything and everybody around us, so that even the angels and reincarnated souls benefit from a complete atonement. May we live to see the day that God Himself redeems us from our current exile, just as He did in Egypt.

Vayeitzei

Climbing the Ladder of Success

The mountaineers faced the Eiger Mountain in the Swiss Alps with awe and trepidation. Having heard that it was nicknamed "Murder Wall," they were concerned that the heavy rock fall would seal their fate. How would they go about reaching the peak safely? Obviously, the right equipment would be necessary. Similarly, we must use the correct tools when climbing the spiritual mountain of success.

At the beginning of this week's portion, *Vayeitzei*, we read that Yaakov lay down to sleep and had a dream (*Bereishis* 28:11-12). In the dream, there was a ladder which was stationed on the ground, its top reaching the Heavens.

Rashi in 28:17 (citing *Bereishis Rabbah* 69:7 the opinion of *Rebbi Elazar* in the name of *Rebbi Yosi Ben Zimra*) informs us that the foot of the ladder stood in Be'er Sheva, its center faced the Temple, and its top was opposite Beis El.

We can, perhaps, understand why the Midrash mentioned that the middle of the ladder faced the Temple, since we appreciate the significance of the *Beis HaMikdash,* but why was it important to reveal that its peak faced Beis El and that its base was in Be'er Sheva? What do these two places signify?

Furthermore, the Midrash (*Bereishis Rabbah* 68:12) says that although Yaakov actually saw a ladder in his dream, the *sulam* then appeared to him as the ramp leading to the outside altar of the Temple. And finally, that it resembled Mount Sinai. What is the significance of these symbols?

(Interestingly, the Hebrew word for "ladder," as written in the text, is *sulam* (spelled *samech, lamed, mem*). These letters can be rearranged to read *semel*, meaning "symbol" or "sign" (see *Ba'al HaTurim* 28:12), indicating that the *sulam* that Yaakov dreamt of symbolized several things.)

We could suggest, in answer to the latter question, that the three perceptions of the *sulam* correlate with the three pillars on which the world was created (*Avos* 1:2), which, in turn, correspond to the three Patriarchs, as follows:

1) The **ladder**, representing **kindness**, correlates with **Avraham Avinu.** Since a ladder is often used as a tool for performing acts of kindness (for example helping someone to reach for something, rescuing people in an emergency, etc.), we could suggest that the ladder symbolizes *chessed*, or *gemilus chasadim*, and therefore represents Avraham, who was consistently benevolent to fellow human beings.

2) The **ramp**, representing **prayer**, correlates with **Yitzchak Avinu.** Yitzchak was brought as an offering to God at the *Akeidah*, and therefore epitomizes prayer, since we are told in the Talmud (*Berachos* 26b the opinion of Rebbi Yehoshua Ben Levi) that *tefillah* nowadays serves as a substitute for offerings. Yitzchak is therefore symbolized by the ramp leading to the Altar in the Temple, where the *Avodah* took place.

3) **Mount Sinai**, representing **Torah** correlates the third Patriarch, **Yaakov Avinu.** We are told in *Bereishis* (25:27), that Yaakov was "a dweller of tents," that is, he was constantly found in the tents of Torah, immersed in Torah study. Yaakov therefore represents Torah, symbolized by Mount Sinai, where the Torah was given to the Nation of Israel.

Thus we see that the *sulam,* in its various forms, corresponds to the three foundations of the world's existence - Torah, *avodah* and *gemilus chasadim;* as well as to the three Patriarchs - Avraham, Yitzchak, and Yaakov.

Parenthetically, one may ask what the difference is between this Mishnah (which states that the world stands on Torah, *avodah*, and *gemilus chasadim*), and the one we find in *Avos* 1:18 which states that the world exists on the three traits of *din* (judgment), *emes* (truth) and *shalom* (peace). Is this a contradiction to the three pillars mentioned in 1:2?

In answer to this question, *Rabbeinu Ovadiah M'Bartenura* encourages us to focus on the difference in language used in the two *mishnayos*. In 1:2, the word ***omed*** is utilized, whereas in 1:18, the word ***kayam*** is employed. *Omed*, stands, indicates that the foundation of the world stands on these things, i.e., that the world was created for the sake of Torah, *avodah*, and *chessed*. However, the word *kayam*, exists, implies that the world would **not** have been created for the sake of *din*, *emes*, and *shalom*; rather, once the world was already in existence, then there was sufficient reason for it to be **maintained** for the sake of these values. The *Tosafos Yom Tov* provides support for this idea as he notes that a version of the Mishnah 1:2 exists which actually uses the word ***nivra***, created, instead of *omed*.

The *Meshech Chochmah* provides a different approach in answering this question as he maintains that Torah, *avodah*, and *gemilus chasadim* are, in fact, synonymous with *emes*, *din*, and *shalom*. The Torah is comparable to *emes*, he explains, as Torah conveys to us the truth!

Gemilus chasadim correlates *shalom* as acts of kindness create peace amongst people. Finally, the *Meshech Chochmah* links *avodah* with *din*, as he points out that the *Sanhedrin* (Court of Law) had to be situated in a place where the outer Altar of the Temple was within their view. (Please note that the *Meshech Chochmah* provides an in-depth, detailed explanation of this connection, which is beyond the scope of this work.) Thus, the *Meshech Chochmah* teaches us that the qualities of Torah, *avodah*, and *gemilus chasadim* (synonymous with *emes*, *din*, and *shalom*) were sufficiently important to warrant not only the creation of the world, but its maintenance as well.

Returning to our original idea, we find another hint to the association between the *sulam* and the *Avos* in the verse following the one in which the *sulam* is mentioned (28:13), where God speaks to Yaakov saying, "I am Hashem, God of **Avraham** your father and God of **Yitzchak**; the ground upon which **you** [Yaakov] are lying, to you I will give it..."

The Torah here refers by name to Yaakov's father and grandfather as well as addressing Yaakov himself. We could therefore suggest that the juxtaposition of these two verses serves as an additional support to the notion that the *sulam* represents the three Patriarchs. Furthermore, as the *Yalkut Me'am Lo'ez* (*Bereishis* 28:13) points out, the ladder stood specifically on three legs, indicating yet again its connection with the three Patriarchs.

One further allusion to the relationship between the Patriarchs and the ladder is gleaned from the numerical value of the word *sulam*. When spelled with a letter *vav* (*samech, vav, lamed, mem*), *sulam* has the *gematria* of 136. Three other words that share the exact same numerical value are ***Tzom*** (*tzadi, vav, mem* - meaning "a fast"), ***Kol*** (*kuf, vav, lamed* - meaning "voice") and ***Mamon*** (*mem, mem, vav, nun* - meaning "money"). What is the significance of these associations?

If we open the *machzor* for *Rosh HaShanah/Yom Kippur* and turn to the section "*Unesaneh Tokef*" in the *Mussaf* service (composed by Rabbi Amnon of Mainz, Germany) where it says: "*U'teshuvah u'tefillah u'tzedakah ma'avirin es ro'a hagezeirah* - Repentance, prayer, and charity cause the evil decree to pass over," we will find written above those three words, three other corresponding words.

They are...

- Above "U'Teshuvah" it says "*Tzom*" (fast).
- Above "*U'Tefillah*" it says "*Kol*" (voice).
- Above "*U'Tzedakah*" it says "*Mamon*" (money).

The *sulam*, with a numerical value of 136, represents *Tzom*, *Kol*, and *Mamon* (as they all share the same *gematria*), which, in turn, correspond to *teshuvah*, *tefillah*, and *tzedakah*. How do these relate to the Patriarchs?

We could suggest that *tzedakah*, like *chessed*, corresponds to our forefather Avraham. *Tefillah* represents Yitzchak, as we explained earlier; and finally, *teshuvah* can be linked to Yaakov because, like the Torah (which is what Yaakov commonly symbolizes), *teshuvah* preceded Creation (see *Pesachim* 54 pg. 54a, *Braisa* quoted there).

So, through the juxtaposition of verses and numerical values, we obtain further support to the idea that the *sulam* represents the *Avos*.

Finally, we read in *Vayikra* (16:3) of God's instructions to Aharon, via Moshe, regarding entering the Sanctuary. Hashem says, "***B'zos** yavo Aharon el HaKodesh* - With **this**, Aharon shall go into the Sanctuary." The *Nachal Kedumim* asks on this verse; with what Aharon was commanded to enter the Holy Temple? What does ***zos*** refer to?

If we take the *gematria* of the word ***zos*** (spelled *zayin, aleph, taf*), he explains, we find that it equals 408, which is the sum of 136 x 3! On a deeper level, God was instructing that Aharon enter the Kodesh with "*zos*-ness" (408), with the cumulative essence of *Kol, Tzom*, and *Mamon*; of *teshuvah, tefillah, tzedakah*; and with the holiness of our Patriarchs - Avraham, Yitzchak, and Yaakov.

When all is said and done, the ladder that is mentioned in this week's portion is always referred to as "*sulam* Yaakov" and never "*sulam* Avraham" or "*sulam* Yitzchak." We could propose, then, that of all three qualities that the Patriarchs represent - *gemilus chasadim, avodah*, and Torah - Torah study, which Yaakov represents, has an advantage over the others. (Please note we are obviously **not** negating the vital importance of prayer and kind deeds!)

The preference of Torah-represented by our Patriarch Yaakov - is alluded to in *Bereishis Rabbah* (76:1 the opinion of *Rebbi Pinchas* in the name of *Rebbi Reuven*), where Yaakov is selected as the choicest of *Avos*. The Midrash brings proof from *Tehillim* (135:4) where King David says, "For

God selected Yaakov for His own." Thus, the ladder which transformed to an image of Mt. Sinai - correlating with our forefather Yaakov - becomes the primary symbol.

Where do we find an allusion to this concept in this week's portion? How do we see that Torah takes precedence over *avodah* and *gemilus chasadim?*

The ideas we will discuss in answering this question will also settle our initial query regarding the significance of Be'er Sheva and Beis El. We learn in *Bava Kama* (82a) from the *Dorshei Reshumos*, that when the Torah mentions the word *mayim* (water) it is simultaneously referring, on a deeper level, to Torah. Be'er Sheva is thus not merely a place, but also symbolizes something far more profound. The word *be'er* means "a well" - i.e. from where water is drawn. As we already mentioned, water symbolizes Torah. Moreover, *sheva* is the number seven which also represents Torah.

The Talmud (*Shabbos* 116a, the opinion of *Rebbi* and *Rav Shmuel Bar Nachmeini* in the name of *Rebbi Yonason*) states that there are actually seven books of Moses and not five. (This is because the book of *Bamidbar* is considered three separate books by our Sages as they deem Ch.10, vs.35-36 - which is cordoned off by two large inverted letter *nuns* as a book in its own right.) Thus, we see that Be'er Sheva, on which the base of the ladder rested, represents Yaakov and, in turn, Torah.

Beis El, on the other hand, at the top of the ladder, symbolizes Avraham Avinu. We read in *Bereishis* (12:8) that Avraham pitched his tent in this exact location. Furthermore, Avraham's home was one of great hospitality and warmth, tantamount to *Beis Kel* - a house of God.

Finally, the center of the ladder which was opposite the *Beis HaMikdash* correlates with Yitzchak Avinu who represents the Temple service (*Avodah*) as we discussed earlier.

When we combine all of this information, we can appreciate the fact that the foundation of life, represented by the bottom of the ladder that rested in Be'er Sheva, is Torah. Everything else, including prayer and kind acts must be rooted in Torah and carried out in a way that is true to Torah values and principles.

We can, thus, conclude that Torah is the greatest vehicle - over and above prayer and kind deeds - which draws us closer to God. This is even alluded to in the name "Yaakov," whose root is *eikev*, meaning "heel." Just like the body rests on the heel, so too are the *mitzvos* based on Torah.

With this teaching in mind, perhaps we could suggest something already mentioned in the *Igeres HaRamban*. That is, whenever we learn Torah, just before we finish our session, let us ask ourselves if we've learned anything that we can apply in our daily living. In this way, not only will we learn about new *mitzvos*, but we will find new methods with which to improve the *mitzvos* we are already doing.

May we be blessed to climb the spiritual ladder, ramp and mountain of success, with all of its meanings, by concentrating on Torah study which propels us constantly from one level to the next, drawing us closer and closer to God.

Vayishlach

My Dear Brother

"Sir," the doctor said to his patient, "If the pain in your leg is that bad, we could just cut it off. Then there would be no more pain." The patient was appalled, "Doc, how can you say that? If I let you cut it off, I won't be able to walk." If this is how we viewed our fellow Jews - as limbs of our bodies - we would never cut them off. Rather, we would treat them well, until they healed and got better.

In this week's portion, *Vayishlach*, we read that Yaakov sent messengers to his brother, Esav, and instructed them to tell Esav, "So said your servant Jacob, '*Im Lavan garti* - I have sojourned with Lavan...'" *Rashi*, citing the Midrash Agaddah comments that with the words, "*Im Lavan Garti,*" Yaakov wished to notify Esav that, despite living with the wicked Lavan, he still kept the 613 commandments of the Torah. This is hinted at through the word "*garti*" (*gimmel, reish, taf, yud*), which has the same numerical value as "*taryag*" (*taf, reish, yud, gimmel*), 613, alluding to the number of *mitzvos* in the Torah.

We may ask why Yaakov considered it significant to inform his brother that he had been observing the *mitzvos* while in Lavan's home. Did he really think Esav would care?

Secondly, how could Yaakov claim that he had kept all the commandments while away from his parent's house, when he clearly could not have been observing at least two: honoring one's parents and living in the Land of Israel?

Before answering this question, we must first understand a principle regarding the fulfillment of a *mitzvah*. The *Shu"t Mahariatz* (in his preface to *Pesach Einayim*, cited in the *Sefer K'Motzei Shallal Rav*) explains that every *mitzvah* corresponds to a specific part of the body. The 248 positive commandments connect to the 248 limbs of a person, while the 365 negative commandments correspond to the 365 sinews. If the function of each *mitzvah* is to maintain the spiritual component of the corresponding part of the body, then failure to keep even one commandment should entail a spiritual shutdown of that corresponding body part! By not keeping even one *mitzvah*, we are essentially lacking a "spiritual limb," so to speak. And yet, it is understood that no Jew can fulfill all of the *mitzvos* because some are specific to Priests, others to Levites, and yet others to Israelites. There are also some which are exclusive to men or women.

This being the case, how are we expected to keep all the commandments of the Torah? Shouldn't we have the opportunity to perform every *mitzvah* in order to live a spiritually complete life?

The *Shu"t Mahariatz* suggests two ways in which we can fulfill all of God's commandments:

1) ***Gilgul*** - Based on the belief that we are reincarnations of previous souls, we can assume that any *mitzvah* that our soul did not experience in one lifetime, could either have been carried out in a previous life, or will be accomplished in a future life. For example, a person may be a *Kohen* in one life and a *Levi* in another reincarnation.

2) ***Achdus*** - Through unity and love of fellow Jews, we can be partners in the fulfillment of *mitzvos* with others. When we became one with each other, as a body is one, then one person's *mitzvah* is credited to another person, just as the entire body benefits when one of its limbs carries out a *mitzvah*.

Focusing on the second approach, the *Shu"t Mahariatz* explains that the *mitzvah* of loving our neighbor as ourselves (*Vayikra* 19:18) offers us the opportunity to accomplish those *mitzvos* which would otherwise be impossible for us to perform. In this way, we gain credit for the *mitzvah* as if we carried it out ourselves. (Note: This does **not** reduce the credit of the primary performer of the *mitzvah*, but rather, the process functions as a candle which can provide light to others without diminishing its own light.)

This idea is alluded to in the words of Rebbi Akiva (cited by *Rashi* in *Vayikra* 19:18, taken from the *Yerushalmi* in *Nedarim* 9:4; also *Toras Kohanim* in *Vayikra* 19:18), who comments on the commandment to love your neighbor as yourself, "*Zeh klal gadol baTorah* - This is a big principle in the Torah." If we read this statement with a comma in between the words *klal* and *gadol*, we could suggest that Rebbi Akiva is saying, "This principle is *gadol baTorah*," i.e. for the "*Gadol*-ness" of the Torah, for the vastness of the Torah. In other words, the commandment of loving another as oneself is the door which offers access to the immensity of the Torah, and all the *mitzvos* that it contains.

Bearing this in mind, we can approach the story found in the Talmud (*Shabbos* 31a) with a renewed perspective. The Talmud there brings the famous incident of the gentile who approached Shammai, and then Hillel, as he wished to convert to Judaism. He requested to convert on the condition that a sage would teach him the entire Torah "*al regel achas*", [standing] on one foot. Shammai rejected his request, whereas Hillel agreed, responding, "What you hate being done to you, do not do to others. That is the entire Torah. The rest is commentary."

The *Shu"t Mahariatz* suggests that this potential convert suddenly realized that he would be unable to fulfill every *mitzvah* in the Torah. Not wanting to rely on a future reincarnation, he therefore requested that he receive all the Torah, "*al regel achas*," which besides its literal meaning, "on one foot," could also be taken to imply "in one cycle," in one *gilgul*, in one lifetime. The gentile wanted the opportunity to perform all of God's commandments within his lifespan! Hillel understood his query and responded accordingly. Yes, there is a way to access all the *mitzvos* in one lifetime; it all depends on consideration and love for one another. It all depends on unity. "*Zohi kol haTorah kula*! - This is the entire Torah!" In other words, that is the way to access all of the Torah!

The *Shu"t Mahariatz* applies this understanding to the first question that challenged Yaakov's claim regarding his fulfillment of all 613 commandments while dwelling in Lavan's house. He suggests that Yaakov actually felt true unity and love for his brother, and wanted this message to be imparted to him. So he instructed the messengers to inform Esav, "*Im Lavan garti,*" meaning "*Taryag mitzvot shamarti,*" implying "Yes, I kept **all** the *mitzvos*, even honoring my parents and living in the land of Israel! How? By truly loving you, Esav, by being connected to you! I fulfilled those commandments through **you**!" Beneath the surface of his words, Yaakov was sending his brother - who in the past sought to kill him - a message of love and unity. This explains why Yaakov sent this message to Esav, as he intended to pacify and appease his brother.

Perhaps, once a day, we could think about a fellow Jew, even one who may seem abrasive to us, and imagine that he is a limb of our very own body. Instead of hating him, we could try to heal him just as we would attempt to cure an infected limb. This exercise may very well change our attitudes towards others.

May we all be blessed to feel true unity and genuine love for each other, so that not only will we live spiritually-complete lives by fulfilling all the *mitzvos*, but also deserve to return to the Land of Israel with our parents and with our family, with the coming of the Messiah, resurrection of the dead, ingathering of exiles, and rebuilding of the Temple.

Vayishlach

It's Deeper Than We Think

In order for intelligence to be directed properly, it must be balanced by an equal measure of humility. We must be acutely aware of our limitations, and realize that understanding may take maturity and more years of study, coupled with experience. We may also have to surrender to the fact that there may be certain areas that we will never be able to grasp, at least not fully, and at least not in this world.

In the beginning of this week's portion we read about Yaakov's return to Canaan after residing twenty years at his Uncle Lavan's home in Charan.

At the outset of his journey, Yaakov sends messengers to Esav in Se'ir - anticipating reconciliation with his twin brother (who, twenty years earlier, wanted to kill him on account of the blessing that he received - see *Bereishis* 27:41), but the messengers return with news that Esav is advancing with 400 men, equipped for war (according to the opinion of *Rashi*).

When Yaakov discovers his brother's intentions, he becomes "greatly afraid and very distressed - ***Vayira*** *Yaakov me'od* ***vayetzer*** *lo*" (*Bereishis* 32:8).

Why does the Torah employ a double expression to describe Yaakov's reaction? Wouldn't it have sufficed to just say that Yaakov was simply afraid? What does the seemingly superfluous *vayetzer lo* (he was distressed) add to our understanding of the situation?

Rashi (based on *Tanchumah* 4, and *Bereishis Rabbah* 76:2) explains that *vayira* implies that Yaakov was afraid that Esav would murder him. The term *vayetzer lo,* however, refers to Yaakov's distress at the thought that he, Yaakov, may be put into the position of having to kill other people (i.e. Esav and his men).

In the words of *Rashi:* "*Vayira - shema yehareg. Vayetzer lo - im yaharog hu es acherim.*"

The *Peninim Yekarim*, cited in *Iturei Torah*, provides us with a deep insight into these *Midrashim* quoted by *Rashi.* He begins by imparting two pieces of information. The first is taken from the Talmud (*Horayos* 13b).

In the days when Rabbi Shimon ben Gamliel was *Nasi* (Prince of the Court), Rabbi Meir was the *Chacham* (Sage), and Rabbi Nasan the *Av Beis Din* (Head Justice), all the students in the study hall would rise as a mark of respect whenever any one of them entered the room.

One day, when Rabbi Meir and Rabbi Nasan were absent, the Rashbag announced to the students of his academy that from this point on, there will be a distinction between the honor that is bestowed upon him - the *Nasi* (which was the most distinguished position) - and the respect shown for Rabbi Meir and Rabbi Nasan who held positions that were lower in rank. From now on, he said, whenever he (*Rashbag*) enters the study hall, every single person should stand up. However, on Rabbi Meir's entrance, only the first row of students should rise. Finally, when Rabbi Nasan enters, only those people within four *amos* of him should rise from their seats.

The next day when Rabbi Meir and Rabbi Nasan returned, they noticed that people were not standing up for them in the usual way. They investigated the matter and found out about the ordinance that Rashbag had passed one day earlier.

Rabbi Meir and Rabbi Nasan considered Rabbi Shimon's behavior haughty and decided to challenge his authority. They were aware that his knowledge of Tractate *Uktzin* was lacking. So Rabbi Meir suggested to Rabbi Nasan that they hold a public debate which would draw attention to Rashbag's weakness in this specific area of Oral Law. Once his deficiency in learning would become known, the Rashbag would be demoted from being *Nasi* and they would be promoted.

Rabbi Yaakov ben Korshai, one of the students, overheard the conversation and was concerned for the honor of Rabbi Shimon ben Gamliel, lest he be publicly disgraced. That night he went out and sat behind the Rashbag's study, expounding the tractate of *Uktzin*, repeating it over and over again. Rabbi Shimon considered this a sign from Heaven that he should familiarize himself with this material, so he proceeded to study *Uktzin* that night and mastered the entire tractate!

The following day, Rabbi Meir and Rabbi Nasan engaged Rabbi Shimon publicly in Talmudic discourse, asking him questions specifically on Tractate *Uktzin*. To their utter surprise, Rashbag expertly answered their questions! (Not only had he learned all the material, but it was also fresh in his mind!)

Rabbi Shimon then understood that Rabbi Meir and Rabbi Nasan had intended to humiliate him, and that had he not learned the material, they would have disgraced him. The Rashbag reprimanded them, saying that they had misjudged the underlying motivation of his edict. They thought that his ruling was for the sake of his personal honor when, in fact, it was for the sake of *Kavod HaTorah*, honor of God's Law.

Consequently, Rabbi Shimon expelled them from the *Beis HaMidrash* and issued a penalty. From that point on, whenever Rabbi Meir said something worthy of being recorded, it should be noted as the opinion of "*acherim* - others" and Rabbi Nasan's observations as "*yesh omrim* - some say." No longer were their sayings recorded in their names.

The second piece of information that the *Peninim Yekarim* cites is from the Talmud (*Gittin* 56a) which talks about Nero the Caesar (certain generals were given the title "*Keisar* - Caesar") who was sent by the Roman Emperor to destroy Jerusalem. On his approach, Nero shot an arrow toward the east, and it fell in Jerusalem. Miraculously, the same occurred when he shot an arrow toward the west, north and south - all the arrows turned around and traveled in the direction of Jerusalem.

Nero then saw a boy standing nearby and asked him to share the last piece of Scripture that he had learned. The boy cited the verse from *Yechezkel* (25:14), "*V'nasati es nikmasi b'Edom b'yad ami Yisrael* - And I will lay my vengeance upon Edom by the hand of my people Israel." Nero understood that this was a Divine sign that Jerusalem was destined to be destroyed, but that the one who carried out its destruction would pay the price. Therefore, he fled and converted to Judaism. One of his descendants was Rabbi Meir.

The *Peninim Yekarim* combines these two *Gemaros* and connects them to the Midrash on this week's portion. As we mentioned earlier, *Rashi* who cites the Midrash explains that Yaakov was distressed (*vayetzer lo*) in case he would have to kill *acherim*, others. If we read into the words of *Rashi* and the Midrash in light of these two *Gemaros* we can derive a profound interpretation.

"*Vayetzer lo - im yaharog hu es* ***acherim.***" Yaakov was troubled lest he kill *acherim* (others). Who are these "*acherim*" referring to?

The *Peninim Yekarim* explains: Yaakov was worried that he would be forced into the position of killing his brother, Esav. Had this occurred, the nation of Edom (Rome) would not have existed. Without Edom, Nero the Caesar would never have been born and with no Nero, the holy *Tanna* Rabbi Meir would not have entered this world. Thus, "*acherim*" refers to Rabbi Meir, just as we learned from the account in *Horayos*!

From this insight we can learn a very powerful lesson about the vastness of Torah, and our approach to its study. Sometimes when we read a Midrash, Talmud, *Rishon*, etc. we can be quick to criticize their interpretations or explanations if they don't make sense to us, or if they seem overly simplified. What we sometimes fail to realize is how much is contained in the simplest of words; from only one word of *Rashi* or Midrash, we uncover hidden treasures!

We must learn to appreciate the immensity of Torah, and train ourselves and our students to delve into the rich words of our Sages with patience and due respect. It is, therefore, crucial that when we cannot understand or fully appreciate an interpretation, we should **not** say, “This doesn’t make sense”; but rather, “I do not yet understand this” or “It doesn’t make sense **to me**” - subtle, but very important, differences in our attitude and approach to Torah study.

May we be blessed to value every single word of God, as well as that of our Sages who explain God’s words, and learn to approach Torah with a renewed appreciation. Let us not be hasty to pass critical judgment, but instead, motivate ourselves to study more and probe deeper in order to truly understand the breadth and depth of the Written and Oral Law.

Vayishlach

3D

Albert Einstein's theory of relativity, published in 1915, predicted how space, time, and motion affected the Earth. By contrast, the Torah discusses how the dimensions of space, time, and Man, who was sculpted from Earth, are interrelated in creating eternity.

In this week's *parshah*, *Vayishlach*, Yaakov wrestles with an angel who injures him in the hip. At the conclusion of this incident, the Torah tells us, "Therefore, the Jewish people do not eat the displaced sinew [of animals] on the hip socket until this very day, since [the angel] struck Yaakov on the hip and displaced the sinew" (*Bereishis* 32:33).

The *Me'or Einayim* teaches that we can understand this prohibition on a deeper level based on the verse, "All of Mount Sinai was smoking (***ashan***)" (*Shemos* 19:18). According to the *Me'or Einayim*, the word ***ashan*** is an acronym for the words ***olam*** (world), ***shanah*** (year), and ***nefesh*** (soul), which in turn correspond to the three mystical dimensions of place (world), time (year), and self (soul).

Our tradition teaches that every human being is composed of 248 limbs and 365 sinews. We may also be familiar with these numbers as corresponding to the 248 positive *mitzvos* and the 365 prohibitions in the Torah. The *Ra'avad*, in his preface to the *Sefer HaYetzirah*, states that these numbers appear not only in human beings (the dimension of self), but also in the dimensions of place and time. Since all three dimensions are hinted to in the word ***ashan***, the qualities of any given dimension are reflected in the other dimensions as well. Let us examine place and time individually to see how this is so.

The dimension of place is exemplified by this world. Many verses in the *Tanach* refer to the Earth as though it were a body. The following verses are examples, "The belly of the Earth" (*Shoftim* 9:37), "The mouth of the Earth" (*Bereishis* 4:11), "The nakedness of the land" (*Bereishis* 42:9). Although these expressions seem to be merely figures of speech, the *Ra'avad* explains that the Earth actually has limbs like a person. The Midrash (*Koheles Rabbah* 1:9) states explicitly, "All that Hashem created in Man, He created in the Earth. Man has a head and the Earth has a head, and so on." Thus, if Man (self) has 248 limbs, then the Earth (place) must also.

The *Zohar* (1:170b) teaches that the dimension of time has sinews. There are 365 sinews in the human body and 365 days in the year. The Talmud (*Makkos* 23b) draws another parallel, stating that there are 365 Torah prohibitions, the same number as the days in a year. The *Me'or Einayim* explains that if the 365 prohibitions were arranged so that each one corresponded to one of the 365 days of the year, then the prohibition against eating the sinew of the hip would correspond to *Tishah B'Av*. The connection lies in the concept of destruction. The sinew of Yaakov's hip was destroyed, and on *Tishah B'Av* the Temple was destroyed.

According to the *Me'or Einayim*, there is a hint to this correspondence in the verse we mentioned earlier. In Hebrew, the verse contains the word "***es.***" "Therefore, the Jewish people do not eat '***es***' the displaced sinew (of animals) on the hip socket..." The word ***es*** signals a direct object; it defies English translation. This particular "***es***" can be interpreted as an acronym for the words ***Tishah Av*** (the ninth of *Av*). In fact, the words immediately preceding this "***es***" inform us how we are to behave on the ninth of *Av*: "Do not eat." The *Zohar* (1:170b) further supports this association by stating that anyone who eats on *Tisha B'Av* is considered as having eaten the forbidden hip sinew of an animal.

What can we learn from all of this? Every place has a particular *mitzvah* - one of 248 - that reflects the best way of serving Hashem there. Every moment of time has a particular *mitzvah* - one of 365 - that reflects the best way of serving Hashem then. Since every **place** corresponds to a unique positive *mitzvah* and every moment of **time** corresponds to a unique prohibition, we **ourselves** must learn how to fulfill the will of God in every place, and at every moment. Should we be involved in positive *mitzvos* and behave proactively? Should we be aware of prohibitions and demonstrate restraint? Since every moment of our lives is an intersection of place and time, we must learn to strike the balance between being proactive and practicing restraint in order to behave appropriately.

Perhaps all three dimensions are hinted to in the word ***ashan*** (smoke) because smoke represents difficult, clouded, confusing situations. These are precisely the times and places that Hashem expects each self to know how to behave according to His Will.

Practically speaking, we can outline a few guidelines for achieving this difficult task.

Awareness: Before entering a given place or situation, recognize that the circumstances contain a unique opportunity for serving Hashem. Ask yourself, "What does Hashem want from me in this place at this moment?"

Guidance: The Mishnah urges, "Make a *Rav* for yourself." (*Avos* 1:6) It is of utmost importance to establish a connection with a Rabbi, Rebbetzin, or mentor who can help guide you through challenging situations. There are three primary things to look for in such mentors: 1. they must be filled with Torah, meaning that their intellectual learning has penetrated their heart and influences their actions; 2. they must have life experience; and 3. they must know you as a unique individual. (Sometimes the best way to develop this personal connection is actually by discussing problems with them!)

Prayer: Ultimately, Hashem is the source of all guidance and support. It is appropriate at every place and time to turn to Hashem and ask for insight and assistance.

May we be blessed to have clear vision so that we can take the right steps, especially in the most challenging and clouded **times** and **places**. May we strike the balance between being proactive and being passive so that Hashem will be proactive with His children and rebuild our Temple, thus turning *Tisha B'Av* into a day of celebration.

Vayishlach

Thinking Outside the Box

There are two types of Jews. One type enjoys putting themselves into a box. This can be most convenient, because by doing so, it is easier for people to define themselves, and there is a certain sense of security that comes with belonging to a particular group. The other type, however, abhor the box. They are completely turned off to the idea of losing one's own unique identity by surrendering their individuality to the greater whole. Who would have thought that by placing ourselves into certain boxes, it actually allows us to live outside of the box?

As Yaakov prepares to meet his brother Esav after being separated from him for many years, he says, "...For with my staff I passed over this Jordan [River] and now I have become two camps" (32:11). In this verse Yaakov stresses that he had a "staff." This staff is also mentioned in last week's portion, when Yaakov was involved in increasing his flock, where it says, "and Yaakov took for himself rods (staffs) of a poplar tree, and the almond, and the plane tree..." (30:37).

In this verse, four different types of staffs are mentioned: staff, poplar, almond, and plane. The *Zohar* comments that these four staffs correspond to the four paragraphs that are written on the parchment of a pair of *tefillin*, and that this comes to teach us that through these four rods, Yaakov fulfilled the *mitzvah* of *tefillin*. The *Arugas HaBosem* asks why Yaakov didn't fulfill the *mitzvah* of *tefillin* the regular way. Why did he have to symbolically perform the *mitzvah* of *tefillin* in such an apparently strange way?

The *Arugas HaBosem* answers that Yaakov saw the future generations of Jews who would be in exile. He saw how his descendants would be very preoccupied making a living, which would bring them to do business in the streets and market places. Yaakov foresaw the challenges and temptations in those places that could lure the Jews astray from the path of Hashem. Therefore, Yaakov prepared the way for them by fulfilling the *mitzvah* of *tefillin* while he was involved in his own livelihood. He did this in order that the power of *tefillin* would continue to be with the Jews throughout all their generations at the time they are involved in their own livelihood.

The power of *tefillin* is that it subjugates our mind and hearts, directing them to the service of God (see the prayer that is recited prior to donning the *tefillin*). Just like Yaakov connected to *tefillin* in the streets after he took off his real *tefillin*, so too, we can connect with the *mitzvah* of *tefillin* in the streets, well after the time we remove our real *tefillin* in the synagogues. The point here is that a Jew can remain strong religiously and spiritually in any kind of environment or situation in which he finds himself.

Perhaps we can add some thoughts about *tefillin* that can stay with us after we remove them. First of all, the straps that bind the *tefillin* to our arms and heads represent the *d'veikus BaHashem* (connection to God) that we always have. Secondly, the *kesher* (knots) of the *tefillin* remind us that we have a constant *kesher* (connection) with God, like a *kesher shel kayamah* (a knot which lasts). This is why the *mitzvah* is called *tefillin*. *Tefillin* (spelled *taf, fey, lamed, yud*, and *nun*) has the same letters as the name Naftali. Naftali means "to join with," as Rachel says "*Naftulei Elokim*" (*Bereishis* 30:8). Menachem Ben Soruk (in *Machberes Tzamid P'sil*, cited in *Rashi* there) says that this means, "I have joined" [with my sister to merit children].

So, whether we wear *tefillin* or see others wearing them, let us take out a moment to remind ourselves of their meaning. One practical suggestion could be: right before taking them off, stop, close our eyes, and consider just how much we are bound to God, at all times. In this way, throughout the day we will be cognizant of God's presence with us and, thereby, act accordingly.

So may we all be blessed with the faith that God is with us always, which will keep us on track no matter what rivers we have to cross, and no matter where we find ourselves.

Vayeishev

To Dwell or Not to Dwell, That is the Question

The shuttle at Newark Airport was most convenient. It allowed the traveling family to get from their gate to the rent-a-car station in a comfortable way, and in a short amount of time. However, during the shuttle ride, one of the children began cleaning the windows and benches. His parents told him that there was really no point in doing that because they were going to be getting off in just a minute. What an incredible lesson they taught their child! This is a teaching we could all put to use: to live with the realization that we should not get too caught up in the comforts of this world, because we are all getting off soon.

This week's portion, *Vayeishev*, begins: "*Vayeishev Yaakov b'eretz megurei aviv Eretz Canaan* - Yaakov settled in the land of his father's sojourning, the Land of Canaan" (*Bereishis* 37:1).

We know that the name of the *parshah* is often derived from the text, as we see in the case of this week's *parshah* where the word *vayeishev*, he settled, appears in the opening verse. However, we may still question the appropriateness of this title since it does not at all reflect the content of the portion, which discusses one of the most unsettling episodes in Yaakov's life!

Parshas Vayeishev deals with the story of *mechiras Yosef* (the selling of Yosef), where the tribes planned to kill Yosef out of jealousy toward him, but ended up selling him to passing traders instead. The brothers then brought Yosef's blood-soaked tunic to their father, who naturally assumed that his son was devoured by wild beasts. This, of course, caused Yaakov great upheaval, anguish, and grief (see verses 37:34-35) - quite the opposite of what *vayeishev* seems to imply!

Secondly, a technical question arises concerning the wording of the opening verse. With regards to Yaakov the passuk says, "*Vayeishev Yaakov*." (The root of *vayeishev* is *yoshev*, meaning to sit or settle). However, in relation to Yitzchak the verse continues, "*B'eretz megurei aviv*." (The root of *megurei* is *gur*, which means to live or sojourn.) Why are two different expressions employed to connote the same idea when the Torah could have used the same word consistently (i.e. either "**Vayeishev** *Yaakov b'eretz* ***yeshuvei*** *aviv*" or "***Vayagor*** *Yaakov b'eretz* ***megurei*** *aviv*")?

The Midrash (cited by *Rashi*, *Tanchumah Yashan*, *Mevo*, 3:13, *Bereishis Rabbah* 84:3, quoted by *Rashi* in 37:2, in reference to 37:1) expounds on the words *Vayeishev Yaakov:* "*Bikesh Yaakov leishev b'shalvah, kafatz alav ragzo shel Yosef* - Yaakov sought to dwell in tranquility [but then] the ordeal of Yosef was sprung upon him."

The Midrash continues: "*Tzaddikim mevakshim leishev b'shalvah. Amar HaKadosh Baruch Hu, lo dayan la'tzadikim mah shemetukan lahem laolam haba, ela shemevakshim leishev b'shalvah ba'olam hazeh* - The righteous seek to dwell in tranquility. The Holy One, Blessed be He, said, 'Is it not enough that the righteous have what is prepared for them in the World to Come that they seek to dwell in tranquility in this world [as well]?!'"

In light of this Midrash, we may ask: What is so wrong with desiring serenity in both this world and the next? Don't *tzaddikim* deserve a calm and peaceful life in *Olam Hazeh* as well as *Olam Haba*? We will answer all three questions based on the *Yalkut Divrei Chachamim* who cites a novel insight from the *Admor* R' Yitzchak Isaac of Ziditchov (cited in the *Sefer Iturei Torah*).

The Midrash says, "*Bikesh Yaakov leishev b'****shalvah*** - Yaakov sought to dwell in **tranquility**." In order to understand this Midrash from a completely different perspective, we must analyze what *shalvah* really means. What is the difference between ***shalvah*** - which means "serenity or tranquility," and

shalom - commonly translated as "peace or harmony"?

The root word of *shalom* is *shalem* (*shin, lamed, mem*) meaning "full or complete." We find this association in *Bereishis* (33:18) where it says, "*Vayavo Yaakov shalem…* - Yaakov came intact…" *Rashi* (citing the Talmud in *Shabbos* 33b and *Bereishis Rabbah* 79:5) explains that *shalem* implies completeness in all aspects of life - physical, financial, and spiritual. *Shalvah*, on the other hand, denotes constriction or limitation of physicality. King Solomon states in *Mishlei* (17:1), "Better a dry piece of bread in serenity (***shalvah***), than a house full of contentious celebrations." The quality of "*shalvah*" is juxtaposed with a description of minimized physical pleasures, suggesting, therefore, they are one and the same - i.e. that the definition of "*shalvah*" is reduced material gain.

Based on this interpretation, the *Admor* suggests that Yaakov wished to dwell in *shalvah*, such that he desired to live a life whose focus lay in the **spiritual** realm and not the material world. Yaakov was content with the basic physical necessities as we find in *Bereishis* (28:20) where he prays for God's protection, and for "bread to eat and clothes to wear," i.e. for life's essentials and nothing more.

This is the perspective of a *tzaddik*. A truly righteous person does not wish to amass wealth and property in this world; but rather, he desires only the bare minimum of material possessions, that which is necessary for survival.

The *Admor* explains that, essentially, Hashem wishes to grant all *tzaddikim* maximum satisfaction both in this world and the next. However, since the *tzaddik* understands that *Olam Hazeh* is transient, he is not interested in benefiting from more than the basic comforts of the physical world; instead, his emphasis lies in obtaining a greater portion in the World to Come.

With this idea in mind, we will now return to the words of the Midrash; "The righteous seek to dwell in tranquility (*shalvah*). The Holy One, Blessed be He, said, 'Is it not enough that the righteous have what is prepared for them in the World to Come that they seek to dwell in tranquility in this world [as well]?!'"

On the simplest level, we read this Midrash as a rhetorical question that implies criticism toward Yaakov, and righteous people in general, for "wanting the best of both worlds." However, if we study the Midrash as a statement, it suggests something entirely different. "The righteous seek to dwell in tranquility (*shalvah*)." God then states: "*Lo dayan latzaddikim mah shemetukan lahem LaOlam Haba*! - **It is not enough** that the righteous have what is prepared for them in the World to Come!" (The inference being, that God wishes to grant *tzaddikim* not only the highest portion in *Olam Haba,* but also the most comfortable and enjoyable life in *Olam Hazeh*!)

However, God sees that this is not what the *tzaddik* wants, as we find in the continuation of the Midrash: "*Ela shemevakshim leishev b'**shalvah** ba'olam hazeh* - But they [the righteous people] seek to dwell in ***shalvah*** in this world." In other words, the *tzaddikim* want *shalvah* - less material comfort in *Olam Hazeh* (the transient, physical world) and instead, a greater portion in the spiritual and eternal realm of *Olam Haba.*

Therefore, God withheld from Yaakov the comforts of this world and blessed him accordingly - by providing him with another trial: "*Kafatz alav ragzo shel Yosef*." Yaakov's desire and sole focus was developing his relationship with God in this world as a precursor to basking in the Divine Light in *Olam Haba.* God, therefore, gave him another opportunity for growth through *mechiras Yosef.*

Based on this new perspective we can now explain, on a deeper level, why the name of the portion *Vayeishev* is, in fact, perfectly appropriate for the material that is discussed within the *parshah.* Although *mechiras Yosef* caused Yaakov great suffering, it ultimately led to a greater *yishuv*, restfulness, in the World to Come. God "sprang on Yaakov the ordeal of

Yosef" because the distress eventually resulted in his obtaining a superior portion in the World to Come.

In light of the ideas discussed, we can also answer the second question concerning why two different expressions are used with regards to Yaakov's settling, versus Yitzchak's sojourning.

"*Vayeishev Yaakov*" refers to Yaakov's desire for *shalvah*, as the Midrash suggests. Based on the *Admor*, the word *shalvah*, used in reference to Yaakov, indicates his concern with matters of spiritual and eternal significance only. *Megurei Aviv*, on the other hand, alludes to the **source** of Yaakov's outlook in life. Yaakov learned to focus on the eternal world from his father, Yitzchak, who perceived himself as a "*ger* - a stranger or sojourner" in *Olam Hazeh*.

Thus, the expressions "*Vayeishev*" and "*Megurei*" actually indicate two sides of the same coin - i.e. permanence of the spiritual world and transience of the physical world.

Finally, based on the deeper reading of the Midrash which proposes that *tzaddikim* are, in fact, **not** interested in the material benefits of this world, we can render our third question irrelevant! We may think that the righteous deserve the comforts of this world and indeed God, in His kindness, would bestow upon them abundant physical blessings **if that is what they actually desired**!

However, since *tzaddikim* recognize the temporary nature of this world and prefer to make do with the minimum in terms of material needs, God rewards them accordingly by presenting them with challenges and hardships in order to allow them to develop themselves and their connection to the Divine even further, thus ensuring them a greater portion in *Olam Haba*.

One way to keep this lesson in mind could be to keep a picture of a *sukkah* on your wall or in your wallet. A *sukkah*, which is a temporary dwelling, is meant to teach us about the transience of this world. Every time we look at it, it will remind us of this reality. Then we could live life accordingly, making the right choices.

May we all be blessed with the type of blessing that we should bestow on our family, friends and people around us: complete ***shalom*** in this world and the next. May we all be blessed further, that if we experience unsettling life situations in this world (as most of us do), then we will connect to the story of the Patriarchs and realize that through our specific challenges, God is providing us with opportunities to grow - just as He granted the same to righteous people throughout the generations. May we, in turn, merit the coming of *Moshiach* and perfect serenity in *Olam Haba.*

Vayeishev

Fort Li

When one finds himself in the palace surrounded by aristocracy, it requires a certain type of conduct. However, when one finds himself in the company of uncouth people, there is an entirely different kind of behavior that must be displayed just in order to protect oneself. Mastering the art of adaptation must be studied in order to ensure our survival.

The theme of this week's portion is about the selling of Yosef. In the beginning of the portion it states, "These are the offspring of Yaakov; Yosef, at the age of seventeen years, was a shepherd with his brothers by the flock..." (*Bereishis* 37:2). One question to ponder is why it was necessary to mention that Yosef was seventeen years old at that time. Of what relevance is this to the storyline, and to our lives?

Furthermore, earlier on, when Yaakov was running away from Esav, he did not go directly to Charan where Lavan lived. Rather, Yaakov hid out in the Academy of Eiver for fourteen years in order to learn Torah (*Rashi Toldos* 28:9, citing *Megillah*, Ch. 1, *Megillah Nikreis*, pg. 17a and *Rashi Vayeitzei* 28:11, citing *Bereishis Rabbah* 68:11. See Sifsei Chachamim, Bereishis. 28:9, #2 who points out that although when Yaakov was younger it says, in the plural, that Yaakov dwelt in tents (Bereishis. 25:27) implying that he studied in two different tents, that of Shem and that of Eiver (*Rashi* citing *Bereishis Rabbah* 63:15), nevertheless, by the time Yaakov ran away from Esav, Shem had already died. Therefore Yaakov went only to the tent or Academy of Eiver).

This too seems difficult to understand. For the first sixty-three years of Yaakov's life, when Yaakov was with his parents, he already studied in the Academy of Shem and Eiver (*Bereishis* 25:27 and *Rashi* there citing *Bereishis Rabbah* 63:15). Why was it necessary to study in the tent of Eiver again for an additional fourteen years?

Rabbi Meir Yechiel from Ostrovtsa explains that during the sixty-three years that Yaakov was with his parents, he learned from the Academies how to be a servant of God amongst Jews like himself. There is a certain mode of behavior that is suitable for a Torah person to maintain when he is in the midst of righteous people. This is what Shem and Eiver taught him at that time.

However, when Yaakov fled that environment of holiness, he needed to learn proper conduct for a Torah person amongst the nations. Especially since Yaakov would be in the company of wicked tricksters like Lavan, he had to learn how to maintain his status as a kosher Jew and not learn from their evil ways.

This was the Torah that Yaakov learned during those additional fourteen years in the Academy of Eiver. Yaakov had to master the art of preserving his holiness even in the most impure settings.

Harav Yaakov Kaminetzky, in his *Emes L'Yaakov*, adds that these two righteous people, Shem and Eiver, were paradigm examples of how to protect one's sanctity even in the face of spiritual contamination. Shem was a son of Noach, who lived through an immoral and corrupt society known as the generation of the Great Flood (*Bereishis* 6:10). Nevertheless, he emerged as a righteous person. Shem, therefore, would be a most suitable mentor to guide Yaakov how to achieve the same goal. We could suggest that even though Shem had died by this time, he had already shared his experiences with Eiver on how to live a holy life even amongst a decadent society. Eiver then shared that information with Yaakov.

Similarly, Eiver himself lived through an unethical and decadent generation who were dispersed after building a tower from which they wanted to rebel against God (*Bereishis* 10:25). In spite of that, Eiver developed into a righteous man. Therefore, Eiver would be a supreme role model for Yaakov to shadow.

This is what Yaakov accomplished when he spent an additional fourteen years in the Academy of Eiver. Yaakov was soaking up the various methods of spiritual fortification that he would need to implement in order to secure his own purity in face of Lavan's culture that was steeped in spiritual pollution.

The Ostrovtsa Rebbi continues to remark that Yaakov foresaw with Divine inspiration that Yosef was destined to leave his family of holy Jews, and spend the vast majority of his life amongst a foreign nation whose inhabitants were decadent. We all know that that place was Egypt.

This is why Yaakov felt compelled to teach Yosef in particular, about the Torah that he received during the additional fourteen years in the Academy of Shem and Eiver. These teachings trained a person how to stay holy even amongst foreign influences. Yaakov did not impart that Torah to his other sons (*Bereishis* 37:3, *Rashi* there citing *Bereishis Rabbah* 84:8).

This is because Yaakov's other children were not going to be exposed to the same sort of spiritual filth that Yosef would have to endure, at least not to the same extent as Yosef. Therefore, there was no reason for Yaakov to share that Torah with them. Yaakov was not playing favorites. Rather, Yaakov was simply carrying out his responsibilities as a father, guiding his children according to their needs.

Now, we all know that according to Jewish custom, we begin teaching our children Torah from the age of three (*Elya Rabbah* 17:3). This tradition can be traced as far back as Yaakov. Yaakov began teaching Yosef when the latter was three years old. Yaakov began to transmit to Yosef how one stays a *kosher* Jew even if one finds himself in spiritual darkness.

It took Yaakov the same amount of time to teach Yosef this Torah as it took him to learn it for himself, fourteen years. This means that by the time Yosef was seventeen years old, he was ready to meet the challenge of maintaining himself as a *kosher* Jew even in the face of negative elements.

This is the relevance of Yosef being seventeen years old at that time. It teaches us that only after he was properly prepared could he overcome destructive obstacles and pitfalls. This lesson may be of paramount importance to us as well. Some of us find ourselves, at times, in circles that are not so conducive to spirituality, to say the least.

How much energy do we need to invest in order to protect our souls? As we mix with the nations of the world and interact with them, are we preserving our unique Jewish identity? Are we a light unto the peoples of Earth? Do we sanctify God's name wherever we go?

We could suggest that the number of years it took Yaakov and Yosef to get ready is not arbitrary. We mentioned above that it took each of them fourteen years. The number fourteen is connected to spiritual protection from outside influences. How so? Let's see.

We have established that it is necessary to shield ourselves from certain cultural influences found internationally amongst the nations of the world. For the most part, the predominant figure which represents the nations is Esav.

Esav's power is described as "*Hayedayim yedei Esav* - The hands are the hands of Esav" (*Bereishis* 27:22). The Hebrew word for hand is *yad*, numerically fourteen. Therefore, it was not surprising, nor was it random, that it took Yaakov and Yosef specifically fourteen years each to guard themselves against the products that were built by the hands of Esav.

One way in which we could fortify ourselves from negative influences would be to study, in depth, the portions dealing with Yaakov and Yosef amongst the nations. As we glean insight into how they maintained their holiness, we will be able to adopt their methods to our circumstances.

May we all be blessed to take the necessary measures to safeguard ourselves against any non-*kosher* influences, and become even more like Yaakov and Yosef, always making a *Kiddush Hashem* wherever we go, whether amongst our own people or amidst other walks of life.

Vayeishev

To Be a Jew or Not to Be a Jew

How children react when their father comes home after an extended trip abroad is very telling. If they run to hide for cover, it is a sign that their father is more of a monarch than a father. But if the children run to the door, and in their excitement, turn their father into a jungle-gym, then it is a sign of a love-based relationship, not a fear-based one.

This week's *parshah*, *Vayeishev*, tells us that Yosef used to convey evil reports to his father about his brothers (*Bereishis* 37:2). *Rashi* (citing *Bereishis Rabbah* 84:7) comments that one of the negative behaviors Yosef observed in his brothers was their eating "*eiver min hachai* - meat taken from a live animal."

No matter how we look at it, this seems highly unlikely. The brothers were all righteous people; we refer to them as "the tribes of God." Could such refined individuals possibly be guilty of such a crime? Furthermore, if they did not commit the acts that Yosef claimed, then it seems that Yosef was a liar and tale-bearer, yet Yosef is also recognized as a *tzaddik*! How can we resolve this difficulty?

The *Parashas Derachim* (*Derech HaAtarim*, first drash) explains that this evil report stems from a dispute between Yosef and his brothers regarding their status as Jews. The brothers maintained that they were complete, full-fledged Jews, whereas Yosef claimed that they still retained the status of Noachides (people bound by the general laws of humanity).

One of the practical differences between Jewish and Noachide law regards the determination of when an animal is fit to be eaten; after slaughtering or after death. Although it may seem that these two situations are equivalent, it is not necessarily so. After an animal is slaughtered, its body may twitch and shake for a few moments until enough blood drains out for the carcass to finally lie still. The cessation of movement may determine death, even if this occurs several minutes after the slaughtering.

Although Jews have many more laws than Noachides, Noachide laws are far more stringent than the equivalent Jewish laws. According to Jewish law, an animal may be eaten immediately after slaughtering; even if its body is still twitching. This inadvertent movement *halachically* has no bearing on the status of the animal. According to Noachide law, however, only actual death permits an animal to be eaten. All movement must cease before an animal may be prepared for consumption.

According to the *Parashas Derachim*, Yosef saw his brothers taking limbs from an animal after it had been slaughtered but before it had stopped moving. According to the brothers (who maintained that they were full-fledged Jews), this was a permissible act. According to Yosef, however, (who considered them Noachides), their act was forbidden.

What lesson can we learn from this technical discussion?

The *Tiferes Shmuel* (vol. 2) explains that Jews and Noachides each have a different type of relationship with Hashem. The Noachide relationship to God follows the model of a servant's relationship to a king. The servant serves the king out of fear, or at best, in order to receive reward. As such, he does only what is expected of him, as any employee would do for an employer. Since Noachides do not go above the letter of the law in their Divine service, Hashem treats them in a comparable manner, i.e. naturally, and does not perform miracles on their behalf.

Jews, however, chose a relationship that follows the model of a child-parent relationship. (Noachides who wish to intensify their level of relationship with Hashem are welcome to do so, just as the Jews did in their collective "conversion" at Sinai.) Jewish service of God is based on love, not fear, and as such, our Divine service often goes above the necessary requirements; as the saying goes, "Where there is love, there is a way." Since Jews are eager to fulfill Hashem's Will, even beyond the letter of the law, Hashem treats the Jewish people in a similar manner and performs miracles for us.

According to the *Tiferes Shmuel*, Yaakov agreed with the majority of his sons that they had the status of full-fledged Jews. This is clear from the fact that Yaakov taught his children all the Torah he had learned from Shem and Eiver (see *Ba'al HaTurim* 37:3). Had Yaakov believed that he and his children had the status of Noachides, it would have been forbidden for him to do this, since the Talmud states (*Sanhedrin* 58b) that a Noachide who involves himself in Torah learning that is not necessary for him, receives capital punishment. Since Yaakov apparently taught his children **everything** that he had learned, it seems that he believed they had the status of Jews.

This will help us understand the Torah's statement that the brothers hated Yosef (*Bereishis* 37:4). We could suggest that Yosef's brothers hated his approach of settling for less in the service of God. They wanted to continually develop a more meaningful relationship with Hashem. Yosef also yearned for this; however, Yosef maintained that the time for this more intimate relationship had not yet come.

At Sinai, we all chose to be God's children, and in turn, God chose to be our parent. Since our relationship is now based on love, we should be willing to go above and beyond the letter of the law. One area in which we can practice this would be prayer. After completing any service of standard traditional prayer, one could say one more prayer or perhaps a Psalm. We will be demonstrating that we are children connecting to God from a place of love.

May we holy brothers and sisters be blessed to develop an unquenchable love for Hashem, so that we eagerly run to serve Him. May Hashem soon reciprocate our love by eagerly and miraculously building our third Temple.

Vayeishev - Chanukah

Beating Around the Bush

To everybody working at the Jerusalem Municipality, Shalom seemed to be a simple man, who did his janitorial job devotedly, keeping the grounds clean. Only when somebody noticed that Shalom would slip away to somewhere secretive each day during the lunch break, did it arouse the curiosity of one of the superiors. One day, the superior decided to follow Shalom. What he saw blew his mind.

Shalom would go to the local grocery store, buy rolls, cream cheese and milk, and then board a bus. Arriving at his stop, Shalom got off, and carried his bags to a Talmud Torah, which was struggling financially. Many of the boys there were orphans. It was during recess, and they were playing, but when they saw Shalom, they all ran to the fence calling out "Shalom Abba." The superior watched Shalom give out the food to the hungry boys, and then returned to his job.

The superior approached Shalom and said that if he ever had to leave a little earlier for lunch, it would be okay, and then offered Shalom some money to buy more food for the boys. Realizing that he had been found out, Shalom begged the superior not to tell anybody what he saw until he died. Years later, during the week of mourning for Shalom, the superior paid a *shivah* call to the family and related this story.

The Midrash (*Pirkei D'Rebbe Eliezer* chapter 38 and in the *Da'as Zekeinim, MiBa'alei HaTosfos*, on *Parshas Mikeitz*, 41:45), says that Yosef married Osnas. The history behind Osnas is that she was in fact Dinah's daughter, birthed after Dinah was violated by Shechem.

Some of the tribes wanted to get rid of Osnas so that the nations should not be able to point at lewdness within the house of Yaakov. Yaakov was not happy with what some of his sons wanted to do with Osnas, and so, Yaakov took her to the desert and hid her under a *sneh* (bush). It is for this reason that she is called Osnas because of the word *sneh*, which appears within her name.

Yaakov then made a medallion on which he engraved the following words "Anyone who marries this person is attaching themselves to the seed of Yaakov." Yaakov gave this medallion to Osnas. Then the angel Michael came down and flew Osnas to Egypt where she was adopted by Potiphar and his wife. Potiphar was the royal butcher. They adopted her because they had no children of their own.

When later on, Yosef came down to Mitzrayim - eventually becoming the viceroy - the Egyptian women would climb the walls to catch a glimpse of his beauty as he was being paraded through the streets of Egypt (*Parshas Vayechi* 49:22). These women would throw their jewelry into Yosef's chariot with the hope that he would take one of the trinkets, which would mean he would marry its owner. Osnas was also there with the other women and she threw the medallion into the chariot. When Yosef saw the engraving contained on it, it caught his attention. And so Yosef married Osnas. Yosef kept the medallion and later used it to prove to his father Yaakov that his sons Efraim and Menashe came from *kosher* ancestry (*Vayechi* 48:9).

Osnas experienced a very colorful life. Shechem was her father; some of the tribes had wanted to get rid of her; Yaakov hid her in the bushes; she was flown to Egypt by an angel; she was adopted by the royal butcher; she became Yosef's wife and the mother of two tribes of Yisrael. Therefore, it is surprising that with all of these events that happened to her, she was named Osnas, after the *sneh*, or bush, in which she was hidden away, which seems to be the most trivial of her experiences. Why indeed was she called Osnas?!

The *Emunas Itecha* says that we all know that the spiritual, primordial, hidden light that God hid away at the time of Creation is actually hidden within the *Chanukah* candles (see *Bereishis Rabbah* 11:2 and the *Bnei Yissaschar, Kislev* 1:6 who cites the *Rokeach* in *Hilchos Chanukah* 2:25). This is hinted to by the fact that just as the hidden light functioned for thirty-six hours during Creation, so too, we light thirty-six *Chanukah* candles altogether by the end of *Chanukah* (excluding the *shamashim*). These thirty-six candles correspond to the thirty-six righteous people in every generation who greet the Divine presence every single day (see *Sukkah* 45b based on Isiah 30:18 the opinion of *Abaye*).

These thirty-six *tzadikkim* are known to be hidden *tzadikkim*. In this aspect, they share a commonality with the thirty-six candles of *Chanukah* which have a hidden element to them as well - the hidden light.

Osnas was one of the thirty-six hidden *tzadikkim*, and her mission in life was to achieve the same thing that *Chanukah* candles are meant to accomplish. Just like *Chanukah's* light is meant to reach the darkest of places, so it was with Osnas. Ultimately, she had to descend to Egypt, the darkest of societies and bring holiness there. Succeeding in this mission meant bringing the Divine presence into the thorniest of circumstances. It is for this reason that God appeared to Moshe in a *sneh*, a bush, hinting to Moshe that "I am with you in your distress" (see *Shemos* 3:2 and *Shemos Rabbah* 2:5 and *Tehillim* 91:15).

This is the reason why of all the possible choices, her name was Osnas, after the *sneh*, bush. This name represented her mission in life, which was to bring the Divine presence into the thorniest of situations. This is why Yaakov brought her to the thorn bush to begin with, not just to hide her from some of his sons, but also to instruct her as to her Divine mission in life: to bring God even into the thorn bush. This meant bringing the light all the way down into the lowest of places. With this mission in mind, we can put a whole new spin on vacation and business trips.

Additionally, if we do one *mitzvah* a day secretly, then with regard to that *mitzvah* we are hidden, just like hidden *tzaddikim* are with respect to most of their *mitzvos*.

May we be blessed thirty-six times over to become true hidden *tzadikkim* and bring spiritual light into a very dark world.

Mikeitz - Chanukah

Take the Hint

The teacher asked her class to find the holiday of *Chanukah* in *Parshas Mikeitz*. The children asked her to give them a hint, so this is what she said...

The holiday of *Chanukah* always coincides with the portion of *Mikeitz*, which we read this Shabbos. Therefore, this week, we will share some insights from the *Iturei Torah* on allusions to *Chanukah* that are derived from the *parshah*.

1) *Parshas Mikeitz* begins in *Bereishis* (41:1): "*Vayehi mikeitz sh'nasayim* - And it was at the end of two years." This phrase is composed of the following letters: *vav, yud, hey, yud; mem, kuf, tzadi; shin, nun, taf, yud, mem.*

The *Hagahos Mordechai* finds a *remez* to the story of *Chanukah* in the acronym of the opening three words of the *parshah*: "*Uv'eis Yochanan Hich'chid Yevanim MiBeis Kodsheinu. Tzivanu SheNadlik Neiros Tamanya Yomi MiChanukah* - And in the time of Yochanan, the Greeks no longer remained in our holy Temple. He commanded us to light candles for the eight days of *Chanukah*" (*Shabbos* 21b).

2) The *Shiltei Giborim* offers another acronym for the word "*Sh'nasayim*" (*Bereishis* 41:1) which hints at the correct positioning of the *Menorah*. "*S'mol ner tadlik, yemin mezuzah* - On the left side (of the doorway) you shall kindle the lamp (i.e. the *Menorah*); on the right side is the *mezuzah*" (see *Shulchan Aruch* 671:7).

3) In *Bereishis* (41:4-5), we read about Pharaoh's dreams. In one dream, seven gaunt and ugly cows consume seven attractive, robust cows; and in the second dream, seven thin and parched ears of grain devour seven

healthy, full ears of grain.

The commentary "*Chanah David*" suggests that the commonality in Pharaoh's dreams - i.e. the weak and lean items consuming the strong, robust ones - hints at the holiday of *Chanukah* which commemorates the downfall of the powerful and mighty enemy, who was delivered into the hands of the weak. (See the "*Al Hanissim*" insertion in the *Amidah* and *Birkas Hamazon* where we thank God for this miracle - "*Masarta giborim b'yad chalashim* - You delivered the mighty into the hands of the weak.")

4) In *Bereishis* (41:34), we read about Yosef's interpretation of Pharaoh's dreams. Yosef advises Pharaoh to appoint overseers on the land, and to prepare Egypt during the seven years of abundance - "*Ve**chimesh** es eretz Mitzraim b'sheva shnei hasava* - And he shall prepare the land of Egypt during the seven years of abundance."

The *Bnei Yissaschar* comments that the word *chimesh* - spelled *ches, mem, shin* - alludes, in its acronym, to the three *mitzvos* that the Greeks wished to abolish: *chodesh* (*Rosh Chodesh*), *milah* (circumcision) and Shabbos.

Furthermore, we find these root letters - *ches, mem, shin* - also appearing in *Shemos* (13:18) where the Israelites' exodus from Egypt is discussed: "*Va**chamushim** alu Bnei Yisrael me'eretz Mitzraim.*" *Rashi*, citing the Talmud Yerushalmi (*Shabbos* 6:7), translates "*chamushim*" as "*mezuyanim* - armed". He then provides an alternative interpretation based on a similar word "*chumash*" which means "one-fifth" and explains that we understand from this elucidation of the text that only **one-fifth** of the Israelites left Egypt; the remaining four-fifths died in the plague of darkness.

If we combine these two insights, we can learn a lesson about the perpetuation of the Jewish people. If, God forbid, we turn our backs on the Torah and *mitzvos* and fail to guard and practice Shabbos, *milah* and *chodesh*, then as a natural consequence we start losing our brothers and sisters through assimilation to the point that, Heaven-forbid, only one-fifth of the Jewish population remains.

However, if we keep all the *mitzvos* - including Shabbos, *milah* and *chodesh* - and understand, and live by, what these commandments represent, then we will ensure the maintenance of our people - all five-fifths of *Am Yisrael.*

5) The *Ner Yisrael* comments that the name of the *Chanukah* holiday appears in *Parshas Mikeitz* (*Bereishis* 43:16) embedded in the words "*Tevach VeHachen* - Slaughter and prepare a meal." The initial letter of "*Chanukah*" (*ches*) is found as the final letter of "*Tevach*" while the word "*VeHachen*"" (spelled *vav, hey, chaf, nun*) provides the remaining letters of "*Chanukah*" when unscrambled. This may allude to the custom of having a festive meal on *Chanukah.*

6) The *Besamim Rosh* in the name of the *Shiltei HaGiborim* points out that the phrase, "*U'Tevo'ach Tevach*" (also in 43:16; spelled *vav, tes, beis, ches; tes, beis, ches*) has a numerical value of forty-four, which is the total number of candles lit over the course of *Chanukah,* when the light of the *shamash* is included.

7) Furthermore, in this week's *haftarah,* which is taken from the book of Zechariah, we read: "*Menoras zahav kulah, vegulah al roshah, shivah neiroseha aleha...*" The prophet Zechariah describes his vision to the angel, "A *menorah* [made] entirely of gold with its bowl on its top, its seven lamps upon it..." (4:2).

The *Iturei Torah* points out that the numerical value of the word "*vegulah*" (*vav, gimmel, lamed, hey*), translated as "it's bowl" is forty-four, also hinting at the number of lights which are kindled in the *gulos,* bowls, that hold the oil!

The following question arises: Why do we light a total of forty-four lights? What message can we derive from this number specifically? The number forty-four in Hebrew is *mem, daled.* When we read these letters in reverse order, the word "*dam*" is formed, meaning "blood." This alludes to the greatness of the *Chashmona'im* (Hasmoneans) who were willing to sacrifice their lives, their blood, for the sake of Torah.

8) In *Bereishis* (43:34), Yosef serves Binyamin five times the amount of food and drink, as the verse says; "*Vaterev mas'as Binyamin mimas'os kulam* ***chamesh yados*** - And Benjamin's portion was five times as much as the portion of any of them."

The *Admor*, Rav Naftali of Rupshitz, finds an allusion in the phrase "*chamesh yados*" (lit. "five hands", but implying "five-fold"), to the *Al Hanissim* prayer where the word ***yad*** (hand) is mentioned five times: - "*Masarta giborim be**yad** chalashim, v'rabim be**yad** me'atim, u'temei'im be**yad** tehorim, u'resha'im be**yad** tzadikim, v'zeidim be**yad** oskei Torasecha* - You delivered the strong into the **hands** of the weak, the many into the **hands** of the few, the impure into the **hands** of the pure, the wicked into the **hands** of the righteous, and the wanton into the **hands** of the diligent students of Your Torah."

9) At the conclusion of *Parshas Mikeitz*, the *Mesorah* informs us of the number of verses in the portion, as it does for every *parshah*. However, exclusive to *Parshas Mikeitz*, we are not only told how many verses there are, but we are also told how many words there are. The *Mesorah* says that it contains 2,025 words. Why is this so? Why is it necessary to know the exact quantity of words in the portion of *Mikeitz*, specifically?

Rav Baruch Epstein explains that the number 2,025 is propitious to *Chanukah*. Each night of the eight-day holiday, we add a new candle. The Hebrew word for "candle" or "lamp" is *ner*, spelled *nun, reish*. The numerical value of *ner* is 250. If we multiply 250 by 8 (for the eight days of *Chanukah*) we reach the number 2,000. If we add onto this value the date on which *Chanukah* begins -the twenty-fifth of *Kislev* - we arrive at a total of 2,025, which is the exact number of words in the *parshah* on which *Chanukah* **always** falls.

(The Vilna Gaon, quoted in *Peninim MiShulchan HaGra,* explains that the *Mesorah* had to inform us of the number of words in *Parshas Mikeitz* because of the uncertainty as to whether the word "Potiphera" (*Bereishis* 41:46) should be considered one word or two. This doubt is resolved once we know the sum total of words in the *parshah.*)

10) In *Bereishis* (41:43), Pharaoh hands the leadership over to Yosef and has him ride in a chariot. The *pasuk* says "*Vayikre'u lefanav avreich* - And they proclaimed before him *avreich.*" *Rashi* cites the *Sifri* where Rabbi Yehudah comments that "*avreich*" refers to Yosef. He explains that this word is actually composed of two separate words: "*av*", meaning "father" or "master," and "*rach*" which is translated "tender" or "young." Thus, Yosef was a master of wisdom even at a very young age.

Rabbi Yose ben Durmaskis accuses Rabbi Yehudah of corrupting the text and, instead, connects the word "*avreich*" to the word "*birkayim* - knees" (they share the same root letters - *beis, reish, chaf*). Rabbi Yose explains: everyone was commanded by Pharaoh to bow down on their knees and prostrate themselves to Yosef who was, at that time, appointed as the new leader, as the conclusion of the *pasuk* verifies, "And he [Pharaoh] appointed him [Yosef] over all the Land of Egypt."

The commentary *Neiros Shabbos* remarks in the name of the Vilna Gaon that the core of Rabbi Yose's conflict with Rabbi Yehudah was the fact that Rabbi Yehudah regarded "*avreich*" as **two** words instead of one. The *Mesorah* informs us of the precise number of words in *Parshas Mikeitz* and thereby endorses Rabbi Yose's opinion over Rabbi Yehudah's. (If "*avreich*" were considered two distinct words, there would be 2,026 words in the *parshah* rather than 2,025, thus ruining the allusion to *Chanukah* which we mentioned in #9.)

May we be blessed with relationships in our lives in which we are able to successfully communicate with one another on the level of *remez*, to the extent that with even one slight nuance we can understand the other's intentions.

May we succeed in adhering to all the *mitzvos* - including *chodesh*, *milah* and Shabbos - and display *mesiras nefesh* in our service of God (i.e. the willingness to sacrifice our lives for the sake of Torah values) so that, in turn, Hashem delivers our enemies into our hands and brings the *Moshiach*, to whom all the nations will bow. Finally, may we deserve the restoration of the Temple and re-kindling of the *Menorah*.

Parshas Mikeitz - Shabbos Chanukah

Burning the Candles from Both Ends

Everybody seemed to be having a great time ice-skating on top of the frozen lake, until the ice suddenly broke under Tuvia's feet. The cracking of ice and splashing of water was heard by everybody. Nobody knew what to do because they were scared to dive in after him. It was only Tuvia's father, who didn't think twice, that jumped in and saved his son from sure death.

Before delving into the portion of *Mikeitz,* which discusses Yosef's rise to power and his brothers' descent into Egypt, let us talk a little bit about this weekend which is Shabbos *Chanukah.* On this Friday we light two types of candles. One type is the *Chanukah* lights and the other type is the Shabbos lights.

There are a number of differences between these two types of candles. For example, *Chanukah* candles should preferably be lit below forty inches from the ground, whereas Shabbos candles should be lit above forty inches from the ground (*Shabbos*, Ch. 2, *Bameh Madlikin*, pg. 21b, the opinion of *Revina*).

Moreover, Shabbos candles may be lit above forty feet from the ground, whereas *Chanukah* lights may not be lit above forty feet from the ground (*Shabbos*, Ch. 2, *Bameh Madlikin*, pg. 22a, the opinion of *Rav Kahana* in the name of *Rav Nasan Bar Minyomi* in the name of *Rebbi Tanchum*).

Additionally, Shabbos candles must be made of superior quality, whereas *Chanukah* candles may be made of inferior quality (*Shabbos*, Ch. 2, *Bameh Madlikin*, pg. 21b, the opinion of *Rebbi Zeira* in the name of *Rav Masnuh*, and some say it was *Rebbi Zeira* in the name of *Rav*).

Also, when it comes to lighting these two types of candles, we must first light the *Chanukah* candles, and only then light the Shabbos candles (*Shulchan Aruch, Orach Chaim, Hilchos Chanukah, siman* 679, citing the *Tur* and the *Bihag*).

Let us explore the inherent difference between these two types of candles which will enlighten us with regard to their discrepancies. The *Toras Avos* (*Inyanei Shabbos*, 69) describes the difference between the essence of Shabbos and the essence of a *Yom Tov* (holiday). What happens to us on Shabbos can be compared to a King and his son, the royal prince.

One day a week the king would summon his son to be with him in the imperial throne room. Similarly, on the Shabbos, the King of Kings, God, calls us, His noble children, to be with Him in His most majestic inner chamber. This means to say that on Shabbos, we are brought to a very high place in order to connect with God.

However, on *Yom Tov*, our bonding with God happens a bit differently. A few times a year, the king would leave his palace to be with his son in his son's home. Likewise, on *Yom Tov*, the Sovereign of Sovereigns leaves His supernal abode in the heavens to be with His children where they live.

The Slonimer Rebbe (in his *Nesivos Shalom* on *Chanukah*) adds a third scenario. Imagine what would happen if the crown prince fell into the bottom of a deep well of water and was in mortal danger. If there was nobody around to save the child, except for his majesty, then the king himself would jump in to save his son-even if the king was wearing his royal garb, which includes the magnificent crown on top of his head.

Such is the circumstance that we found ourselves in on *Chanukah*. During the Syrian-Greek attack on Jews and Judaism, we fell spiritually, to the lowest of dark places. In fact, the Torah describes the Greek exile as "Darkness." (See *Bereishis* 1:2, and the *Bereishis Rabbah* 2:4 citing the opinion of *Rabbi Shimon Ben Lakish* based on *Yirmiyahu* 4:23 and *Esther* 6:14)

By Hashem stepping in to rescue us, the message was clear. Basically, God said to us that we are His children (*Devarim* 14:1), He is always with us in our times of distress and darkness (*Tehillim* 91:15), and that we are never banished from Him (*Shmuel II* 14:14).

Therefore, when we light the *Chanukah* candles at nightfall when it is dark, God is saying to us that He is with us even during the darkness of our lives. Since *Chanukah* is celebrated when the nights are the longest, the message is that God's light is with us to comfort us even during the darkest chapters of our lives.

This explains why the *Chanukah* candles are *kosher* even if they are made of inferior quality. It teaches us that even if we feel that we have become spiritually inferior; nevertheless, God's light will still come down to warm us. This is further illustrated by the materials used in lighting the candles.

When lighting with oil, there are three components. They are: *ner* (the flame), *p'sil* (the wick) and *shemen* (the oil). The acronym of these three Hebrew words spells *nefesh* (soul). This teaches us that the light of *Chanukah* will illuminate our souls. But, it is even deeper than that.

There are five parts to the soul. In ascending order they are: *nefesh* (soul), *ruach* (spirit), *neshamah* (soul), *chaya* (life), and *yechidah* (oneness). (See *Devarim Rabbah* 2:37, the opinion of *Rebbi Simon*, and see *Bereishis Rabbah* 14:9.)

The lowest part of the soul is *nefesh*. This level represents our base animalistic urges. Yet, we are being shown by the three components of the candles that the light of *Chanukah* reaches all the way down even to the level of *nefesh*.

This also explains why *Chanukah* candles should preferably be lit below forty inches from the ground. The Talmud teaches us that the Divine presence never descends into the area of forty inches from the ground (*Sukkah*, chap.

1, pg. 5a, the opinion of *Rebbi Yosi*). However, the one exception to this rule is *Chanukah*.

By lighting the candles under the forty inches, we are being told that God's light does lower itself even into that area. The message is clear. Even if we have fallen to the lowest of places, God is there for us.

By lighting the candles outside, (*Braisah* in *Shabbos*, chap. 2, *Bameh Madlikin*, pg. 21b) we are being told that Hashem is with us even on the streets, where a person can stoop to very low and far places. Since the majority of *Chanukah* is celebrated during the weekdays, we learn that God is with us even in the mundane.

Unlike *Chanukah* which lifts those who have fallen to the lowest places, and which brings close those who have drifted to the furthest of places, Shabbos is a day which takes holy people, who have worked on themselves, to even higher places.

This is the reason that Shabbos candles must be made of superior quality. It teaches us that the Shabbos day takes self-made superior people to even greater heights. Now we can also understand why it is acceptable for the Shabbos candles to be above forty feet. We learn from this that the Shabbos day elevates spiritual people to even higher plateaus.

However, when we celebrate both *Chanukah* and Shabbos together, we achieve completeness. The two types of candles complement each other. The *Chanukah* candles lift those who have fallen to the lowest depths, and then the Shabbos candles raise them to the highest of places.

This is why we light the *Chanukah* candles before the Shabbos candles. First, we light the *Chanukah* candles to reach out to people in the places that they find themselves, which may be the lowest of the low. Only then do we light the Shabbos candles, which bring us to the highest of the high, into God's Royal Throne Room.

In this respect, Shabbos *Chanukah* is the greatest Shabbos of the year, because on this Shabbos everybody can reach the highest of levels.

We could add that in many ways, this is precisely what happened with Yosef and his brothers when they descended into Egypt. Egypt was an immoral and decadent society. So impure was Egypt that it was practically impossible for one to receive prophesy there.

Yet, when push came to shove, and the Jewish people were about to disappear, God Himself came all the way down to save us (*Shemos* 3:8). This means that the Divine presence descended even below the forty inches from the ground.

One catalyst which helped this process to occur was Yosef and his family. Yosef's mission was to bring purity even into the midst of spiritual pollution. Yosef achieved this by refraining from sinning with Potifar's wife, who tried to seduce him (*Bereishis* 39:8).

Yehudah's mission was to bring Torah even to the core of spiritual filth. He achieved this when he established a Torah academy in Egypt's district of Goshen (*Bereishis* 46:28, *Tanchumah* 11, *Bereishis Rabbah* 95:3, the opinion of *Rav Chanina*).

Slowly but surely, Yaakov and his family turned a corrupt Egyptian society into a spiritual oasis. To do that, they had to be a light unto the nation. This was not just any light; they had to be like *Chanukah* lights.

We could suggest that this is why Yosef compared himself and his brothers to flames of a candle (*Bereishis* 50:21, *Megillah*, chap. 1, *Megilla Nikreis*, pg. 16b, the opinion of *Rebbi Binyamin Bar Yefes* in the name of *Rebbi Elazar*). Perhaps, the secret behind that comparison was that he likened himself and his family to *Chanukah* candles. This means that just as the *Chanukah* lights have the power to bring the glow of holiness to the most decrepit of cultures, so too do we have that strength.

It was nothing short of a *Chanukah* miracle transforming a country of darkness into a pocket of light. This is why the Torah calls the Jewish district of Egypt "Goshnah" (*Bereishis* 46:28). That name is spelled with four Hebrew letters: *gimmel, shin, nun, hey*. They are the very same letters found on a *dreidel*! They stand as the acronym for "*Nes gadol hayah sham* - A great miracle happened there." (See the *Bnei Yissaschar*, by Reb Tzvi Elimelech of Dinov, in his *Ma'amarim* on *Chodesh Kislev-Teves.*) This indicates what a miraculous feat it was to bring holiness into the most impure of places.

Let's take a moment to gaze into the *Chanukah* candles and into the Shabbos lights and think about their implications. This will help us absorb this teaching, and will whisk us away from the bottom to the highest of places!

May we all be blessed to ignite the *Chanukah* flame within us, even into the darkest parts of our personalities; illuminate our souls, so that this Shabbos we all reach the highest of spiritual places; and experience such closeness with God that we bask in His holy, warm glow.

Chanukah

Don't You See?

"But Mommy," asked the little girl, as they passed by a blind person, "How can she have a smile on her face? She can't see anything!" "My little precious one," replied the mother, "some people can see more without their physical eyes than others who have 20/20 vision, and that is something to be happy about." The little girl didn't quite understand what her mother was trying to say, until she learned this upcoming piece of Torah.

The Talmud (*Shabbos* 21b) tells us the *Chanukah* story in short: "When the Syrian-Greeks entered our Temple they made all the oil impure. When the Hasmoneans were victorious and regained control, they checked the Temple and found only one remaining flask of oil with the High Priest's seal still intact. There was only enough oil to light the *Menorah* for one day, but a miracle occurred and the lights remained lit for eight days. So the next year, the Sages instituted those eight days as a holiday of praise and thanks to God."

This Talmud implies that one of the prime efforts of the Greeks in their military campaign was to defile Jewish oil; this is strange behavior, to say the least, because every army moves strategically in order to humble the enemy. For example, first you cut off the enemy's water supply, then you would blow horns to frighten the enemy, and afterwards the actual attack begins (see *Rashi*, *Shemos* 8:17 citing *Tanchumah*). What was the strategic move behind making Jewish oil impure?

The Slonimer Rebbe says that the Greek's actual battle was to spiritually darken the eyes of the Jewish people. They understood that a military victory could not occur until this objective was achieved. For example, the Talmud (*Nedarim* 64b) says that someone who is physically blind is compared to a dead person. This means to say that although all the other faculties are working, being blind alone is tantamount to death. So it is with someone who is spiritually blind; he, too, is considered to be dead. Which means that, even if he or she observes all the *mitzvos*, spiritual blindness alone is tantamount to spiritual death.

What does it mean to have spiritual blindness? In order to understand this, let us first define what spiritual vision is. Spiritual vision means recognizing that "there is no one else besides Him" (*Devarim* 4:35). This means that a person recognizes that God's light is what illuminates the entire Creation, that the whole world is an extension of Godliness, and also that Hashem sustains everything. In other words, it is a state of recognition that God is behind everything; wherever I go, and whatever I do, I am always with God.

Spiritual blindness however, is just the opposite. This is when one does **not** recognize that there is nothing else other than Him. When one doesn't have the awareness that God's light illuminates all of Creation, and one doesn't realize that the whole world is an extension of Godliness, and one does not see that God is sustaining everything. In other words, this is a state where one does not see God behind everything; and, therefore, this person is disconnected from Hashem. Since spiritual blindness is tantamount to death, it would be safe to say that one of the purposes of man's creation is for him to achieve spiritual vision; because without it, everything else is meaningless.

The Jewish people's survival has always been dependent on this vision, and the Greeks understood that if they could spiritually blind us, then the Jews would be considered dead and lost (God forbid). At that point the destruction of the Jews would be an inevitable reality (God forbid). So again, the Greek's primary objective was to darken the eyes of the Jewish people (see *Bereishis Rabbah* 2:4 expounding on *Bereishis* 1:2 for support of the idea that the Greeks are hinted to in the Torah with the Hebrew word *choshech*, darkness).

The Slonimer Rebbe points out that the primary function of the *menorah's* light is to illuminate the eyes of the Jewish people. Through the light of the *menorah*, a Jew can come to see that nothing exists besides God. This is because the primordial light, known as *Ohr HaGanuz,* begins to shine once again in our world during the *Chanukah* holiday.

A hint to this idea is that this primordial light functioned for thirty-six hours (see *Bereishis Rabbah* 11:2), and over the course of *Chanukah* one will have lit altogether thirty-six candles (excluding the *shamashim*). The Midrash says that this supernal light enables one to see from one end of the universe to the other. This could mean that this light enables us to see through every creation, and realize that it is God who is the ultimate source of everything.

This explains the Greek strategy in their military campaign. If they could succeed in darkening the eyes of the Jewish people to the point where we don't see God in our daily lives, they would have rendered the Jewish people as dead and lost (God forbid). The Greeks knew that the Jewish oil used for lighting the *menorah* contained the "DNA" of this spiritual light. Their objective was to contaminate that very oil so that we would not be able to perceive God in every facet of light through it. They almost succeeded. It was that one remaining flask that kept the Jewish fire burning.

One practical way to reconnect with this special light would be the following. When we light the *Chanukah* candles, we tap into that one remaining flask, and we bring the *Ohr HaGanuz* into the world. So after lighting the *menorah*, and after singing the *Maoz Tzur*, let us sit by the *Chanukah* candles, and gaze into their light. Let the holiness be absorbed into our systems, and think about how we got to this point in our lives. Let us try to see how God has been guiding us every step of the way.

So may we all be blessed with vision to realize that nothing exists outside of God, and thus remove the darkness from our lives and from the world, bringing an end to war once and for all.

Parshas Mikeitz - Zos Chanukah

The Speed of Light!

There are times in life that God shines His light upon us. At those times, we can accomplish a lot in a short amount of time. We need to be aware of these moments and take advantage of them.

In this week's portion, after Pharaoh had his dreams and was not satisfied with the various interpretations rendered, he sent for Yosef. He was brought hastily out from the dungeon; he shaved himself, changed his clothes, and came before Pharaoh (41:14). The *Zohar* (vol. 1, pg. 194b) says that the Hebrew word *Vayiritzuhu*, "as they brought him hastily" should be read as *Vayiritzaihu* which means "and He appeased him," teaching us that God appeased Yosef.

What is the connection between the written word (and he was hastened) to the spoken word (and he was appeased)? The *Maharal* in *Ner Mitzvah* tells us that the number seven represents nature because in seven days God created the natural world. The number eight is that which transcends nature. The big difference between that which is natural and that which is transcendent, is that all of nature is limited either in place or in time. However, that which transcends nature is unlimited, and not bound by the laws of time and place.

As a matter of fact, there is a world that is called the World of Eight and it is from that world that "unlimited-ness" is drawn. For example, any miracle that stems from the World of Eight is not bound by time, and we find that those salvations happen very quickly. In our exodus from Egypt, it says that everything was done in haste (*Shemos* 12:11), and it says, "Egypt imposed itself strongly upon the people to hasten to send them out of the land" (*Shemos* 12:33). This is followed by "they could not delay" (*Shemos* 12:39), and this is why the holiday is called *Pesach* because that word means to "jump" (see *Rashi*, *Shemos* 12:11).

In other words, the miracle pushed time aside. What should have taken a long time happened instantaneously, because the miracle that transpired when we left Egypt came from the World of Eight. When this process begins to happen, it is a propitious time for us to "cash in," meaning that when the gates of the World of Eight are opened, we are capable of advancing our spiritual growth with record-breaking speed.

The *Emunas Itecha* says that this explains the connection between the words "and they hastened him" and the words "and they appeased him." Yosef realized that since he was brought out from jail so hurriedly, his personal salvation stemmed from the World of Eight, which meant that he could tap into that energy and grow physically and spiritually at an Earth-shattering speed. In this way, Yosef was appeased with this opportunity which made all his suffering in Egypt worthwhile.

The miracle of *Chanukah* also stems from the World of Eight. This is especially so of the eighth day of *Chanukah*, when the miracle reached its zenith, as the oil which could naturally last only for one day transcended nature and lasted for eight days. The first seven days of *Chanukah* are not quite yet connected to the World of Eight because the first seven days are still connected to the number seven, and are, therefore, still part of the natural world.

However the eighth day of *Chanukah* brings the holiday into a whole new dimension, the World of Eight. It is then that we witness the full power of transcendence. This teaches us about the opportunity we all have to grow in leaps and bounds spiritually, in just a short amount of time. This is why the eighth day of *Chanukah* is named *Zos Chanukah* which means, "This is *Chanukah*" because this is the real *Chanukah*. This awareness should encourage us to take advantage of this time, and utilize every moment of the day.

Practically speaking, any sudden worldly, physical or financial success, or any success that exceeds our expectations, can be utilized for spiritual advancement as well. So, next time a promotion comes our way, let us use that moment as an opportunity to increase our spiritual studying as well.

For instance, those periods would be ideal for taking on a new practice that enhances our Torah study or *mitzvah* observance. Who knows, maybe if we behave this way, Hashem will send us another milestone of achievement in order to benefit from the heightened *avodas Hashem* to which it leads.

So may we all be blessed with unlimited-ness that descends from the World of Eight, allowing us to obtain the ability to absorb a lot of holiness at the speed of light.

Vayigash

Put Your Money Where Your Mouth Is

The *Rosh Yeshiva* told R' David that if he wouldn't reproach Nassan so harshly by raising his voice, and instead approach him more delicately, with a smile on the face, and a pat on the back, he would find Nassan more willing to listen.

In this week's portion, *Vayigash*, Yosef reveals his true identity to his brothers (*Bereishis* 45:3). A few verses later (in 45:12) Yosef, as if to prove the authenticity of his revelation, says, "Your eyes see… that it is my mouth that is speaking to you."

The Midrash (*Bereishis Rabbah* 93:10) expounds on this verse and explains that with the words, "Your eyes see," Yosef intended to communicate to his brothers that he was circumcised. With the second part of the verse, continues the Midrash, Yosef wished to point out that he was speaking "*Lashon HaKodesh* - the Holy Tongue," i.e. Hebrew.

Two questions arise with regard to this Midrash. Firstly, how does Yosef's speaking *Lashon HaKodesh* prove his identity? The Ramban on this verse (45:12) informs us that many of the Egyptians spoke Hebrew because of business trading between Egypt and its neighboring country, Canaan, where Hebrew was the vernacular. Secondly, the Midrash tells us that Yosef wanted to draw attention both to the fact that he was circumcised and to the fact that he was conversing in Hebrew, the holy language. What is the connection between these two things, and what message do they convey?

Before we can answer this question, says the *Tiferes Shmuel* (in *Cheilek Aleph*), we must first analyze several verses from *Parshas Vayeishev*. We are told (*Bereishis* 37:4) that Yosef's brothers "were not able to speak with him in peace." Later in the text (37:8) it says that his brothers continued to hate Yosef, "on account of his dreams, and on account of his words." Perhaps we can understand that Yosef's brothers were jealous of his dreams and consequently hated him, but what did Yosef **say** to them, besides for the recounting of his dreams, that fuelled their hatred?

To answer this question, we have to first appreciate the nature of *tochachah,* rebuke. The Torah instructs us in this *mitzvah* in *Vayikra* (19:17) where it says, "You shall reprove your fellow, and do not bear a sin because of him." The *Tiferes Shmuel* asks on this verse: What is the connection between rebuking a friend, and being innocent of sin?

On a simple level we can understand this verse to mean that if we witness someone about to transgress, but fail to rebuke him, then on some level, we are held accountable for his wrongdoing. If, however, we reprove a transgressor and alert him to his potential misdeed, then the recipient of the rebuke has the opportunity to refrain from carrying out that sin. By rebuking another, therefore, we are preventing others from transgressing and, in so doing, averting sin ourselves.

There is a deeper understanding of this verse, however, expressed by the *Tiferes Shmuel*, which will help us to answer several of the questions raised so far. He begins by differentiating between two types of rebukers:

Rebuker number one is described as a person who reproaches others from a place of **love**. This rebuker genuinely cares about his fellow friend, just as a parent cares for a child, so that when he witnesses someone about to transgress, he rebukes the person out of concern and compassion, as he is unable to stand at the sidelines and watch the other commit spiritual suicide! Regarding this type of rebuke, Shlomo HaMelech (*Mishlei* 27:5) says, "*Tovah tochachas megulah me'ahavah mesutares* - Better is revealed rebuke than hidden love." On a simple level, we can understand this to mean that it is better for a person to rebuke a transgressor directly than to merely love the sinner in his heart. In other words, although it is praiseworthy to love someone else, it is far more beneficial for the transgressor to be rebuked, since it allows him the opportunity to mend his ways!

The *Tiferet Shmuel*, however, understands this verse on a deeper level. The *pasuk*, he explains, can be read as a question: "*Tovah tochachat megula*? - What type of open rebuke is good? *Me'Ahavah mesutares* - [the type that stems] from a hidden love [within the heart of the rebuker]."

Rebuker number two is described as someone who rebukes another from a place of **hatred**. In this situation, a person publicly reprimands the transgressor, emphasizing his shortcomings and mistakes, with the aim of disgracing him. It is likely that the rebuker in this instance will **claim** to love and care for the other, but only to preserve his own image. He will pretend to care for the other and claim that his words of rebuke are for the other's benefit, but deep down, he actually intends to crush the other's self-image and cause him despair.

Based on this information we can now understand the verse in *Vayikra* 19:17. There, we are told to rebuke our fellow man... "*velo sisa alav chet*." Although this phrase is commonly translated as, "and do not bear a sin because of him," it can also be read as "but do not burden him (the person you are rebuking) with [his] sin." In other words, refrain from placing the burden of sin on the transgressor to the point that he will feel so guilty and ashamed of his misdeed that he will end up feeling completely hopeless and inept. This type of rebuke can only emanate from a place of hatred.

The *Tiferet Shmuel* says, after establishing the two types of rebukers, we can now address the episode described in *Parshas Vayeishev* from a new perspective. He explains that Yosef suspected his brothers of being involved in inappropriate actions including immorality and eating limbs from a live animal (see *Rashi* on *Bereishis* 37:2), so he decided-out of love and concern for his brothers-to rebuke them directly. This proved to be unsuccessful;

so, seeing no other choice, he proceeded to deliver a *dibah ra'ah'*-an evil report-to his father (*Bereishis* 37:2). The *Tiferet Shmuel* explains that Yosef's brothers misunderstood his intentions and perceived his actions as an expression of animosity towards them.

We can now understand the verse (*Bereishis* 37:4) which tells us that "the tribes were not able to speak with Yosef in peace - *Lo yachlu dabro l'shalom*." If we place a comma in between the words *yachlu* and *dabro*, we can read the statement as, "*Lo yachlu* - [Yosef's brothers] could not tolerate; *dabro l'shalom* - his [Yosef's] way of speaking in peace;" i.e. the way Yosef would use loving words, pretending that he was rebuking them out of love.

Although Yosef **was** coming from a place of love, his brothers perceived him as Rebuker Number Two! They thought that Yosef hated them and that he wished only to cause them disgrace. They could not tolerate the way Yosef would (so they thought) "hide behind the wings" of the *mitzvah* of *tochachah*, in order to maintain his innocent image! This is what fuelled their hatred. This interpretation also settles the query as to what the text is referring to when it informs us that Yosef's brothers hated him because of his dreams and because of his **words**. What words did Yosef utter that upset his brothers? Based on this insight, we can explain that Yosef's brothers could not bear the way in which he would speak to them with loving and caring words, while inside (so the brothers thought) feeling pure hatred and intending to bring shame upon them to the point of despair.

Although we have answered several of the queries raised, we have yet to answer the questions concerning the Midrash and Yosef's intention to inform his brothers that he was speaking *Lashon HaKodesh* and that he was circumcised. How did this prove his identity and what messages do these ideas convey?

The *Tiferes Shmuel* states that the "*Bris HaLashon* - the Covenant of the Tongue (speech)," and the "*Bris HaMeor* - the Covenant of the Skin (circumcision)" are like two "inseparable partners." He explains that a person who misuses his tongue in speaking inappropriately, will ultimately end up defiling his *Bris HaMeor* by acting immorally. This idea is supported by a verse in *Koheles* (5:5) which says, "Do not allow your mouth to cause your flesh to sin."

Included in the definition of inappropriate uses of speech are: *lashon hara* (speaking disparagingly of another even if it is entirely truthful), *rechilus* (tale bearing, even if the information is true and not derogatory), *motzi shem ra* (speaking fabricated negative information about another), *sheker* (telling lies) and *nivul peh* (speaking in a lewd manner).

We can now connect this concept to the issue of Yosef's rebuke to his brothers. If, indeed, Yosef's words did stem from a place of hatred, if he actually misused his tongue by speaking *lashon hara*, then it should have led him to ultimately falter in the realm of his *Bris HaMeor* by behaving immorally. So, after revealing his identity to his brothers, Yosef urges them to notice that he is circumcised. Although, as we are told in the previous *parshah*, *Mikeitz*, that the Egyptians were also circumcised (see *Rashi* on 41:55 where he cites the *Bereishis Rabbah* 91:5), there was a notable difference between their circumcision and Yosef's circumcision.

The tribes were unique in their righteousness and holiness. They were able to distinguish between a person who was circumcised versus one who, as well as being circumcised, also **abides by and lives up to what the circumcision represents**, i.e. guarding oneself from immorality. Yosef therefore encouraged his brothers to use their holy eyes and gift of Divine inspiration to detect that he had, indeed, lived up to the message of circumcision - that he did not engage in immorality; therefore proving, retroactively, that his words of rebuke back home in Canaan were indeed sincere and came from a place of love.

We explained that Yosef, as the Midrash describes, wanted to make his brothers aware that he was speaking *Lashon HaKodesh*. In other words, he wished to prove his identity with the fact that he was conversing in Hebrew. However, as we questioned earlier, how can this verify his identity if many of the Egyptians also spoke Hebrew?

The *Tiferes Shmuel* points out that Yosef did not intend to convey this information in order to prove his identity. He had already identified himself (45:3)! Rather, Yosef wanted to notify his brothers that he spoke only *Lashon HaKodesh*, **holy words**, pointing out to his brothers that the *tochachah* that he gave to them back home was genuine; that his words were *kadosh*, coming from a holy, loving place.

To prove this point, he urged his brothers to see his "circumcision," the Divine Light, which confirmed that he had guarded the *Bris HaMeor*, and therefore verified, retroactively, that he had kept the *Bris HaLashon* too. By conveying this message, Yosef enlightened his brothers, making them aware of their misunderstanding, and therefore enabling them to do *teshuvah* and finally make peace between one another.

May we all be blessed to keep our mouths clean, not only hygienically but spiritually too, keeping away from all forms of negative speech so that we are protected from defiling other parts of our body. May we master the art of rebuke, that it should emerge only from a place of sincere care and love for another (only this type of rebuke will be received well), so that, ultimately, we will merit the reinstitution of the Temple and the arrival of the *Moshiach*.

Vayigash

Planting the Seeds

Yitz's rock makes ripples in the river after he threw it in. Yitz's father, who was standing by, said to him, "Son, just as the rock made waves in the water, so do we cause domino-effect ramifications with our actions."

In this week's portion, *Vayigash*, it says "And God spoke to Israel in a night vision and He said, 'Yaakov, Yaakov,' and he said, 'Here I am'" (*Bereishis* 46:2). In the next verse it says, "And He said, 'I am the God, God of your father; have no fear descending to Egypt, for into a great nation I will establish you there.'"

The *Zohar* on these verses says that it was absolutely necessary for Yosef to go down to Egypt first, in order to *kasher* Egypt from its impurity and immorality. Yosef was best suited for this job because according to the *Kabbalah*, Yosef connects with the Kabbalistic Sphere of *Yesod* (Foundation) which corresponds to the sanctity of circumcision. When Yosef withstood the advances of Potiphar's wife (*Bereishis* 39:8-10), he paved the way for his family to be able to survive in Egypt, and not be influenced by its impurity. Then, Yaakov and his family could accomplish in Egypt what they did best, which was to extract holy sparks which had fallen into the darkness of Egypt.

The *Alshich* adds to this by pointing out that Yosef commanded the Egyptians to undergo circumcision (see *Rashi*, *Mikeitz* 41:55 citing *Bereishis Rabbah* 91:5) in order to weaken the lustful passions of the Egyptian society. Yosef worked to improve conditions spiritually in Egypt for twenty-two years. The number "twenty-two" is not arbitrary because it corresponds to the twenty-two letters of the Hebrew alphabet. Each year Yosef worked at planting, so to speak, a different letter in Egypt, in order to pave the way for

Yaakov and his family to survive in Egypt on their mission to extract the sparks of holiness.

However, when Yaakov began his descent into Egypt, he was concerned about the overwhelming impurity found there. It is for this reason that Hashem (God) told Yaakov "Have no fear descending to Egypt." The word "*merdah*" can be divided into two parts. The first letter *mem* stands for "*mi'gezeiras*" which means "from the decree of," and the remaining part of the word (*reish, daled, hey,*) which numerically equals 209, refers to the 209 years the Jews experienced Egyptian slavery.

The *Alshich* does not conform with the accepted number of years that the Jews experienced Egyptian bondage, which is 210. This is because the last year that the Jews were in Egypt, God struck the Egyptians with the plagues that lasted about a year, and for all practical purposes, the slavery had stopped. Although the Jews were physically in Egypt for 210 years, the *Alshich* does not count the last year as part of the years of slavery because the Jews were not subjected to slavery in that year.

The reason Hashem told Yaakov not to fear Egypt and its impurity was because of what it says in the very next verse: "I will descend with you to Egypt and I will also certainly bring you up" (*Bereishis* 46:4). This meant that the Divine presence would be with the Jewish people in their exile.

This message speaks to us until this very day. Namely, that God is with us in the darkest chapters of our history on a national level, and Hashem is with us individually in our most difficult and challenging situations. This thought should permeate our minds, hearts, and souls at all times so that we never lose hope.

Additionally, every time we turn our eyes away from gazing at something inappropriate, we add a level of holiness to ourselves and to our surroundings. One less look a day is already embarking on the road to purity. This ensures that God's presence will dwell amongst us.

So as we "*Vayigash*" (approach) the darkest months (such as *Teves*, which has the longest nights of the year), may each and every one of us be blessed to find the greatest light in our Torah study and in our prayers which are made up of the twenty-two holy letters of the Hebrew alphabet. Thus, we will experience the final redemption, and realize, retroactively, that God was with us the entire time.

Vayigash

I Am With You

Moishy was skipping and jumping as he made his way down the sidewalk. He didn't have a care in the world. He didn't even look both ways before crossing the street, all because he was holding his father's hand. Daddy is taking care of me; what could possibly go wrong? If we could be more like Moishy, how much more calm life would be.

In *Parshas Vayigash* (46:3) God says to Yaakov, "I am God, the God of your father, fear not going down to Egypt, for a great nation I will make of you there." The *Ohr HaChaim HaKadosh* asks: what was Yaakov afraid of? If his fear was that the Egyptian exile was going to begin, with all its pain and suffering, then how did God alleviate Yaakov's concerns by saying, "Don't fear, for I will make you into a great nation there." So what that he will become a great nation? That still doesn't address the subject of Yaakov's fear, i.e. all the pain and suffering?

The verse (*Tehillim* 137:1) says, "By the rivers of Babylon, there we sat, and also wept when we remembered Zion." This verse is describing the Jewish nation's descent into the Babylonian exile. The *Zohar* (volume 2, pg. 2b, at the beginning of the *Parshas Shemos*) points out that at that time, the Jewish people were very broken. This was not because of all the pain and suffering that they would have to endure. On the contrary, the Jewish people have the strength to persevere through whatever tortures the nations throw at us.

Rather, the *Zohar* says, the Jewish people were very broken because they thought (as they began the first of their four exiles) that this meant they would become very distant from God. This thought is something which the Jewish people could not tolerate. They were only comforted when Yechezkel the prophet revealed to them what was happening in Heaven at that time. God was saying to his entire entourage of holy angels, "What are you all doing here? My beloved children are going into the Babylonian exile and you are all just sitting around? Get up, pack your bags, and go with them to Babylon, for I am going to Babylon." So the Holy One, Blessed Be He, with His myriad of angelic hosts went to Babylon with the Jewish people. When the Jewish people heard that God was with them, they were no longer concerned with the exile whatsoever, because they knew that God had not forsaken them.

The Slonimer Rebbe suggests that just like the Jews on the way to Babylon thought God had left them, so too Yaakov Avinu on his way down to the Egyptian exile was afraid that God was forsaking him and his family. As long as Yaakov was living in *Eretz Yisrael*, Yaakov felt a special closeness to God because it says (*Devarim* 11:12) that the eyes of God are always on the Land of Israel. However, now that Yaakov would be leaving the Land, he thought there would be a great distance between himself and the Divine. This can be compared to a child who walks with his parents. As long as the parent is holding the child's hand, the child doesn't have a concern in the world. However, the moment the parent lets go of the child's hand, that is when the child begins to get frightened.

This is analogous to Yaakov. As long as he was in Israel he felt as if he was walking with his Parent in Heaven's hand. But now that he would be going to Egypt, he felt as if his Parent had let go; this was the cause of his concern. God alleviated his fears when He said to Yaakov, "I will go down with you into Egypt" (46:4), meaning to say, "I will not forsake you."

Just as when a King's child falls to the bottom of a pit; if there is nobody around to rescue the little Prince, the King will go down himself to rescue the child. Even in the midst of Egyptian impurity, we were called God's firstborn child (see *Shemos* 4:22), and there was nobody who could have saved us, not even the angels (due to the fear that even they would be negatively influenced by Egyptian society), so God Himself, the Parent, went down to the bottom of the pit to rescue His child.

The reason why God is with us during the darkest of exiles is because God knows that even when a Jew sins, in the depths of his heart he has such remorse, and his heart is so broken because he is moving further away from God. God recognizes that even though a Jew feels broken at the time of sin, he still cannot stand up to the temptation. This is why God is so close to us even at our lowest moments. This is not only true with an exile on a national level, but it even holds true for an exile on an individual level. This means that if a Jew feels that he is going through his own personal *Mitzrayim* - meaning that one is going through dark, difficult, and challenging times - he has to realize that God is with him in those low places.

When we feel that we have drifted far away, we should say the following words, “Dear God, I know that You are with me. Thank You for taking care of me. I love you, too!” This declaration will help us feel reconnected and lift our spirits as well.

May we children be blessed with the knowledge that God, our Parent, is holding our hand with an understanding of where we are coming from, which will give us the strength to persevere, no matter what difficulties we seem to be experiencing.

Vayigash

Do It Anyway

Shmuel wasn't in the mood to take his medication, but so what? He knew he had to take it anyway. Doing what we have to do isn't dependent on our mood; it's dependent on our responsibility.

In this week's portion, *Vayigash*, we read about the emotional reunion between Yosef and his father, Yaakov. The verse (46:29) says that Yosef "fell on his father's neck and wept excessively." *Rashi* cites the Midrash Aggadah which points out that Yaakov did not fall on his son's neck and neither did he kiss him. Instead, while Yosef embraced his father, Yaakov recited the "*Shema.*"

Why did Yaakov choose this particular time to say the *Shema*? Hadn't he already recited it that morning, before continuing his journey to Egypt?

The *Emunas Itecha* resolves this difficulty by conveying the deep significance of the *Shema* prayer. He cites the "*Sefarim HaKedoshim*" (mystical sources) which state that the greatest expression of Divine service is *mesiras nefesh*, self-sacrifice. The willingness to die in order to sanctify God's name is addressed in the first verse of the *Shema.* As we declare the oneness of God, "Hashem ***echad,***" we affirm our commitment to His sovereignty (*Kaballas ol malchus shamayim* - accepting the yoke of Heaven), and have in mind our readiness to give our lives in order to sanctify His name.

The *Emunas Itecha* explains: for twenty-two years, Yaakov mourned Yosef - his most beloved son (*Bereishis* 37:3) - and thought that he had been killed by a wild beast (37: 33). Yaakov was completely inconsolable. To him, the thought of life without Yosef was more painful than the idea of death itself. Therefore, the notion of *mesiras nefesh* - of surrendering his life for God -

was not much of a challenge for Yaakov in this condition.

However, once Yaakov discovered that Yosef was, in fact, alive and was reunited with him after a long and arduous era of bereavement, his existence suddenly regained value and meaning. At that point, Yaakov actually felt **alive** and desired to live once again. (See 45:27 where Yaakov's spirit is revived after hearing that Yosef is living, "*Vatechi ru'ach Yaakov avihem,*" and the name of next week's portion which is entitled "*Vayechi* - he lived," also alluding to this point.)

It is for this reason, the *Emunas Itecha* explains, that Yaakov said the *Shema* exactly at the moment of reunion with Yosef. All the time that Yaakov was grieving, he was unable to serve God in its fullest sense because his *mesiras nefesh* (willingness to die for God) was not totally authentic, due to his emotional state at that time. After all, if one feels that life is not worth living in the first place, God forbid, how hard would it be to be prepared to die?

Once Yaakov saw Yosef with his own eyes, however, he experienced an immediate emotional and psychological transformation; life suddenly became meaningful and extremely precious, once again. This explains why **specifically at that moment** Yaakov engaged in the recitation of the *Shema* - the one prayer in which we declare our readiness to die for God's sanctity. Only when we truly **love** and **desire** life can we actually serve Him with genuine *mesiras nefesh*. This is termed "*avodah bi'shlemusah,*" service of God in totality.

This idea is hinted at in the verse following the poignant encounter (46:30) as Yaakov says to Yosef, "Now I can die." Yaakov understood that only once he had seen Yosef and regained his will to live, could he truly be in the position to sacrifice his life for God with complete sincerity.

We can derive a crucial lesson from this insight. Sometimes, when we perform a *mitzvah* or kind deed, we do so because we are in the mood, or because it makes us feel good. Similarly, we may refrain from certain negative actions simply because we have no desire or temptation to carry them out in the first place. Both these cases exemplify a type of *avodas Hashem* that cannot be defined "*avodas Hashem bi'shlemusah*" because, in truth, it is more of a self-service than Divine service.

A practical example of the first case (i.e. performing a good deed for alternate reasons other than *ratzon Hashem* - God's Will, can be illustrated in the following scenario: One day, as I am walking down the street, I stumble across someone who is obviously in desperate need of help. There's a woman sitting on the ground with a small child by her side, both in tattered clothing. My emotions are aroused. I feel sorry for them and their hopeless situation and, naturally, I place some coins by their side. It's the least I can do!

As I continue on my way, I notice another woman who is peculiar-looking and a little on the rowdy side. She approaches me and shakes a cup right in front of my face. Rather than empathize for this beggar, I feel intruded and irritated. I think to myself, "Why should I give my money to this random person who invades my space and makes me feel uncomfortable?!"

Clearly, the difference between these two cases is the outward behavior of each of the beggars and my subsequent perception of, and reaction to, the situation. In reality, I don't know which of them needs more help. In truth, I should feel equally duty-bound in both cases to offer assistance because the *ratzon Hashem* obligates me to help the poor and needy as much as I can, **regardless** of my feelings, mood, thoughts, opinions, judgments, reactions, etc.

I am not referring to cases where one may be in real physical danger. Obviously the priority in these situations is to protect oneself. Here we are discussing the attitude or behavior of people in need that may "rub us the wrong way," regarding which, the Torah makes no distinction in terms of our obligation to help them.

Of course, I am in no way suggesting that we should become robots who completely suppress our emotions in order to carry out the will of God. On the contrary, our feelings and desires are extremely important! We should empathize with people in need; we should be excited to do the *mitzvos*. What I am pointing out, however, is that we must learn to differentiate between the feelings we experience and the **reason** that we should execute the particular *mitzvah*. We do not give charity **because** we feel sympathy; we do not learn Torah **because** it is inspiring; but rather, for the sole reason that it is God's Will.

Avodas Hashem that is authentic and complete is demonstrated in situations when we conquer our negative mind-set, and execute a positive *mitzvah* which we, originally, had no interest in performing, or felt would be too difficult to carry out. Similarly, genuine Divine service is evident in circumstances when we crave to commit negative actions but successfully overcome our desires in recognition of God's Will.

For instance, honoring parents is a positive commandment from the Torah that obligates us to respect our parents even at times when we feel pestered by them or embarrassed by something they say or do, etc., and not just when circumstances are smooth. As servants of Hashem, we should try our utmost to always help our parents and respect them at all times and in all situations.

Finally, if we develop a desire to behave according to the Torah and train ourselves to do *mitzvos* and refrain from *aveiros* even when it is hard for us, we will eventually transform our will so that it conforms with God's Will. Then we will thereby fulfill the Mishnah (*Avos* 2:4) which states; "Do His Will as if it was your's, so that He may do your will as if it was His. Nullify your will before His, so that He may nullify others' will before yours."

We should be encouraged by the fact that even after we overcome a specific conflict between our personal desire and God's Will, and succeed in aligning our will with His, God will credit us **every single time** we do that particular deed that was once difficult for us, as if it were a struggle each time!

May we be blessed to serve Hashem in totality by doing what we are supposed to even when we don't want to, and by withholding ourselves from negative actions when we would rather give in to temptation. May this second nature become first nature so that we learn to love what God loves and despise what He despises. And in so doing, may we develop the right tastes, and thus enable ourselves to appreciate and enjoy the ushering in of the *Moshiach*, *Olam Haba* and all that comes with it.

Vayechi

Life After Death

I think it's pretty safe to say that most of us feel that the necessity of going to a cemetery is a grave situation. But when you think about it, the grave is just a doorway that we eventually have to go through - and please God, one day, we will return to this world through that same entrance.

At the beginning of this week's portion, *Vayechi*, we are informed that Yaakov lived in the land of Egypt for seventeen years (*Bereishis* 43:28).

The Midrash in *Bereishis Rabbah* (96:5) compares Yaakov Avinu with Rabbi Yehudah HaNasi who lived in Tzipori for seventeen years. What is the deeper significance of this association, besides the fact that they sojourned for the same length of time in these locations?

We will be able to answer this question in light of a Talmud in *Kesubos* (103a): When the time neared for Rabbi Yehudah HaNasi to pass on, he requested that his sons enter his room, and then instructed them, "Take care that you show due respect to your mother. The light shall continue to burn in its usual place, the table shall be laid as usual, [and my] bed shall be spread in the usual way."

The Talmud then explains the reasoning behind each of his instructions. With regard to the final two orders, the Talmud says that even after his passing, Rabbi Yehudah would return home every Friday night and, therefore, wanted his sons to take responsibility for setting the table and making his bed. According to the *Gilyon HaShas (citing Sefer Chassidim, Ch. 1129)* Rabbi Yehudah appeared in full Shabbos attire and recited *kiddush* for the entire household, exempting them in the *mitzvah*.

The Talmud continues: One Friday night a neighbor came to the door, and was speaking in a loud voice. The maidservant quietly asked the visitor to lower her tone out of respect for the Rabbi (Rabbi Yehudah HaNasi) who was sitting in the house. Once Rabbi Yehudah HaNasi became aware that word of his visits was out, he no longer returned home out of concern that people would degrade previous *tzaddikim* who did not have the privilege of revisiting their homes in the physical world.

We see from this account that Rabbi Yehudah was still obligated in *mitzvos* even after physical death, so much so that he was able to perform *kiddush* on behalf of others. How was this possible? Does bodily death not mark the end of the period when we are able to serve God, and gain merits though Torah study and fulfillment of His commandments?

The *Emunas Itecha* explains that Rabbi Yehudah, during his life in *Olam Hazeh* (the physical world), valued the *mitzvos* and the personal growth that they provide to such an extent that he was able to continue growing even after death. He regarded each and every commandment as a precious and unique opportunity for personal and spiritual development. Moreover, he was able to maintain this awareness and utilize these opportunities successfully.

Consequently, even after his soul left his body, he merited the ability to continue growing and developing spiritually through the *mitzvos*, as the Talmud in *Berachos* (64a, citing *Rabbi Chiya bar Ashi* in the name of *Rav*), says: "The scholars have no rest either in this world or in the World to Come; as it says, 'They go from strength to strength…'" (*Tehillim* 84:8).

The *Emunas Itecha*, citing the *Koheles Yaakov* in the section *Erech Rebbe*, says that the soul of Rabbi Yehudah HaNasi was a reincarnation of a "spark" from Yaakov Avinu's soul. This is hinted at in Rabbi Yehudah's title, *Nasi* (prince), spelled *nun, shin, yud, aleph*. These letters form the acronym for the phrase; "*Neshamah shel Yaakov Avinu* - Soul of our Patriarch Jacob" or, "*Nitzutz shel Yaakov Avinu* - Spark of our Patriarch Jacob."

If Rabbi Yehudah - a spark of Yaakov's soul - reached a level in *Olam Hazeh* that enabled him to continue doing *mitzvos* even after physical death, then surely Yaakov Avinu - the **source** of Rabbi Yehudah's soul - also continued to be *chayav* (obligated) in *mitzvos*, and also revisited his household each week to say *kiddush* for his family. Yaakov valued the personal growth that the *mitzvos* provided to such a degree, that even after death, he was still capable of growing.

The Talmud (*Taanis* 5b) provides support to this idea as it recounts the dialogue between Rabbi Yochanan and Rabbi Nachman concerning the perpetuation of Yaakov's life on Earth. Rabbi Yochanan declared the famous words, "*Yaakov Avinu lo meis* - Jacob, our Patriarch did not die." Rabbi Nachman disputed Rabbi Yochanan's assumption, based on the simple fact that we know Yaakov died and was bewailed, embalmed, and buried. In defense of his position, Rabbi Yochanan quoted Yirmiyah (30:10), wherein both Yaakov Avinu and his children "Yisrael" are mentioned, and are likened to one another. The Sages expound that just as Yaakov's descendants (Yisrael) are alive, so will he (Yaakov) be alive.

Although Rabbi Yochanan derived evidence from the Torah to support the fact that Yaakov is living, we are still unable to reconcile this view with the fact that Yaakov died and was buried! (See *Bereishis* 49:33 & 50:13.)

The *Emunas Itecha* resolves this seeming contradiction as he explains that in reality, Yaakov **did** die. However, it is considered **as if** he never died because his obligation in *mitzvos* continued, to the extent that he was able to also exempt others, in accordance with Jewish law.

Now we can appreciate even more the Midrash that connects Yaakov Avinu with Rabbi Yehudah HaNasi. During the time that Yaakov lived in Egypt, he continued to improve and develop himself through the *mitzvos*, even as his life was drawing to a close. Similarly, Rabbi Yehudah HaNasi - a reincarnation of Yaakov - worked on his *avodas* Hashem and grew from the *mitzvos* during his stay in Tzipori.

This idea is alluded to, and also further emphasized, in the number of years that Yaakov and Rabbi Yehudah spent in Egypt and Tzipori, respectively. Seventeen is the numerical value of the word *tov*, good, indicating that both Yaakov Avinu and Rabbi Yehudah HaNasi spent the seventeen years, in their respective places, productively.

We can also lead a growth-oriented life through *mitzvos*. Choose one *mitzvah*, and study about its inner meaning. Then, when we perform it, we can grow from it.

May we be blessed to approach Torah study and the performance of *mitzvos* with the necessary sincerity and seriousness, which will cause us to improve ourselves and develop from one level to the next. Consequently, may we be blessed to live forever (*Vayechi*) - even after death - and witness the resurrection of the dead, when the Patriarchs will recite *kiddush* for their children, i.e. **us**, and continue to sanctify us more and more.

Vayechi

Ko-Existence

Avi's first trip to Israel was great. He spent his year learning in a *yeshiva.* Avi felt that all the learning he did back in the States simply did not compare to the quality of Torah study in the Holy Land. Avi felt that the Torah literally came alive in Israel. The people, places, and events that he studied about, happened right here. The year flew by, and Avi had to go back, and visit his parents. This was also exciting for Avi; after all, he hadn't seen his parents the entire year.

The scene at the airport was a heartwarming one, filled with lots of hugs, kisses, and tears. This reunion reminded Avi of another one that he had studied about in the *yeshiva.* In that story, the son hadn't seen his father for twenty-two years. Yes, there were hugs, kisses, and tears, but there was also another element that occurred, the recitation of *Shema.* It baffled Avi and got him thinking.

This week's story deals with Yaakov's death and burial (*Bereishis* 49:33 & 50:13). Just before Yaakov passed away, he calls for his children to gather around his bed (*Bereishis* 49:1-2). Yaakov's intention was to reveal to his sons what would happen at The End of Days (*Bereishis* 49:1).

However, right before Yaakov revealed this most coveted secret, the information was taken away from him by God. Yaakov, fearing the worst, said to his children that perhaps the reason why the facts were taken away from him was because one or more of his children were wicked.

After all, Yaakov reasoned, my grandfather Avraham had a Yishmael. My father Yitzchak had an Esav. Maybe I, too, fathered unrighteous children who are not deemed worthy of this information.

Yaakov's sons responded by saying, "*Shema Yisrael Hashem Elokeinu Hashem Echad* - Hear O Israel, Hashem our God, Hashem is One." They explained themselves by saying that just like there is only One God in Yaakov's heart, so too, there is only One God in their hearts.

When Yaakov heard what his children said, he responded with the words, "*Baruch Shem Kevod Malchuso L'Olam Va'ed* - Blessed is the Name of His Glorious Kingdom forever and ever."

The Sages grapple with how we should conduct ourselves when we recite the daily *Shema*. To say the "*Baruch Shem*" sentence would be an affront to Moshe because he did not include that sentence in the Torah and to delete that sentence would be a slight to Yaakov because he did say it.

The way the Sages resolve this issue is that we should say it, in order to show respect for Yaakov; however, it should be said quietly in deference to Moshe (see *Pesachim*, Ch. 4, *Makom Shenahagu*, pg. 56a, the opinion of *Rebbi Shimon Ben Lakish*). This discussion leads us to another episode.

Earlier, when Yaakov finally arrived in Egypt and saw Yosef for the first time in so many years, Yosef fell on Yaakov's neck and cried (*Bereishis* 46:29). Yet, Yaakov does not cry on Yosef's neck, because Yaakov was reciting the *Shema* (*Rashi* citing the *Midrash Aggadah*).

This is a bit perplexing. If the time to recite the *Shema* was at hand, then Yosef should have recited it as well. But, if it was not the time to recite the *Shema*, then Yaakov should not have said it.

The *Chasam Sofer* (*Parshas Vayigash*, in the paragraph *Vayar Eilav*) answers this by suggesting that it was indeed the time to recite the *Shema* and both Yaakov and Yosef did indeed say the *Shema*. However, Yosef only said the verse of *Shema*, whereas Yaakov also said the verse of *Baruch Shem*.

Therefore, it took Yaakov a little bit longer to complete his recitation than it did for Yosef. During the extra time it took for Yaakov to recite the *Baruch*

Shem, Yosef fell on his father's neck and cried.

Once again, we see that Yaakov was involved in the recitation of the verse *Baruch Shem.* Let us explore a deeper understanding of this pattern.

The *Ohr Torah* (cited in the *Lekach Vihalibuv*) explains that Esav represented the power of evil in the world which tries to conceal God's existence. Perhaps we could suggest a support for this idea by mentioning that Esav's grandson was Amalek (*Bereishis* 36:4 & 36:12).

Amalek's philosophy was that everything that happens in this world is just a coincidence (*Devarim* 25:18 and *Rashi* there). In other words, according to Amalek's way of thinking, there is no Divine intervention.

Where would Amalek have received this training, if not from the house of Esav, which tries to hide God's existence. Moreover, we could suggest that this philosophy of concealing God's existence in the world is hinted at in Esav's very essence.

When Esav was born, the Torah describes him as having an "*aderes sei'ar*" - a "cloak of hair" (*Bereishis* 25:25). Perhaps one reason why the Torah shares this with us is because it is a message about who Esav was. The nature of hair is that it covers up what is underneath it. Therefore, at his very core, Esav represented a view that attempts to conceal the truth.

The *Ohr Torah* says that Yaakov, Esav's brother, was the antithesis of this approach. Yaakov represented the holy power of revealing God's essence and majesty in the world. Yaakov and Esav struggled spiritually about this throughout their lives.

The *Lev Aryeh* on the Torah cites the *Arizal,* who teaches that there are two verses which represent God's magnificent revelation and control over the world. One is the *Shema* and the other is the *Baruch Shem.*

However, there is a difference between them. The *Shema* signifies the revelation of God's essence above, in the Heavens; whereas the *Baruch Shem* epitomizes the revelation of God's essence down here on Earth.

Yaakov fought against Esav's world view by occupying himself in the recitation of *Shema* and *Baruch Shem*. This is hinted at when the Torah records Yaakov's instructions to his messengers before sending them to Esav.

Those words were, "*Ko somrune la'adoni Esav* - So shall you say to my master Esav" (*Bereishis* 32:5); and "*Ko amar avdecha Yaakov* - So says your servant Yaakov" (*Bereishis* 32:5). Both of these statements begin with the word "*ko*" (so).

Ko is made up of two letters: *kaf* and *hey*. Together, they have the numerical value of twenty-five. This number is special because there are exactly twenty-five letters in the *Shema* verse. This indicated that Yaakov would battle Esav by reciting the *Shema*, which would strengthen God's revelation above.

But the word "*ko*" does not appear only once; it is found two times, as we mentioned before.

The second *ko* (twenty-five) represents the amount of letters contained in the second verse *Baruch Shem*. This shows that Yaakov would battle Esav by reciting the *Baruch Shem*, which would strengthen God's revelation below.

Actually, the *Baruch Shem* verse only has twenty-four letters in it. However, according to the *Arizal*, in the future, one letter will be added to the *Baruch Shem* verse. That letter will be a *vav* at the beginning of the sentence, making it *Ubaruch Shem*. Thus, there will be twenty-five letters eventually.

We could add that this explains our custom today. God's sovereignty is not yet completely revealed on Earth. This is why we recite the *Baruch Shem* verse quietly. The *Baruch Shem* is connected to the world below. Since God's Presence is not completely felt down here, we say the *Baruch Shem* quietly as if to say that we do not yet experience God's revelation in totality.

However, we still say the *Baruch Shem* expressing our hope for the day when God's Presence will be recognized by all. In the future, when the revelation will be whole, the letter *vav* will be added, because the *vav* is a "connecting" letter, and as such represents the "connection" that will exist between the upper and lower worlds; namely, that both will be permeated by God's Presence.

We could go a little further to say that God's revelation will only come to fruition when God's people live in the Promised Land. This is why Moshe did not include the *Baruch Shem* in the Torah.

Moshe spent his entire life outside the land of Israel. Therefore, the ultimate revelation was not yet actualized. Thus, the *Baruch Shem* verse was omitted from Moshe's Torah.

However, Yaakov lived most of his life in Israel and was eventually buried in Israel. Since Yaakov was closer to God's complete revelation, he did say the *Baruch Shem* verse. This will shed light on why Yaakov said the *Baruch Shem* when he met Yosef.

The names of the tribes were etched into the onyx stones, worn on the shoulder pads of the High Priest (*Shemos* 28:10). Six names were scratched into each stone. *Rashi* (citing *Sotah*, Ch. 7, *Eilu Ne'emarin*, pg. 36a) comments that the tribes Reuven, Shimon, Levi, Yehudah, Dan, and Naftali were found on the first stone, whereas the tribes Gad, Asher, Yissachar, Zevulun, Yosef, and Binyamin were engraved on the second stone.

The tribes were listed in chronological order of birth. When all the tribe's names are together, there are fifty letters. When divided in this way, there are twenty-five letters in each set.

The twenty-five letters on the first stone represents the first verse, *Shema,* which has twenty-five letters. The twenty-five letters on the second stone represents the second verse, *Baruch Shem*, which has (or will have) twenty-five letters.

This comes to teach us that when all the tribes are unified, then God's revelation will be felt throughout the entire world. This will happen when we are all "gathered" into our Holy Land, Israel.

This is why, when all his children were "gathered" around Yaakov (who represented Israel - and such was his name), there was unity amongst them. How apropos that both verses, *Shema* and *Baruch Shem,* were uttered at that time, which demonstrated the revelation of God that they could accomplish together.

However, as long as Yaakov thought that Yosef was dead, Yaakov concluded that there was lack of unity, and thereby the structure of fifty letters was destroyed. This meant that the revelation above and below, represented by the *Shema* and *Baruch Shem* verses, would never come to be.

In Yaakov's mind, God's revelation in this world looked pretty bleak. After all, one of the tribes was missing, meaning that complete unity was absent, thereby undermining total revelation.

Therefore, during all those years, Yaakov only recited the *Shema* verse, but omitted the *Baruch Shem* verse. This expressed Yaakov's thinking. God's Presence may be felt above, but it will never be realized completely below.

We might add that Yosef's name appeared on the second onyx stone. Therefore Yosef was connected to the second verse, *Baruch Shem.* With Yosef thought to be gone, Yaakov no longer bothered to recite the second verse, *Baruch Shem.*

However, when Yaakov saw that indeed Yosef was still alive, he not only recited the *Shema,* but also included the *Baruch Shem.* With Yosef back, there could be unity. The second onyx stone was activated, and therefore, the second verse is once again relevant because total revelation is once again possible.

Now all the tribes were unified, and all their names were fused together. This would ensure that God would be recognized by all.

Practically speaking, let's try to put more intent into the recitation of the *Shema.* Before we say the *Shema* it would be advisable to study it and then concentrate on new ideas that we pick up along the way when we actually say the *Shema.*

May we all be blessed to recite the *Shema* and *Baruch Shem* each and every day with intent, may we be committed to revealing God in this world through our actions, and thus defeat the forces of Amalek and Esav who try to suppress the knowledge of God's existence in our lives.

Vayechi

High Hope, High Hope

Hope is the feather that makes the soul soar high. Hope is the thing by which all can be accomplished. So let our hope shape our future.

In this week's *parshah, Vayechi*, Yaakov tells his children, "Gather around, and I will tell you what will happen to you at the End of Days." (*Bereishis* 49:1) *Rashi* (citing *Pesachim* 56a) explains that Yaakov wanted to reveal to his children the date of *Moshiach*'s arrival, when suddenly the Divine presence left him and he no longer remembered the date. As a result, Yaakov had to speak about other things, so he blessed his children. Apparently, Yaakov sinned by wanting to disclose the date of *Moshiach*'s arrival, since the Divine departs from a person only when something is amiss. What exactly was wrong with Yaakov's desire?

The Midrash (*Bereishis Rabbah* 98:20, in the name of R' Yitzchak) states, "Everything is with hope. Pains and suffering are with hope. Sanctifying God's Name is with hope. The merits of the Patriarchs are with hope. The desire for the Coming World is with hope. Grace is with hope. Forgiveness is with hope, as it says (*Bereishis* 49:18), 'For Your salvation I hope, Hashem.'" The *Nesivos Shalom* adds that this verse-taken from this week's *parshah*-also implies that the future redemption will be achieved with hope. Let us elaborate.

All good things can be accomplished through hope. When we place our complete hope and trust in Hashem's salvation, extraordinary results can come about. Whether we hope to endure pain, to deserve the merits of the Patriarchs, to find favor in everyone's eyes, or to usher in the Messianic Era, the very act of hoping indicates a complete dependence on Hashem. This is what creates the energy for these events to happen. The *Nesivos Shalom* writes that one who believes and trusts in Hashem and hopes for salvation will obtain it. Even if we are not worthy, the hope itself will make it happen.

We can add to this that *emunah* (belief) and *bitachon* (trust) are the building blocks of Judaism - literally the *Aleph-Beis* (in Hebrew, the initials of *emunah* and *bitachon* are *aleph* and *beis*). Imagine a one-year-old child, sitting and crying in the hope that someone will come to feed or change him. Could any healthy parent in the world possibly ignore the cries of his child? The child hopes and completely depends on being cared for by the parents - and as a result, the parents' response is immediately forthcoming. The child's hope actually brings about the parents' care.

Based on this idea, the Chortkover Rebbe explains what Yaakov did wrong. A verse in Isaiah (60:22) describes the arrival of *Moshiach* with the words, "I am Hashem; I will hasten it in its time (***b'itah achishenah***)." The Talmud (*Sanhedrin* 98a) cites R' Yehoshua ben Levi, who notices an apparent contradiction in the verse. How can it be that *Moshiach*'s arrival will be ***b'itah*** (at the appointed time) yet also ***achishenah*** (hastened)?

The Talmud resolves this problem by explaining that, if the Jewish people deserve redemption, the arrival of *Moshiach* will be hastened (***achishenah***). However, if the Jewish people do not deserve redemption, *Moshiach* will arrive at the appointed time (***b'itah***) anyway. Since Yaakov wanted to reveal the appointed time of *Moshiach*'s arrival, he apparently felt that the Jews would never deserve a hastened arrival of the End of Days. As a result, he was punished by the departure of the Divine presence. It seems that Yaakov should have believed more strongly in the power of hope, which is capable of bringing *Moshiach* before the appointed time. Even if our Torah study, prayer, acts of kindness, and other *mitzvos* are all sorely lacking, hope itself can enable us to obtain our dreams.

Later in the *parshah*, we see that Yaakov realized his mistake. In his blessings to his children, he says, "For Your salvation I hope, Hashem"

(*Bereishis* 49:18). We could suggest that the Divine presence returned when Yaakov said these words, because his acknowledgment of the power of hope rectified his earlier mistake. With the return of the Divine presence, Yaakov once again knew the date of *Moshiach*'s arrival - but he did not reveal it because he saw that there was no need. Through the power of hope, salvation can come earlier than we deserve.

It would be a good practice to recite the twelfth Tenet of our Faith every single day. There is says, "I believe with complete faith in the coming of the *Moshiach*." Then, slow down and with a hopeful heart say the next part of the sentence, "And even though he may tarry; nevertheless, I hopefully wait for him to come." The amount of hope we put into this sentence may just seal his coming. This is all for national redemption. However, for our personal salvation, when we are going through difficult times, we should become accustomed to say "*Lishu'asecha kivisi Hashem* - For Your salvation I hope, Hashem."

May we be blessed with hope, that we will find grace and forgiveness in each other's eyes, resulting in unity among the different groups, and thus deserve the hastened arrival of *Moshiach*.

Vayechi

Talk Ain't Cheap

When the mouth behaves like an oyster, and clams up, we are sure to find a precious pearl on the inside...the tongue.

This week's portion, *Vayechi*, not only concludes the book of *Bereishis* but also brings us to the period of time known as *Shovevim* (which, in its Hebrew form, serves as the acronym of the six Torah portions that follow *Vayechi: Shemos, Va'eira, Bo, Beshalach, Yisro, Mishpatim*). The Arizal teaches us that these weeks are special because during this time, we can fix inappropriate conduct; meaning we can increase the holiness in our lives (see the *Be'er Heitev, Orach Chaim* Ch. 685:2, in the laws of *Meggilah* citing the *Arizal* in his commentary to the Torah). Although all the tribes are mentioned in this week's portion when Yaakov blesses them, there is one tribe which is given special attention, and that is Yosef.

Yosef is called a *tzaddik*, a righteous person (see *Zohar* vol. 1, pg 45a). There is a verse in *Mishlei* (10:25) that says, "A *tzaddik* is the *Yesod* (foundation) of the world." It is known Kabbalistically that *Yesod* is the name of one of the spiritual spheres that is linked to the place of circumcision, which represents sanctity of circumcision. So, if Yosef is a *tzaddik* and a *tzaddik* is *Yesod*, then Yosef represents *Yesod*. This means that Yosef personified sanctity of circumcision. We all know that he overcame the advances of Potifar's wife (see *Vayeishev* 39:8-13), and he wouldn't so much as look at the Egyptian women when they climbed the walls to catch a glimpse of his beauty. (See *Vayechi* 49:22 & *Bereishis Rabbah* 98:18; see also *Parshas Shemos*, essay number 2, for further elaboration on this topic.)

The *Emunas Itecha* cites the *Sefer HaYetzirah* which says that, "Sanctity of tongue leads to sanctity of circumcision; and impurity of tongue (i.e.

gossip, derogatory speech, making fun of others, embarrassing somebody) leads to impurity of circumcision." There is a hint that these two ideas are connected, for there is a type of *lashon hara* called *avak* (meaning the dust) of evil speech, when nothing negative was said explicitly, but rather was insinuated (see *Bava Basra* pg 165a). The acronym for *avak* in the Hebrew stands for "*os bris kodesh* - the sign of the holy circumcision." This teaches us that if a person defiles the tongue, it will lead to defiling the sanctity of circumcision.

It is interesting to note that the Hebrew word for mouth, *peh,* has exactly the same numerical value as the Hebrew word for circumcision, *milah* (each word equals 85). It is also interesting that the Hebrew word *milah* has an alternative translation of "word," showing the connection between the words that we speak and the effect it has on the place of circumcision.

We could suggest that this could explain why the prohibition against *lashon hara* is found specifically in *Parshas Kedoshim* (*Vayikra* 19:16), conveying to us the message that by guarding our tongue, we imbibe *kedushah* into our being.

This explains why Rachel deserved to have a son who excelled in sanctity of circumcision. When her father, Lavan, pulled a fast one by switching Rachel with Leah to marry Yaakov, Rachel was silent so her sister would not be embarrassed. This silence on Rachel's part is sanctity of tongue, which led her to have a child who excelled in sanctity of circumcision (see *Bereishis Rabbah* 84:9 and the *Matnos Kehunah* there). This is how the portion of *Vayechi,* which focuses on Yosef, helps us prepare for the weeks of *Shovevim.*

Perhaps we could suggest a way of improving our speech. Try sitting down each day for one minute with the resolve not to say even one word, no matter what, not even for the sudden phone call. This will train us to be more careful in general with our speech. This will impress upon us the power that words yield. Then we will be well on the way in our journey of holiness as well.

So may we all be blessed at this time of year with a solid foundation comprised of holiness of tongue and holiness of skin, bringing the world to a heightened level of sanctity.

Sefer Shemos

Shemos - Pesach

Down Time

There is something extremely comforting to people who are going through a low ebb in their life. The following paragraphs reveal that secret.

This week we begin not only a new portion, but also a new book, both entitled *Shemos* (lit. "Names"; the book is also known as *Sefer Shemos*). In *Parshas Shemos* we read about the harsh enslavement and bitter affliction that the Jews suffered in Egypt under the cruel direction of Pharaoh and his men.

The Chernobyler Rebbe writes in his monumental *Meor Einayim* that in order to understand why the Egyptian exile occurred, we must refer to a verse (*Yechezkel* 1:14) where it mentions the *chayos* (creatures) that "ran and returned." The *Meor Einayim* interprets this description of the prophet *Yechezkel's* vision as an allusion to exile. He explains that everybody has to experience low points in life in order to elevate the souls that are already in those low places, and are unable to climb out of the depths on their own.

This can be illustrated by the following metaphorical scenario: Imagine you are standing on a rooftop, and while looking down to street level, you notice the glimmer of a precious stone, all the way down in the gutter. In order to rescue the jewel, you must descend from the roof, climb down all the stairs, leave the building, enter the street, walk over to the drain, bend down and stick your hand in the dirty gutter in order to remove the gem and bring it back up with you.

We can connect and expand this metaphorical scenario in relation to our own life situations. Sometimes, we are "on the rooftop" (i.e. experiencing a high point in life) and may see jewels down in the gutter (i.e. other people suffering lows), but not pay close enough attention to attend to the situation and rescue them. When we feel "on top of the world," we tend to - albeit unintentionally and completely not maliciously - overlook certain people who may be going through difficult times.

However, when a sudden low falls upon us and we feel subdued and down, it is surprising to see with whom we strike up conversations. When we are feeling a little less confident than usual and slightly more vulnerable and defenseless, we find ourselves wanting to connect to others in similar situations. Some of us will even leave our "rooftops" and go down into the streets to connect to those feeling low and depressed and, in so doing, "pick up the jewels from the gutter", i.e. lift others out of their misery. Once our spirits improve and we "get back to ourselves" by whatever methods we know succeed for us, we can simultaneously bring others - who may never have experienced the "highs" of life, and therefore wouldn't know how to escape their despair - with us.

Thus, whenever we undergo dark and difficult phases within our lives, let us bear in mind the potential opportunities hidden within those specific periods and take advantage of them. In fact, we learn from the *Ba'al Shem Tov* and the *Meor Einayim* just how valuable these opportunities are.

The *Ba'al Shem Tov* says that *tzadikim* (righteous people) are agents of the Divine. The *Meor Einayim* cites a Talmud (*Yoma* 19a) as support to this idea, where it states that *Kohanim* (priests) are agents of God. Furthermore, we find (Shemos 19:6) that the People of Israel are charged by God to be "a kingdom of *Kohanim*" which, in context, means a nation of ministers rather than literal priests. If we apply this definition of *Kohanim* to the Talmud, we conclude that the Jewish people as a whole are expected to assume the role of agents of the Divine.

We can connect this concept to the ideas discussed earlier. When we feel "down in the dumps" and defeated, it may just be that God has selected us to carry out a special mission. He may want us to forge a connection with others who are in low spirits or in God-forsaken places, and bring them relief from their unfortunate situations. We must experience "lows" in order to genuinely relate to and connect with others in similar circumstances, and for them to successfully receive and accept our assistance and attention.

Two things are gained by this experience:

1) We cannot help another unless we relate to them and understand what they are going through.

2) Only once we are able to truly relate to others, will they be open to receiving our help. Through this process, we help to build both ourselves and other people.

The *Meor Einayim* says that the purpose of the Egyptian Exile - when *Bnei Yisrael* fell to the lowest of depths and experienced life in the "gutter" - was to redeem precious jewels, special Jewish souls. Which souls could he be referring to? (The *Meor Einayim* does not specify who these souls were.)

We could suggest based on the Arizal that the precious souls were reincarnations of souls from the *Dor Haflagah*, Generation of the Dispersed. (The *Dor Haflagah* is the generation after the *Dor HaMabul*, Generation of the Flood). They are referred to in this way because they were scattered (*Haflagah*) all over the Earth following the building of the city and tower of Bavel.) We derive support for this idea through the method of *gezeirah shava* (where two separate verses sharing the same word are drawn together to derive various conclusions).

After the story of Noach and the flood, the Torah relates the incident of the building of the Tower of Bavel. In *Bereishis* (11:3-4), we read that the people used mortar (*chomer*) and bricks (*levenim*) to build the city and tower, which, they intended, would reach the Heavens and would thus "make a name" for themselves. In *Shemos* (1:14), we see that the Egyptians embittered the lives of the Jews with hard work, mortar (*chomer*), and bricks (*levenim*) - the exact same materials! We can conclude from this *gezeirah shava* that the exile in Egypt served as a *tikkun* (rectification) for the Generation of the Dispersed, who rebelled against God.

The Arizal seems to imply that every Jewish soul in Egypt was a reincarnation from the *Dor Haflagah*. However we could propose that, based on the fact that the Jewish population in Egypt was far larger than the entire human population of the *Dor Haflagah*, only a percentage of the Jews in Egypt were actual reincarnations of souls from the Generation of the Dispersed. Firstly, the *Dor Haflagah* came just after the *Dor HaMabul* - when almost the entire population was destroyed. Secondly, the Jews experienced a population boom in Egypt (see *Shemos* 1:7,12,20).

When we couple the teaching of the Arizal with the proposition mentioned above, the message of the *Meor Einayim* intensifies. We learned from the Chernobyler Rebbe that, at times, we must fall in spirit and descend to "low" and dark places in order to rescue souls that exist there, and that this was the purpose of the Egyptian exile. Based on the Arizal and our suggestion, we learn that sometimes an entire people may need to descend to "low," God-forsaken places, often at great sacrifice and loss, in order to rectify the souls that already exist in those depths. The entire Jewish people came down to Egypt and suffered greatly under the Egyptians for the sake of a number of souls - precious jewels - that required *tikkun*.

Perhaps we could suggest a way of applying this lesson to our Jewish living. The next time we feel a little bit down, give someone a call. Maybe the way we are feeling will help us to be more sensitive to another person's situation. Try to help in any way you can. There is no doubt that this will likely lift your own spirits. But this time, as you climb the ladder of spirituality, you will be bringing someone else up along with you.

May we be blessed with the awareness to realize the special mission that God is sending us on when we experience "down" times. When we feel "low" and are despairing, let us take on the role of His personal agent and execute our extremely crucial duty of bringing others who are less fortunate out of their misery. May we, thus, deserve that God come down and elevate us from our depths in exile to the highest of heights, bringing true redemption and salvation on both the personal and universal levels.

Shemos

We Are What We Eat, and We Become How We Eat

We could argue that every president and prime minister is connected to Kabbalistic sphere of *Malchus* (sovereignty). If only they realized how close *Malchus* is to the sphere called *Yesod* (foundation), how differently they would choose to run their country.

In this week's portion, it is written, "And there rose up a new King over Egypt who knew not Yosef." According to one opinion in the Talmud, (*Sotah,* pg. 11a) this verse does not mean that he was actually a new king, but rather it was the same Pharaoh who renewed his decrees, and made them harsh against the Jewish people.

There are many lessons to be learned from this opinion. One of them is pointed out by the Slonimer Rebbe, who says that Pharaoh did not know the quality of Yosef, because Yosef is called a righteous person (*Zohar* vol.1, pg. 45a), and a righteous person is called the *yesod,* or foundation, of the world (*Mishlei* 10:25). This means that Yosef is connected to *Yesod,* which is the Kabbalistic sphere that represents sanctity of circumcision. This sphere is very "good" (the Hebrew word for good is *tov*), and therefore this means that Yosef was very "*tov.*"

The *gematria*, or numeric value, of the Hebrew word *tov* is seventeen; this was precisely how old Yosef was when he was sold to the Egyptians and stood up to the temptations which risked ruining his sanctity of circumcision (see *Bereishis* 37:2). If you multiply seventeen by nine (representing the ninth sphere, *Yesod*), the result is 153; if you then add three points for the three Hebrew letters in the word *tov*, you arrive at the number 156, which is the exact numerical value of the name "Yosef". The reason we multiplied seventeen by nine specifically is because the sphere called *Yesod* is the ninth sphere, when you count the Kabbalistic spheres from the top to the bottom.

Basically, if we take Yosef's age, seventeen (which is *tov*) and multiply it by the ninth sphere, then we come up with the numerical value of Yosef, teaching us that Yosef was very good (very *tov*) when it came to what *Yesod* represents - the sanctity of circumcision. Pharaoh, the king (*Malchus*), did not know Yosef. Meaning that *Malchus* did not know about *Yesod.* In other words, Pharaoh was unaware and disconnected from the holy lifestyle that Yosef represented (see the *Be'er Mayim Chaim*).

Pharaoh's harsh decrees were a direct result of the ruination of the sanctity of circumcision. The Arizal says that this is hinted to when God tells Avraham that his "seed" will be slaves (*Bereishis* 15:13). Because of sinning with seed, i.e. lack of holiness, will his descendants be slaves. One reason why ruination of circumcision's sanctity brings on the exile is because they both share a commonality of feeling: a distance from God.

In *Likutei Torah* by Reb Chaim Vital, it says that the ruination of the sanctity of eating brings about the ruination of the sanctity of circumcision. In the past, we spoke about how the ruination of the sanctity of the tongue leads to the ruination of the sanctity of circumcision; this week, however, we are talking about how eating habits play a role in sanctity of circumcision. Last week, we focused on what comes out of the mouth, whereas this week, we focus on what goes into the mouth (Refer to *Parshas Vayechi, "Talk Ain't Cheap,"* for further understanding of this issue). There is support for the fact that eating habits play a role on the sanctity of circumcision.

Yisro says to his daughters, "Call that man who saved you so that we can eat bread together" (*Shemos* 2:20 and see *Bereishis* 39:6). *Rashi* comments that Yisro meant to say that maybe that man will marry one of you. We see from here that the Torah, in describing the attraction between husband and wife, expresses itself with eating. This proves that there is a direct connection between eating patterns and conduct in the area of circumcision.

Ruination of the sanctity of eating is not just achieved by non-*kosher* food, but even by over-indulgence in *kosher* food. The Egyptians succeeded in luring the Jews into the lustful passions of eating. (See *Bamidbar* 11:5 where it says that the Jews in the desert complained about the Manna and they reminisced about the fish, melon, onions, leeks and garlic that they ate in Egypt.) As a result, the Jews also over-indulged with their lustful passions regarding the place of circumcision; as it says, "the Jews were fruitful and increased abundantly, and multiplied and grew exceedingly" (*Shemos* 1:7).

The Hebrew word for "exceedingly" or "over-excessively" is *me'od,* which the Midrash says is a word that hints at the evil inclination (*Bereishis Rabbah* 9:7). This teaches us that the Jewish people weren't just interested in building families, but they were with their spouses for the lustful passion aspect.

Jewish souls come from a world of delight, which is why Jews seek delights in this world. If a Jew doesn't find a permissible and holy venue for those pleasures, then he or she can so easily fall into obtaining those desires in a prohibited way.

Shabbos affords us the opportunity to engage in physical activities that give us pleasure for the right reasons, and not for sake of indulgence (*Shabbos* 118a, citing *Yeshaya* 58:14). For example, on Shabbos we are empowered to eat in order to have strength to serve God and to raise the sparks of holiness in the food. On Shabbos we are afforded the opportunity to engage in relations for the right reasons, i.e. to save oneself from sin, to give pleasure to others, or to raise righteous children, etc.

This is why we find that Moshe instituted observing Shabbos for the Jewish people in Egypt (*Shemos Rabbah* 1:18) so that the Jewish people would be able to elevate all their mundane activities and direct them to the service of God, and thus deserve to be redeemed. Because, through Shabbos the Jews would be able to sanctify their eating habits, and this would then sanctify their conduct in the place of circumcision. Then they would feel very close to Hashem which would bring about the redemption - which is by definition, closeness to Hashem.

May we all be blessed with sanctity of eating and in fixing sanctity of circumcision, and subsequently deserve to be redeemed from our current exile, and experience closeness to Hashem at a time which will be likened to Shabbos, with unlimited spiritual delight.

Shemos

Underfoot

If we only knew how holy the places in which we find ourselves are, we would take advantage of every moment and situation that presented itself to us.

This week's portion deals with the story of the Burning Bush (*Shemos* 3:1-4). Basically, Moshe (Moses) is shepherding Yisro's flock, when he sees a bush that is on fire; and yet, it is not being consumed (*Shemos* 3:2).

Curious, Moshe turns to see what this is all about, when suddenly, he hears God's voice saying, "Do not draw near, take your shoes off of your feet because the ground upon which you stand is holy." (*Shemos* 3:3-5) Then, Hashem introduces Himself by saying, "I am the God of your father, the God of Avraham, the God of Yitzchak, and the God of Yaakov" (*Shemos* 3:6).

One shocking aspect of this episode is God's instruction to Moshe not to draw near. Why not? At Mount Sinai, Moshe did get close (*Shemos* 19:20). This is especially difficult in light of the fact that the burning bush was on Mount Sinai (Yonasan Ben Uziel, *Shemos* 3:5).

If Moshe was allowed to get close on Mount Sinai at the time that the Torah was being given, then why not get close now, on the same mountain, when God appeared to him?

Furthermore, if God prevented Moshe from coming close to the bush, then why did God go on to command Moshe to take off his shoes? Since the ground he was walking on was holy, Moshe had to remove his shoes.

But, God stopped Moshe in his tracks before he got to the bush. So the Earth

Moshe stood on was not holy, and there was no need to remove his shoes. Why then did God demand that Moshe take off his shoes even though he was far from the bush? (See *Ramban, Shemos* 3:5.)

The *Chofetz Chaim Al HaTorah* (*Shemos* 3:5) teaches that often the *yetzer hara* (evil inclination) has us think that it is too difficult to study Torah and perform the *mitzvos* (commandments) in the places that we find ourselves.

The "place" could be geographical or situational, meaning where we are at in life. Either way, the *yetzer hara* injects thoughts into our minds and hearts which preach despair.

At times, we can hear those thoughts echoing in our heads which say that it is futile to serve God in this place. If only we were in a different place, it would be more conducive to getting close to God.

However, this is simply not true. Because wherever we find ourselves, and whatever the circumstances, we can get close to God through Torah and *mitzvos*.

The story of the Burning Bush is a source of this powerful lesson. Moshe saw that the fire on the bush was not a natural one because the branches were not being burned. Moshe understood that God's Divine presence rested on the bush.

Moshe, wanting to connect and get even closer to God, runs to the bush. God stops him and says, "No. You do not have to be here next to the Divine presence in order to be close with Me. You can stay there, far from the concentration of Divine presence, and still be close to Me."

God went on to support this point by telling Moshe to remove his shoes. The message was clear: every place in which you find yourself in is holy. Holiness can be found anywhere. Closeness with the Almighty can be achieved in any place.

This is because God can be found in every place and in every moment. The only thing we need to do is remove the barriers that prevent us from cleaving to God. Those barriers are negative and impure behaviors.

Once we stop damaging and destructive behavior, we remove the partitions that separate us from God. This is what God hinted to when He said to Moshe, "remove your shoes." In other words, remove the walls that cause distance between us. Then, closeness with God will happen naturally.

As the *Beis Aharon* once said, "It is not the place which prevents us from clinging to God, it is the person" (*Parshas Vayeitzei, Vayifga Bamakom*).

In short, there are sparks of holiness to be found in all places. All we need to do is dig and we will find them. Before we embellish this concept, let us introduce several ideas.

Prior to the sin of eating from the forbidden fruit, God's Divine presence was found even on Earth, and it was easy to connect with Him. However, once Adam and Eve chose to partake of the forbidden fruit, the Divine presence left the Earth and went up to the sky. In turn, the Earth was cursed (*Bnei Yissaschar* in *Agra D'Pirka* #304 citing the *Maharam Cheigiz* in *Mishnas Chachamim* on *Bereishis* 3:6, and *Bereishis Rabbah* 19:7 on *Bereishis* 3:8, the opinion of *Rebbi Aba Bar Kahana*, and *Bereishis* 3:18).

However, God left behind sparks of holiness that can be tapped into if we work at it. This explains why the Patriarchs were so involved in digging wells. On a deeper level, they were teaching us that we can still access those holy sparks. All we have to do is dig (*Shevilei Pinchas* citing the *Sfas Emes, Parshas Toldos*, in the name of the *Chiddushei Harim* on *Bereishis* 26:18).

Again, the message is that God can be found in every place. This is why God is called *HaMakom* (The Place). To teach us that He can be found in all places (*Bereishis Rabbah* 68:9, the opinion of *Rav Huna* in the name of *Rav Ami*, on *Bereishis* 28:11).

This is also why, when Yaakov ran away from Esav, his brother, it says that Yaakov came upon "The Place." It meant that Yaakov had a rendezvous with God right before leaving the Promised Land. God's message to Yaakov was, even outside the Land of Israel you will still be able to find Me (*Shevilei Pinchas*).

Every place in the world stems from the Torah. After all, God looked into the Torah and created the world. It must be that every place stems from a different chapter in the Torah. (Rav Baruch of Medziboz in *Botzinah D'Nehora*, *Parshas Shoftim*, the paragraph that begins *Ki Yifla*, based on *Bereishis Rabbah* 1:1, the opinion of *Rav Hoshaya Rabba*.)

This means to say that no matter what place we find ourselves in, we have a mission to accomplish there, and we can get close to God from that area. In every place, we can connect with "The Place."

This is the deeper meaning behind the statement, "One should be exiled to a place of Torah" (*Avos* 4:18, the opinion of *Rebbi Nehorai*). This means that sometimes one needs to travel to a faraway place in order to connect with the Torah found in that place, because that Torah is connected to the root of that person's soul.

When God taught Moshe the lesson that God can be found even in the place one is already standing, by telling him to remove his shoes, Moshe began to digest what he had just heard. In order to drive the point home, God went on to introduce Himself to Moshe as the God of Avraham, Yitzchak, and Yaakov.

God meant to say, "Look at the Patriarchs. They were busy with digging wells, teaching us that God can be found anywhere. You too, Moshe can find Me anywhere. Therefore, take off your shoes and dig to find Me in any situation or circumstance in which you find yourself."

The fact that God is called "Place" teaches us something else - that God decides in which "place" each and every one of us will be found. Therefore, Yaakov need not fear that he was going to Charan or Egypt. Either way, Hashem has a job for Yaakov to do in that place.

This is why, when visiting a mourner, we customarily say, "*HaMakom yenachem eschem* - The Place [God] will comfort you." The reason why the name "*HaMakom*" is used for God in this scenario is because this is the only source of comfort we could give to a mourner.

By using the name "*HaMakom,*" we remind ourselves that it is God who decides the place in which a person lives. The same God Who decided that the person live on Earth, now decided that the person live in Heaven.

When we take off our shoes at night, we should stop for a moment and think that the place we are in is so holy. Our homes are filled with so many opportunities to do *mitzvos*. This moment of contemplation can set the tone for how we behave in our homes.

May we all be blessed to remove the barriers that separate us from God, and search for Him by digging, and to successfully find Hashem right beneath our feet.

Shemos

Grounded

We have all heard about the importance of being grounded; however, in the following paragraphs we are going to discover an entirely new dimension of what this means.

In this week's *parshah*, *Shemos*, Hashem appoints Moshe to lead the Jewish people out of Egyptian slavery. According to *Rashi* (*Shemos* 3:11), Moshe has two immediate questions about his task: "Who am I to bargain for the Jewish people's release?" and "By what merit do the Jewish people deserve a miraculous redemption?" Although we can understand that Moshe might be a bit daunted by his appointed task, why does he assume that the Jewish people don't even deserve to be redeemed? Since Hashem decided to release the Jews, surely they are ready to leave!

The *Tiferes Shmuel* (vol. 1) explains Moshe's reasoning based on the verse, "Moshe was very humble, more than any person on the face of the Earth" (*Bamidbar* 12:3). This humility manifests itself in Moshe's first question: "Who am I to bargain for the Jewish people's release?" He assumes that there must be other, worthier people who could accomplish the task more satisfactorily. If there are no such people, then his second question stands, "By what merit do the Jewish people deserve to be redeemed if he, the choicest of them all, feels so unqualified for the task?"

According to the *Nesivos Shalom*, Hashem uses the Burning Bush to explain why He will redeem the Jewish people even if they have no merit whatsoever. The bush represents the Jewish people. The fire that surrounds the bush represents the burning passions and impure lusts of the Egyptian society. When Moshe notices the bush (*Shemos* 3:3), he wonders why it is not consumed by the flames. According to the *Nesivos Shalom*, Moshe understood the symbolism of the bush and the fire. His bewilderment, on a deeper level, was regarding how the Jewish people were able to maintain their identity in the face of all the burning temptation that surrounded them.

Perhaps we could suggest how Hashem addressed Moshe's concern about the Jews being undeserving. When Hashem speaks to Moshe at the bush, He says, "The place (*Makom*) upon which you are standing is holy ground" (*Shemos* 3:5). The word *Makom* is one of Hashem's names, since Hashem is the ultimate Place. As the Midrash teaches (*Bereishis Rabbah* 68:10), God is not in the world; rather, He is the Place where the world resides!

We can, therefore, interpret this scene to mean that the Jewish people, represented by the bush, are rooted in holy ground. We are fundamentally attached to Hashem, the Place and the Source of everything. Hashem is particularly invested in us because of this deep connection we have to Him. The redemption of the Jews from slavery, thus, did not depend on the Jewish people's merit. Hashem planned to redeem us anyway, because of our deeply-rooted relationship to Him.

Maybe we could add that it is for this reason God created us from the ground (*Bereishis* 2:7). The ground represents the dimension of *Makom* (Place). This, in turn, refers to God who is called *Makom*. By creating Man as originating from the ground, God is teaching us that our roots are in Hashem Himself, who is the *Makom* of the world. This is why the name of all humanity is Adam (*Bereishis* 1:26), to remind us that we come from the *adamah* (ground). (The name Adam is the root of the word *adamah*.) This collective name, Adam, is a constant reminder that we are eternally linked to God.

Since we belong to the human race, then, by definition, there are inevitably going to be periods when we feel distant from God and overwhelmed by difficulties. Perhaps we could suggest an exercise during those times in order to maintain strength and hope. On days like that, our mantra has to be, "I am a *Ben Adam*, meaning a *Ben Ha'adamah*, meaning a *Ben Hashem*" (a child of God). "I am forever connected to God and He is eternally providing me the courage to move on." This can keep us centered in face of the most chaotic of times.

Even when we feel surrounded by burning fires of temptation, may we be blessed to recognize our deep connection to God and Hashem's unconditional love for us. May this be a source of encouragement and energy that will help us feel supported in every circumstance we encounter.

Va'eira

As the Pendulum Swings

It is precisely when the circumstances of our lives begin to shift in an unfavorable direction that we should be hopeful that good news is waiting for us right around the corner.

This week's portion begins by telling us that God spoke to Moshe and told him that He had appeared to Avraham, Yitzchak, and Yaakov (*Shemos* 6:2-3). *Rashi* comments that when the verse says that God appeared to Avraham, Yitzchak, and Yaakov, it means that God appeared to the *Avos* (Patriarchs).

This *Rashi* has puzzled scholars for centuries. Once it says that God appeared to Avraham, Yitzchak, and Yaakov, isn't it obvious that He appeared to the *Avos*? That is who the *Avos* are. What is *Rashi* adding by his comment, which seems to be completely redundant?

The *Aron Eidus* suggests an interpretation based on a fascinating and intriguing passage in the Talmud.

The passage begins by citing a verse that says, "You are our Father, for Avraham has not known us, and Israel has not recognized us; You, God, are our Father, our Redeemer, forever is Your Name" (*Yeshaya* 63:16).

Rabbi Shmuel Bar Nachmeini in the name of Rabbi Yonasan offers an insight to explain this prophecy. In the future, God will say to Avraham, "Your children have sinned against Me." Avraham will respond, "Master of the Universe, wipe them out and sanctify Your Name."

God then says to Himself, I had better go to Yaakov because he had suffered the pain of raising his family and therefore he might be merciful on them. God then said to Yaakov, "Your children have sinned." Yaakov responded,

"Master of the Universe, destroy them and sanctify Your Name."

God said to Himself, "There is no logic to the grandfather (Avraham), and there is no advice from the grandson (Yaakov)." So, with no other option left, God went to Yitzchak and said, "Your children sinned against Me."

Yitzchak responded and said, "Master of the Universe, are they my children and not Your children? At the time that the Jews said, 'We Will Do' before they said 'We Will Hear' (*Shemos* 24:27), You called them 'My First Born Child' (*Shemos* 4:22), and now they are my children and not Yours?"

Furthermore, Yitzchak argued, how much could they have sinned already? What is the average lifespan of a person - seventy years? (*Tehillim* 90:10). Subtract the first twenty years, during which a person does not get punished for his sins (*Bamidbar* 14:29), and we are left with a maximum of fifty years of sin.

Subtract twenty-five years from that because half of the time it is night, when people are sleeping and cannot sin, and we are left with a maximum of twenty-five years of sin.

Subtract twelve and a half years from that, when people are tending to their basic needs such as prayer, eating, and using the bathroom and are too busy to sin, and we are left with a maximum of twelve and a half years of sin (if they use every spare moment to sin).

If You, God, can tolerate and carry that amount of sin, fine. If not, then let half be on me and half be on You. And if You want the burden of sin to be completely on me, then that is also fine, due to the merit of giving my life to You [at the time of the Binding of Yitzchak] (*Bereishis* 22:10).

When the Jewish people heard that, they opened their mouths and said to Yitzchak, "You are our father" (*Yeshaya* 63:16). Yitzchak said to them, "Before you praise me, praise The Holy One Blessed Be He."

Then Yitzchak showed God to the Jewish people, and they saw Him with their eyes. The Jews lifted their eyes toward the Heavens and said, "You, God, are our Father, our redeemer, forever is Your Name" (*Yeshaya* 63:16). (See Tractate *Shabbos*, chap. 9, *Amar Rebbi Akiva*, pg. 89b.)

This story seems a bit strange because we all know that, Kabbalistically speaking, Avraham and Yaakov come from the side of kindness and mercy, whereas Yitzchak comes from the side of strict justice. Therefore, how could it be that the "sweet" Patriarchs come down hard on the Jews, whereas Yitzchak, the "tough" Patriarch, is the one who comes to the Jewish people's defense?

To explain this, the *Aron Eidus* points out an important pattern that we find throughout the Torah. Whenever the side of harshness pushes its outer limits and becomes extreme, that is precisely when the opposite extreme, mercy, is awakened and begins to pull the pendulum back the other way.

One example of this is the *Sanhedrin*, The Jewish Supreme Court. When all of the judges decide unanimously that a litigant is guilty, which is an example of extreme strict justice, that is precisely when he is set free. (This is an example of compassion. See *Sanhedrin*, chap. 1, *Dinei mammonos bishloshah*, pg. 17a, The opinion of *Rav Kah*ana).

Another example of this is the *Metzora*, a person smitten with spiritual leprosy. Yet when he is completely covered with the *tzara'as*, the spiritual skin disease, which is extreme harshness, is he declared to be pure, which is mercy (*Vayikra* 13:13).

The message is clear. Whenever starkness reaches its peak, that is when compassion is stimulated. Not only is the side of mercy aroused, but, once it is activated, it even has the power to transform the harshness into mercy.

This clarifies our story. In the End of Days, strict justice will reach such an intense level that even Avraham and Yaakov will behave very much out of character by prosecuting the Jewish people, sentencing them to death, God forbid.

When that happens, it is a demonstration of severity reaching its maximum potential. That is precisely when the side of kindness is stirred. However, it is motivated to such a degree that it has the strength to alter harsh justice, changing said justice into compassion itself.

The kindness overcomes the strictness to the point that it converts harshness into compassion. That is why Yitzchak, of all people, will be able to defend the Jews. This is because Yitzchak will be transformed from a prosecuting attorney into a defending attorney.

The *Aron Eidus* says that this idea is hinted to at the beginning of our portion. The first verse reads "*Vayedaber Elokim* - And God spoke" to Moshe (*Shemos* 6:2). The verse could have as easily said, "*Vayomer Hashem* - And God said..." However, the choice of words, "*Vayedaber Elokim,*" carries with it the connotation that God spoke to Moshe harshly (see *Rashi* and *Rabbeinu Eliyahu Mizrachi Shemos* 6:2).

This means that there was a lot of harsh justice going on at that time. But, it is precisely because of that harshness that the side of mercy was aroused. That is why that very verse concludes, "*Vayomer eilav ani Hashem* - And He said to him, I am God." The choice of these words, "*Vayomer*" and "*Hashem,*" implies that the tide was turned back, towards the side of mercy.

The side of mercy increased to such an extent that even well-known and established paradigms of harshness were transformed into softness. This is hinted to in the first word of the next verse.

That word is "*Va'eira* - And I appeared" (which happens to be the name of our portion). The numerical value of *Va'eira* is 208. This number is propitious because it has the exact numerical value as the Hebrew name "Yitzchak" (see the *Ba'al HaTurim*, *Shemos* 6:3).

This teaches us that when things got so heavy, to the point that God spoke harshly with Moshe, the side of softness kicked in to such a great degree that even Yitzchak began to defend the Jewish people.

The title "*Avos,*" Patriarchs/Forefathers, denotes compassion. After all, the nature of a father is one who is expected to have compassion. That is why, in the story above, the Jewish people turned to Yitzchak calling him "father" once they saw his compassion for them.

This will illuminate *Rashi*'s remark. The verse said "And I appeared to Avraham, to Yitzchak, and to Jacob." *Rashi* commented on that, that God said, "And I appeared to the *Avos*." We wondered what *Rashi* added, since it is obvious that Avraham, Yitzchak, and Yaakov were the *Avos*, Patriarchs.

The *Aron Eidus* answers that *Rashi* meant to say that even Yitzchak became one of the *Avos*, meaning that even Yitzchak moved over to the side of compassion implied by the title "*Avos*." This is all the more meaningful when we remember that the numerical value of the word *Va'eira* is the same as the name Yitzchak.

Once harshness reached its peak, softness hit back even harder, transforming strictness into sweetness. This is the depth of *Rashi* connecting the word "*Va'eira*" (208-ness/Yitzchak-ness), to the "*Avos,*" which represents compassion.

When I saw this piece in the *Aron Eidus*, it made me wonder what relevance this has to the rest of the portion. I also wanted to know how this applies practically to our lives.

Perhaps we could suggest the following. At this point of the story, the Egyptian Exile pretty much reached its peak. The Jews had fallen to the forty-ninth level of impurity. It looked as though they would never escape their predicament. All hope was lost. Pain and suffering reached its zenith.

The lesson that God wanted to teach Moshe now was that precisely when things appear to be bleakest is when salvation is going to come. God wanted Moshe to share this message with the Jews in order to give them hope and comfort.

Indeed, that is exactly what happened. Just when the Jews least expected to be rescued, the plagues began to kick in. The Jews learned that their existence was not about to end, but rather it was the end of Egyptian Sovereignty, and the beginning of Jewish nationalism.

The lesson for us is poignant. Sometimes in our own lives we feel that we are at the end. We cannot fathom how the situation could ever change for the better. We feel that there is no place to turn.

It is precisely when things seem to be at their worst, that the ray of hope begins to shine. We must always remember that it is darkest before dawn. When the gloom of night reaches its peak, the force of light is kindled and happiness is on the way.

We should remember that when we fall to the bottom of the barrel, there is only one place to go - and that is... up! History repeats itself. This is what happened to our great, great grandparents in Egypt and it still holds true for you, for me, and for everybody today.

When all seems lost, we can begin to find ourselves and God in our lives. Calling out to Him, just as our ancestors did, is one sure way of reconnecting with God, and then, just as our forefathers were freed from bondage, so too, will we be freed.

May we all be blessed with hope, and the comfort of knowing that no matter what we are struggling with in life, the future holds a more promising tomorrow.

At our darkest moments, may we be blessed with deliverance and feel God's warmth surrounding us, filling us, nurturing us, bringing us all back together with our compassionate fathers: Avraham, Yaakov, and even Yitzchak.

Va'eira - Pesach

Living Jewishly

Our hearts should swell with Jewish pride, especially when we think of who we are, how far we have come, and how much we have accomplished with all the odds stacked against us.

In this week's *parshah, Va'eira,* Hashem speaks to Moshe and tells him to say to the Jewish people, "I am Hashem, and I will take you out from under the burdens of Egypt; and I will save you from their service; and I will redeem you with an outstretched arm and great judgments. And I will take you to Me for a people, and I will be a God to you…." (*Shemos* 6:6-7). This passage uses four separate expressions of redemption. Surely any one of these expressions alone would have sufficed to convey Hashem's promise to redeem the Jewish people! Why are all four necessary?

The *Nesivos Shalom* explains that these four promises are not merely expressions of redemption; rather, they represent four separate redemptions (see *Talmud Yerushalmi*, *Pesachim* 10:1). These four redemptions can be understood as four stages of redemption that were needed to completely liberate the Jews from Egyptian Exile.

The Jewish people in Egypt had fallen to the lowest possible spiritual level. The Midrash (*Shocher Tov*, on *Tehillim* 114) compares the enslaved Jewish nation to a fetus within the womb of an impure animal, based on the verse, "…to take for Himself a nation from amidst a nation" (*Devarim* 4:34). The Jewish people were living "inside" the Egyptians. Their identity was completely meshed with the corruption and immorality of the Egyptian society.

According to the *Nesivos Shalom,* since the situation was so severe, the first stage of redemption was for the Jews to be taken out from the darkness and impurity of their surrounding culture. Nevertheless, they were still slaves to their inner drive toward negativity (*yetzer hara*). The second stage, then, was to be saved from this servitude. The slave mentality cannot be so easily eradicated, however. Even after being saved, the Jewish people were still subjugated to the side of negativity. It was this subjugation from which Hashem redeemed the Jews. The final redemption was for Hashem to take the Jews as His nation.

When we look carefully at the progression of these four stages, we see the Jewish people slowly moving away from their Egyptian neighbors and defining their own identity, gradually transforming from Egypt's possession to Hashem's. This process enabled the Jews to grow into themselves and recognize their unique identity as a people.

The ten plagues (seven of which are found in this week's *parshah*) are a concrete example of this process. As the plagues progress, the Jews' separation from the Egyptians becomes increasingly clear. This distancing from other nations is not a blanket condemnation; rather, it entails a rejection of those secular influences that are destructive to spiritual growth or antithetical to Torah values. This process of separation helps crystallize the Jewish people's unique identity.

The *Ibn Ezra* (on *Shemos* 8:28, citing R' Yehudah HaLevi) notes that the plagues progressed from the bottom up. The first two plagues, blood and frogs, involved water which flows to the lowest places on Earth. The next two plagues, lice and wild beasts, took place on land - one step higher than water. The following plagues, livestock epidemic and boils, were caused by airborne disease - one step higher than land. The plagues of hail and locusts involved clouds (the locusts formed a cloud of their own) representing the highest level even beyond that, in the celestial realm. And the death of the first born affected people's very souls, coming from beyond the furthest galaxies, from under the Throne of Glory.

The Midrash (*Shemos Rabbah* 9:10) explains that during every plague, the Egyptians were stricken, while the Jews were spared. However, the Jews who completely identified themselves with the Egyptians were not saved (*Shemos Rabbah* 14:3). They died during the Plague of Darkness. Their desire to become like the Egyptians ultimately resulted in their sharing the same fate.

We can learn from the process of the Jews' redemption from Egypt how valuable it is for us to maintain a unique identity and not to align ourselves with value systems that are antithetical to Torah. Even the non-Jewish prophet Bilaam recognized this when he described the Jewish people as "a nation that dwells alone, and is not reckoned among the nations" (*Bamidbar* 23:9). This quality of separateness (not to be confused with superiority) is actually the source of our strength as a nation. While other nations rise and fall, we are still here to tell the tale. The degree to which we preserve Jewish identity is the degree to which that identity will preserve us.

Perhaps we could suggest an application of this teaching. Let us try to adopt just one item that identifies us with the holiness of the Jewish people. It could be a small change of dress into something a little more modest or a more refined manner of speech. Every small step in this direction liberates us from being consumed by cultures which are antithetical to Torah values.

May we be blessed to succeed in separating ourselves from any philosophy that is counterproductive to spiritual growth. And through building ourselves gradually, may we merit seeing our enemies destroyed from the bottom up, so that we will soon be redeemed from this dark exile.

Va'eira - Pesach

Scoring a Ten

So much is available today with just the touch of a button. The Torah also teaches us that the entire world is literally at our fingertips.

In this week's portion, *Va'eira*, God says to Moshe, "and I will harden the heart of Pharaoh and I will multiply my signs and my wonders in the land of Egypt" (*Shemos* 7:3). In this verse God informs Moshe that He is going to bring plagues on the Egyptian Empire. Most of the plagues are found in this week's portion (seven to be exact) and the remaining three are mentioned in next week's portion, *Bo*, making the sum total ten plagues.

One might wonder why God brought specifically ten plagues upon Egypt. Why not five or six, or maybe just one blow to knock them out?

One approach in explaining why there were specifically ten plagues is based on the teachings of the *Be'er Mayim Chaim*, which is as follows: According to the *Kabbalah*, there are ten *sefiros* which are really ten worlds that teach us how to serve God in sanctity and purity. The Egyptians, through their impure and immoral conduct, tried to ruin these ten *sefiros*. From the ten *sefiros*, God took revenge on the Egyptians by producing ten plagues (one plague emanating from each *sefirah*), which punished the Egyptians.

Additionally, the Jewish people deserved that the ten plagues would emanate from the ten *sefiros* and crash down upon the Egyptians. This is because the Jewish people lived by the sanctity of these ten *sefiros* (see *Shir HaShirim Rabbah* 4:2 which says that the Jews did not assimilate with the Egyptians, and also see *Shemos Rabbah* 1:28 where Moshe gave the Jews Shabbos, which empowered the Jewish people with the ability to sanctify themselves even in the areas of permissibility).

We could suggest that this holy conduct of the Jews fixed a slight lacking of sanctity that was found in Yosef. Yaakov blesses Yosef by saying, "and the fingers of his hands were flexible" (*Bereishis* 49:24). The Talmud addresses this (*Sotah* 36b): "Ten drops were lost to Yosef when they came out of his ten fingers at the time Potifar's wife tried to seduce him."

The Jewish people, living by the sanctity of the ten *sefiros,* rectified the ten fingers of Yosef. This is why the Jews merited God to say, "and I will place My Hand (*Yadi*) against Egypt" (7:4). If we change the vowels of the word *Yadi* to read *Yadai,* it turns the singular word "my hand" into the plural form "my hands." This is a hint at God's two hands (so to speak); and when you have two hands you get ten fingers. The ten fingers of God are the ten *sefiros*, which produced the ten plagues that smote the Egyptians.

This all happened because Jews lived by the sanctity of the ten *sefiros*, whereby Yosef's ten fingers were repaired. Thus, the Jews merited for God to use His ten fingers, as it were, to hit the Egyptians with ten plagues. This is why there were specifically ten plagues, due to the holiness of the ten *sefiros* by which the Jewish people lived. To live by the ten *sefiros* is not just to maintain the sanctity of mouth and the sanctity of circumcision (as we mentioned in the previous two portions); rather, it is to sanctify every facet of life. This includes activities such as sleep, conversation, sightseeing, sports, etc., thus fulfilling the verse (*Mishlei* 3:6), "in all of your ways know Him."

May we raise our two hands and ten fingers to bless each other so that we dedicate our entire lives to the service of God.

Va'eira - Pesach

For the Fear of God

There are some people to whom it is easy for us to say "no"; however, when we feel reverence for somebody, it becomes increasingly difficult to turn him down. This is an attribute that we could all use wisely to our advantage.

This week's portion, *Va'eira*, recounts seven of the ten plagues that God brought upon Egypt. Before the seventh plague of hail, Hashem told Moshe to inform Pharaoh as follows.

"So said Hashem, the God of the Hebrews: 'Send out My people so they may serve Me. For this time I shall send all My plagues against your heart, and upon your servants, and your people, so that you shall know that there is no one like Me in all the world'" (*Shemos* 9:13-14).

Yonasan ben Uziel explains (9:14) that God was relaying to Moshe that through the plague of hail, the Egyptians will understand that all of the plagues were sent by God and not brought about by other people's magical powers.

A couple of questions arise:

1) Firstly, how did the plague of hail convince the Egyptians that the plagues were not caused by sorcery? What was specific to this plague that forced them to recognize God as the Power behind all the plagues?

2) Secondly, we find earlier in the *parshah* (*Shemos* 8:15) that Pharaoh's sorcerers had already acknowledged God by the third plague of lice, when they declared, "It is the finger of God!" If the Egyptians already recognized His involvement by the third plague, what additional understanding and

awareness did they obtain through the seventh plague of hail?

The *Emunas Itecha* says that the aim of the seventh plague was to eradicate the people's rebellion against *malchus Shamayim* (the sovereignty of God) by strengthening their *yiras Hashem* (fear of God).

We see (*Shemos* 9:27) that this goal was achieved, as Pharaoh finally admitted to Moshe and Aharon after the plague of hail, "Hashem is the Righteous One, and I and my people are the wicked ones!"

The *Emunas Itecha* explains that during the seventh plague, along with the physical downpour of destructive hail, came a spiritual downpour of *yiras Shamayim*, i.e. a flow of energy that engendered in the Egyptians fear and awe of the Divine.

This insight helps answer our initial questions. It was not so much the actual hail that caused Pharaoh and the Egyptians to realize God's omnipotence, but rather the surge of *yiras Shamayim* that enveloped the atmosphere during the miraculous hailstorm. This downpour of *Yiras Shamayim* ultimately enabled the Egyptians to see that God - and not the sorcerers - is the only real all-powerful being, the true "Almighty."

The *Emunas Itecha* points out that, although by the plague of lice the Egyptians already began to acknowledge God's involvement in the plagues, this recognition was on an intellectual level only. Up until the seventh plague, Pharaoh and his men recognized the hand (or finger!) of God but did not arrive at complete acknowledgment and understanding of His supremacy and awesomeness on an emotional level.

The plague of hail, however, with its downpour of *yiras Shamayim*, helped Pharaoh and the Egyptians to allow their intellectual acknowledgment of God's existence to seep into their hearts. This was to the extent that the dread of God was felt by each Egyptian, in every fiber of his existence. The plague of hail thus served to bridge the immense gap between intellect and emotion.

We learn from here the crucial role that *yiras Shamayim* plays in the journey toward recognizing God and His involvement in the world. Only once we attain genuine awe of God can we begin to sincerely love Him and execute His Will.

One way to enhance our *yiras Shamayim* would be to write on an index card: "Where did I come from, to where am I going, and before Whom am I going to have to give an accounting?" (*Avos* 3:1). Keep this card on the dashboard of the car or on the fridge. Every time we think of this reality, we will have increased our *yiras Shamayaim*.

May we be blessed with *yiras Shamayim*, to respect God by accepting the yoke of Heaven, so that we deserve to witness the time when God's sovereignty will be clearly recognized by all.

Bo - Pesach

Blinded by the Light

When we were children, we were attracted to sweets. Only with maturity did we develop an appreciation for other tastes. The same holds true for spirituality. Sometimes it's an acquired taste; but once we develop it, we won't be able to get enough of it.

This week's *parshah, Bo,* discusses the Plague of Darkness. The Midrash (*Shemos Rabbah* 14:2) questions the source of this darkness and cites one opinion that says that the darkness came from the heavenly spheres Above. This is puzzling. How can the light and purity of the Divine realm contain any darkness at all? Furthermore, even if there is darkness Above, it is surely spiritual darkness and why would Hashem share this darkness with the Egyptians?

The *Tiferes Shmuel* (vol. 1) and the *Nesivos Shalom* (citing the *Toldos Yaakov Yosef*) explain that the darkness experienced by the Egyptians was actually Divine Light. For wicked people, intense spiritual light is blinding, the same way a person is momentarily blinded when walking out of a dim room into the bright sunlight. The eyes of wicked people are not accustomed to holy light, and therefore the Egyptians experienced this light as darkness!

This idea is supported by the Talmud in *Nedarim* (pg. 8b, the opinion of *Reish Lakish*, based on *Malachi* 3:20) that in the future God will take the sun out of its box. The righteous will be healed by it, but the wicked will be judged by it. The same light will heal one and yet be painful to another.

The Torah tells us (*Shemos* 15:22) that after the Jewish people's redemption from Egypt, they journeyed for three days in the desert without water. The Talmud (*Bava Kama* 82a) teaches that Scriptural references to water often correspond to Torah. Therefore, it interprets this passage on a deeper level as meaning that the Jewish people traveled for three days in the desert without Torah. The story continues, "They [the Jewish people] came to Marah, but they could not drink the waters of Marah because they were bitter" (*Shemos* 15:23).

The *Nesivos Shalom* explains that since the Jewish people went for three days without Torah, they were no longer able to "drink" from it, since it tasted "bitter" to them. When a person is unaccustomed to Torah and spirituality, it can taste extremely unappealing.

The *Rambam* (*Hilchos De'os* 2) elaborates on this idea. To a person who is physically ill, bitter foods can taste sweet, and sweet foods can taste bitter. According to the *Rambam*, the same is true of one who is spiritually unwell. Such a spiritual invalid may have a craving for what is bad and actually be unable to tolerate goodness.

This is how we can understand the Plague of Darkness. No darkness came down into Egypt - only an outpouring of Divine Light. This light blinded the Egyptians, who were too spiritually ill to tolerate it. The Jews, however, "had light in their dwelling places" (*Shemos* 10:23). Since they were less spiritually ill than the Egyptians, they were able to perceive the light as it truly existed.

There is an idea that *Gehinnom* (Purgatory) is not a separate place from Paradise; rather, it is merely a different experience of it. For some people, spending eternity immersed in Torah study and spirituality is an indescribable delight. For other people, who spent their lives chasing after material desires, this same situation is experienced as dreadful suffering.

May we all be blessed to accustom ourselves to the spiritual elements of this world, so that when we reach the World to Come we can appreciate its light. May our tastes mature for what is really sweet in this world, so that we can appreciate true beauty and holiness when we reach the ecstasy of Paradise.

Bo

To Feel or Not to Feel

Knowledge is great, but when it's teachings reach our heart, then it is truly the best.

In this week's portion, *Bo*, God commands *Bnei Yisrael* in the *mitzvah* of *Rosh Chodesh*, the new month (*Shemos* 12:2). This is reminiscent of *Rashi*'s commentary on *Bereishis* (1:1) who, citing Rabbi Yitzchak, asks why the Torah began with the account of Creation and not with the first *mitzvah* that God commanded Israel (i.e. *Rosh Chodesh*). *Rashi* explains that the story of Creation establishes God as the Sovereign of the world, and thus serves to refute the claims made by other nations that the Land of Israel was stolen by the Jews, since the entire Earth, including Israel, is God's property and He decides who will possess it.

We may ask what is unique about *Rosh Chodesh* that it was the first *mitzvah* ever commanded to the Children of Israel, and also that it could have been the opening words of the Torah?

In the concluding verse of *Parshas Bo* (*Shemos* 13:16), we learn about another *mitzvah*: *tefillin*. The pasuk says: "And it shall be a sign upon your arm and as *totafos* between your eyes." We deduce from the chronology of the text (both in *Shemos* 13:16 and in *Devarim* 6:8) that the *tefillin* of the arm (*tefillin shel yad*) is donned before the *tefillin* of the head (*tefillin shel rosh*). (See *Menachos* 36a.) Why is this the case? What is the significance of this particular order?

We will be able to answer these questions based on the *Maharal* (*Gevuros Hashem*, Ch. 60) who says that the three *matzos* which adorn the *Seder* table on *Pesach* represent the three Patriarchs, while the four cups of wine correlate with the four Matriarchs. Why does the *matzah* represent the

Patriarchs and the wine, the Matriarchs? Why not the reverse? Why not have 3 cups of wine to represent the Patriarchs, and four *matzos* to represent the Matriarchs?

To explain these associations, the *Maharal* points out the essential difference between men and women. Males tend to connect more with the *mo'ach* - the mind, i.e. knowledge, intellectual understanding, and reasoning. Conversely, females are usually more attuned to the *lev* - the heart, i.e. instincts, feelings and emotions.

Matzah - which is formed from grain - represents knowledge. We learn this from the Talmud (Berachos 40a) which equates the developmental stage of eating grain to the stage of attaining "knowledge;" "A baby does not know how to call out 'Abba' (father) until he has tasted the taste of grain." Thus, matzah corresponds to the mind, which, in turn, represents the Patriarchs.

Wine, on the other hand, symbolizes emotions. When we drink wine (perhaps a little more than we are used to), our intellectual capacity is diminished and our feelings come to the surface. The consumption of wine causes a person to express his or her true inner feelings. Thus, wine is associated with emotions and, therefore, represents the Matriarchs.

According to the *Emunas Itecha*, a person who serves God with "*hergesh*" (feeling) is superior to one who approaches Him with the mind or intellect (*da'as*). The *Emunas Itecha* offers the following example to illustrate this point.

A person may believe that the *Geulah* (redemption) will occur, but if he accepts this on an intellectual level only, then he is likely to despair if the situation seems bleak or hopeless. However, if this knowledge seeps into his heart and he feels and believes very deeply that it will happen, then even in the most dire of circumstances, he will never lose hope. The latter individual may not be able to explain or describe how the *Geulah* will actually come about, but he has a deeply-rooted feeling within his heart that it will-and this is what maintains his *emunah* (faith).

Based on the ideas from the *Maharal* and the *Emunas Itecha*, we can answer our initial questions. The *mitzvah* of *Rosh Chodesh*, the new month, is dependent on the moon. Unlike the sun which emits light, the moon receives light. Similarly, as the *Kli Yakar* says in *Bereishis* (1:31), the male is the provider during intimacy (like the sun which produces light) and the female is the receiver (comparable to the moon that receives light). Thus the moon - which is the essence of the *mitzvah* of *Rosh Chodesh* - is likened to women, who represent *hergesh.* (Interestingly, an association is often made between a person's mood and the lunar cycle, emphasizing further the connection between the moon, women and *hergesh.*)

The fact that the *mitzvah* of *Rosh Chodesh* could have been the opening verse of the Torah emphasizes the superiority of the message of this commandment, i.e. the importance of connecting with our heart and deep feelings. There are times in life when we experience a lack of clarity, when things do not "add up" or make sense, and the only way we can gain some understanding and hope is if we tap into our heart and listen to our inner voice. This is the lesson we learn from the moon and the *mitzvah* of *Rosh Chodesh.*

The order in which we don the *tefillin* also stresses this point. The Talmud infers from the order in the verses - which mention the arm before the head - that the *tefillin shel yad* must be donned before the *tefillin shel rosh.* This is because the *tefillin* of the arm represents the heart, while the *tefillin* of the head correlates with the mind. This *mitzvah,* therefore, reminds us to direct our emotions toward God and to always connect with our inner feelings.

One way to tap into our emotions would be the following. When something happens in our life, whether sweet or bitter, we should ask ourselves not only "what we think," but also "how do we feel." Contemplation in answering that question can keep us in touch with our emotions.

May we be blessed to tap into our inner voice and cling onto the hope and faith that eventually all our difficulties - both on an individual and national level - will be resolved.

Bo - Pesach

One Small Step for Man; One Giant Leap for Mankind

A wise man is not just one who learns from everybody, but one who even learns from the animals.

In this week's portion, *Bo*, Moshe tells Pharaoh that, "when the slaying of the firstborn happens, there will be a great outcry (*tze'akah*) throughout all of Egypt" (*Shemos* 11:6). When this plague actually took effect, there was indeed a great outcry throughout Egypt (*Shemos* 12:30). One could ask why it was necessary for the Torah to stress, not just once, but twice, that there would be a great outcry throughout Egypt. Crying out is a natural consequence of the damage that happened in Egypt. Therefore, the crying out is not the primary aspect, but rather the secondary aspect. The actual plague is the primary aspect. So why would the Torah stress the crying out?

The Midrash (*Devarim Rabbah* 2:1) points out that there are ten expressions used for prayer. The second one is called *tze'akah*, which means to cry out or scream out. The *Emunas Itecha* says that the listing in the Midrash goes in ascending order, paralleling the ten Kabbalistic spheres, which are listed in descending order. This means that the first expression of prayer corresponds to the lowest *sefirah* which is the tenth one, but the second expression of prayer corresponds to the ninth Kabbalistic *sefirah*. Since the second expression of prayer is *tze'akah*, this means that it is connected to the *sefirah* called *yesod*. We all know that *yesod* on the Kabbalistic charts corresponds to the reproductive organ, which means that *yesod* represents sanctity in the area of circumcision.

The Arizal in *Pri Eitz Chaim* (21:7) points out that the word *tze'akah* was used in removing the frogs (*Shemos* 8:8). So if *tze'akah* is connected to *yesod*, and *tze'akah* was used by the frogs, it must mean that there is also a connection between frogs and *yesod*. We could suggest that just like the ten expressions of prayer were in ascending order, so too were the ten plagues in ascending order; and just like the ten expressions of prayer paralleled the ten *sefiros*, so too did the ten plagues parallel the ten *sefiros*. Therefore, the first plague corresponds to the lowest, tenth *sefirah*, and the second plague (the frogs) corresponds with the ninth *sefirah* which is *yesod*. This would support the words of the Arizal.

The *Zohar* (volume 2, pg. 36a) states that the plagues were indeed plagues to the Egyptians. However, those very same plagues served as a healing for the Jewish people. Based on all this, we could suggest that since the frogs correlate to *yesod*-sanctity of circumcision-the frogs served to hit the Egyptians in this area, while simultaneously healing the Jews in this regard. The Egyptians had to refrain from relations throughout the duration of this plague of frogs, because the frogs not only entered their homes but even made their way into the bedrooms and onto the beds themselves (see *Shemos* 7:28). This made relations a virtual impossibility.

On the other hand, the Jews learned a valuable lesson regarding circumcision from the frogs. It is stated, "The frog (in singular) came up and covered the land of Egypt" (*Shemos* 8:2). Rebbi Akiva taught how this plague came to be. One frog indeed leaped out of the water, as is implied by its singular form; however, frogs covered the land of Egypt when this one huge frog gave birth to all the rest of them (see *Sanhedrin* 67b). From this Talmud we see that the frogs came from the place of *yesod*.

Rashi, however cites a different Midrash (see Rebbi Akiva's opinion *Sanhedrin* chap. 7 *Arba misos* pg. 67B; *Tanchumah Va'eira* #14) which says that when the Egyptians saw this monstrous frog they attempted to kill it by beating it; however, every time they hit it, swarms of frogs came forth. The obvious question is, if the Egyptians saw that every time they hit the frog things got worse, why didn't they just stop hitting the frog?

The *Birkas Peretz* answers, "This is the way of anger. Once a person gets angry, he will find it very hard to stop himself, as people do not behave rationally when they allow anger to consume them. The Egyptians were incensed when the direct opposite of their efforts occurred, and so they kept hitting it anyway." We could add that these two approaches compliment each other. That is, just like with anger, "once it starts it's hard to stop," so it is with *yesod*, which is from where the frogs emanated. Once a person starts to allow free reign in these areas, it is going to be very hard for him to stop.

As the Talmud says, "There is a small organ to man; if he starves it, it will be satiated; but if he tries to satiate it, it will be hungry" (*Sukkah* 52b). We learn all this from the fact that the frogs spread from the reproductive organ of the mother frog in such a way that it could not stop. This is how the frogs taught the Jews the urgency of taming the area of circumcision, because if we don't, it will devour us.

As long as the frogs were present, they forced the Egyptians, and taught the Jews to understand the necessity of curbing an immoral appetite. In the absence of the frogs, there is only one other thing we have left which corresponds to *yesod*, and that is *tze'akah*. When Moshe attempted to remove the frogs, he didn't have to cry out in order to do so because God already guaranteed that he would remove them. So why did Moshe cry out when it came time to remove the frogs?

It is because Moshe understood that in the frogs' absence, there would no longer be a constant healing, teaching us to live lives of sanctity and purity. This is why Moshe cried out in prayer; in order to ask God for assistance in strengthening ourselves in this area and, simultaneously, teaching the Jewish people that the only way we can get a handle on this area of life is through prayer. However, not just any type of prayer, but rather the type of prayer represented by *tze'akah*, which means to shout it out.

May we follow the frogs' example and shout it out, in order that we burn up our fiery passions and stand on a solid foundation.

Bo - Pesach

The Beauty of the Beast

Not only are we supposed to learn from the animals, but sometimes we are even supposed to act like animals.

As God smites the Egyptians with the final three plagues in this week's portion, we are commanded to bring the *Korban Pesach*, the Paschal Lamb, to celebrate our redemption from the cruel hands of our persecutors.

Over the millennia, many lessons have been gleaned from this offering. However, this year I found a new approach that I would like to share with you.

The *Aron Eidus*, points out how embarrassing, and dangerous, it must have been for the Jews to fulfill this charge. Imagine going to the local marketplace to purchase a sheep, *schlep* it all the way home, and then tie it up to your bedpost.

Remember that this animal is worshipped by the vast majority of this country's citizens. Think of all the nasty looks that the Egyptians shot at their foreign minority, whom they despised.

Don't forget that the Jewish people's homes were not secure from their Egyptian counterparts. Any Egyptian could enter any Jewish home at will. Picture how uncomfortable the Jews must have felt when asked what they were doing with their country's deity.

To add insult to injury, the Egyptians would remind the Jews that they themselves were idolaters, worshipping the same gods that the Egyptians did (see *Rashi Shemos* 12:6 citing the *Mechilta*). "Now, suddenly, you're becoming so religious with your God?" the Egyptians would torment.

This was the test that God put His people through prior to extracting them from the decadent society in which they found themselves. Hashem wanted to see if the Jews were willing to serve Him even when it would be difficult and downright embarrassing.

In order to fortify ourselves with the strength to do God's Will, even when it is humiliating, we must take a lesson from the animals. Just as animals feel no awkwardness in doing what they have to do, even in public, so too, do we need to cultivate that disposition in the line of duty.

There is a passage in the Talmud from where this is learned. The verse says, "*Adam ubeheimah toshi'a Hashem* - You, God, save both man and beast" (*Tehillim* 36:7). Rebbi Yehudah said in the name of Rav that this verse refers to people who, although they may be as bright as "*Adam,*" they nevertheless make themselves like the "beast" by removing from themselves humanistic knowledge (i.e. consciousness of one's surroundings that could lead to mortification) that could prevent us from serving our Creator.

When we strip ourselves of awareness that creates embarrassment, then we have become like the beast, and then we are deemed worthy to be saved like the beast. In other words, when *Adam* (man) becomes like a *beheimah* (animal), then Hashem will save him (*Chullin*, chap. 1, *HaKol Shochtin*, pg. 5b, and *Rashi* there).

When it comes to the service of God, we need to do what is necessary even in the face of those who mock our religious practices. Just like an animal goes about its business even though people are laughing at it, we too must resolve to carry out the Divine will no matter what.

Just like an animal does not feel shame and couldn't give a care about what people say about it, so too we should not be concerned with what people think and say about us. As long as we are doing the right thing, we should not worry about public opinion.

In this respect, we are to become equals with the animals. This idea is hinted to elsewhere. One verse says, "You shall not see the ox of your brother or his sheep or goat cast off, and hide yourself from them; you shall surely return them to your brother" (*Devarim* 22:1).

The other verse says, "You shall not see the donkey of your brother or his ox falling on the road and hide yourself from them; you shall surely stand them up, with him" (*Devarim* 22:4).

The *Aron Eidus* suggests that the words, "your brother" in these two verses does not only refer to the owner of the ox and donkey; rather, it also refers to the ox and donkey themselves. Meaning, that when it comes to *mitzvos* that are similar to these two commandments, (returning lost items and helping another load and unload), we should see ourselves as animals.

We should imagine that the ox and the donkey are our "brothers." Sometimes we hesitate in doing a *mitzvah* because we think that a certain commandment is beneath our dignity. By envisioning the animals as our brothers, we will remove the feeling of embarrassment that could be experienced when *schlepping* things in a public place.

This is one of the primary lessons that we can extrapolate from the commandment of bringing the Paschal Lamb as an offering. God said to Moshe and Aharon that they should tell the Jewish people, "*V'yikchu lahem ish seh l'veis avos, seh labayis* - They shall take for themselves, each man, a lamb or kid for each father's house, a lamb or a kid for the household" (*Shemos* 12:3).

Another way to read the words "They shall 'take' for themselves (*ish seh*)," is that each and every person must "take" or "acquire" for himself the character trait of a *seh*, an animal. Meaning that just as the animal does not feel shame and does what is necessary, we too must not feel disgrace and should do what we have to in the service of God.

This is why the verse says, "*l'veis avos* - for their father's house." A deeper understanding of these words is that we are expected to reach the level of our *Avos* (Patriarchs), Avraham, Yitzchak, and Yaakov. Nothing stopped them from carrying out God's Will.

The entire civilized world at that time may have ridiculed them for their beliefs and practices, and yet they were steadfast in their faith. Nothing could shake them from the truth. They held on tenaciously to God's law.

This is further hinted to in the words "*l'veis avos* - for their father's house." These two words are spelled with seven letters: *lamed*, *beis*, *yud*, *saf*; *aleph*, *veis*, *saf*. The numerical value of these two words is 845, the same numerical value as the words "Avraham Avinu, Yitzchak Avinu, Yaakov Avinu."

This drives the point home. At the time we were commanded to bring the Paschal Lamb, in spite of public humiliation, we were being asked to live up to the Patriarchs' expectation and live by this philosophy. The Jews at that time succeeded in following the Patriarchs' footsteps by going through with this *mitzvah*.

How awesome it is that the Almighty endowed within us the ability to mimic the positive qualities found in the animal kingdom to overcome the obstacle of inhibition. The only way to cultivate this lesson would be to put it into practice. One example would be to *daven* at an airport terminal even if you are the only recognizable Jew there. Just doing this will give us the thick skin to not be concerned with onlookers.

May we all be blessed to emulate our forefathers with the humility and courage to do what's right even in face of taunting opposition, and thus merit to celebrate Passover in our newly built Temple in Jerusalem.

Beshalach

That's So Sweet

The test of a good person is how sweet he is.

In this week's portion, *Beshalach*, it says that Pharaoh sent away the people (*Shemos* 13:17). The Midrash (*Shemos Rabbah* 20:2) points out that ultimately God sent the Jews out of Egypt, not Pharaoh; however, we learn from the verse that Pharaoh escorted the Jews out of Egypt. The Hebrew word meaning "to escort" is *melaveh*, which also means "to attach" (see *Bereishis* 29:34 and *Onkelos* there). The *Ohr Gedalyahu* says that this teaches us that Pharaoh did not only escort us out of Egypt, but Pharaoh was still connected to us as we left Egypt, meaning the Jewish people still had some connection with Pharaoh and the Egyptians.

You can take the Jew out of Egypt, but taking Egypt out of the Jew wasn't as easy. We could suggest that the ways of Pharaoh and the Egyptians were ways of bitterness (*Shemos* 1:14). These people were not very nice to say the least; they were tough, hard, callous, insensitive, and cruel people; meaning, their ways were bitter. The Jews were affected by that society and, to some degree, became bitter as well. This is why God led the Jewish people through the wilderness (*Shemos* 13:18).

In leading the Jews on this path, Hashem was trying to transform *Bnei Yisrael* into sweet people. This is evident in the variety of ways God provided the manna for us while on this path (*Shemos* 16:4-36). Although the manna tasted like whatever the eater wanted it to taste like (*Yoma* 75a), which in itself is sweet, there were only five things that the manna could not taste like: cucumbers, melons, leeks, onions, and garlic (*Bamidbar* 11:5). This is because those tastes don't agree with nursing women and their babies (see *Rashi* there, citing the *Sifri*). This is such a sweet consideration and sensitivity to another's needs. God's vision of transforming the Jews into a sweet people seems to be the thematic idea of this portion.

For example, the Jews came to a place called Marah and found that the only water there was so bitter, it was not fit for human consumption. Hashem told Moshe to throw a tree into the water. When he did, the water miraculously turned sweet (*Shemos* 15:23-25). This was a prime lesson for the Jewish people to move away from being bitter people and move towards being sweet people. At Marah, God also gave us Shabbos (*Shemos* 15:25 and *Sanhedrin* 56b). It was given at this location, because Shabbos represents serving God in a sweet way since everything about Shabbos is sweetness.

Ultimately, this path led us to receive the Torah itself. Through the study of Torah, one becomes attached to God (see *Shabbos* 105a on *Shemos* 20:2). God is described as the merciful and compassionate One (*Shabbos* 133b on *Shemos* 15:2); so when we attach ourselves to God, we are attaching ourselves to the source of sweetness. Remember, if it's not sweet, it's not Torah. As it says (*Mishlei* 3:17), "Her ways are the ways of pleasantness and all her paths are peace."

One exercise in becoming even sweeter people could be to go out of our way and give somebody a heartfelt smile or a sincere compliment. You could say, "I just wanted to let you know I truly admire....about you." It's such a sweet thing to say, and it goes a long way.

May we all be blessed that all of our Torah study and *mitzvah* performance be done in a sweet way so that we become sweet people, and thus, merit ushering in a time where every day will be as holy as the Shabbos day, when we engage in drinking the sweetest waters and munching on the sweetest manna (or should we just say "mann-ching").

Beshalach - Shvii Shel Pesach

When Push Comes to Shove

"Putting your money where your mouth is" means to make your actions match your beliefs.

In this week's portion, *Beshalach*, we read about the Israelites crossing the *Yam Suf* - the Red Sea (*Shemos* 14:22). The *Yalkut Shimoni* (no. 234) cites two opinions regarding what occurred immediately prior to the sea splitting. Rabbi Meir holds that each tribe contended to be the first to jump into the sea. Rabbi Yehudah, however, says, "*Lo kach hayah hama'aseh* - this was not what occurred." The tribes, he explains, did not wish to enter the sea and argued over who would jump in first, as each one suggested that the other go in first. This is the exact opposite of Rabbi Meir's opinion!

How can these two diametrically opposed opinions be reconciled? What really happened at the *Yam Suf*? Were the tribes eager to jump into the sea or not?

The *Torah L'Da'as* (vol.1) states that the opinions of Rabbi Meir and Rabbi Yehudah are, in fact, not at all contradictory. He explains that as the tribes approached the *Yam Suf*, they were motivated to jump in. Each of the tribes wanted to be the first to enter and verbalized this desire - just as Rabbi Meir maintains. However, when the time came to act, the tribes, one by one, backed out - as Rabbi Yehoshua describes.

The *Torah L'Da'as* shows how Rabbi Yehudah's words complement the opinion of Rabbi Meir. Rabbi Yehudah states, "*Lo kach hayah hama'aseh* - this was not what occurred in actuality." In other words, although the tribes initially wanted to jump in (which is what Rabbi Meir's opinion refers to), when the time came for *ma'aseh*, action, they failed to follow through. Thus,

Rabbi Yehoshua's opinion supplements and enhances the view of Rabbi Meir.

We learn from here the importance of putting our teachings into practice. We may have many good ideas and lengthy discussions about our goals and aspirations, but the real test is transferring those thoughts and words into action. As they say in the vernacular, "Actions speak louder than words."

One way of getting us into shape would be to discuss and decide to take on a small *mitzvah* and then jump in and do it. Eventually, we will be able to build up our spiritual muscles and carry out even more difficult tasks.

May we all be blessed to practice what we preach in the service of God, no matter what it takes. May we, in turn, deserve that God take action and build the *Beis HaMikdash*, ushering in a new era of protection, peace, and love.

Beshalach - Shvii Shel Pesach

Communication and Relationships

Sometimes, if we plan ahead, we can actually circumvent uncomfortable and downright dangerous situations.

This week's *parshah*, *Beshalach*, describes the Splitting of the Sea and the Jewish people's miraculous rescue from Pharaoh's army. The Torah recounts the situation as it appeared to the Jews just before the Splitting of the Sea: "Pharaoh approached; the Children of Israel raised their eyes, and behold, Egypt was traveling after them, and they were very frightened; the Children of Israel cried out to Hashem" (*Shemos* 14:10).

The Jewish people were surrounded on all sides. In front of them was the raging sea; on either side, they were confronted with desert and ferocious wild animals; and behind them, rapidly approaching, was the bloodthirsty Egyptian army. HaRav HaGaon Rav Chaim Pinchas Scheinberg, *zt"l*, once explained that this whole desperate situation was contrived only in order for the Jewish people to cry out to Hashem. God loves us and wants to hear from us so much, that when we don't communicate with Him, He may create a situation in which we are cornered for the sole purpose of prompting our prayers.

We can use a practical analogy to illustrate this point. When a student goes abroad to study for a year, he may get so involved in his Torah learning and his other activities that he forgets to call home regularly. Eventually, he may get so caught up in his life abroad that weeks can go by without a letter or a phone call to his parents. Although his parents would dearly love to hear from him, they don't want to nag or hassle - so, when they can no longer stand the silence, they take a different approach, and purposely do not mail his monthly allowance. When the student realizes that he has no money, the first thing he does is pick up the phone to call home!

The student's parents did not withhold the money as a punishment. Rather, they used it as a tactic to re-establish a relationship with their son, because they love him so much.

According to Rav Scheinberg, it's possible that the Jewish people could have circumvented the entire desperate situation at the sea if they had "cried out to Hashem" (Shemos 14:10) with equal intensity before the circumstances demanded it. Had they realized the ultimate goal of establishing a connection with Hashem, perhaps they would not have been forced into a corner at all.

Ideally, it would be a good practice to speak to God, once a day, in our own words and say to Him, "Hashem, I want to have a close relationship with You, so here I am opening communication. I recognize that You are my Parent and that You love me. So, God, I love You, too." We just may be able to avoid difficult circumstances with this type of dialogue.

Just as the Jewish people were redeemed then, so may we be redeemed from our current crushing situation, when we are surrounded on all sides and don't know which way to turn. May we be blessed to constantly communicate with the Divine in an intimate and powerful way; thus, meriting to circumvent fear and tragedy, and soon usher in the final Redemption.

Beshalach - Shabbos Shirah

Whistle While We Work

It's a miracle! What's a miracle? What's ***not*** a miracle? Everything is miraculous.

One of the most dramatic and amazing events in human history, takes place in this week's portion. I am referring to the incredible miracle that has become known as the "Splitting of the Sea" (*Shemos* 14:21).

Immediately following this incident the Jews sang one of the most famous songs ever to be sung - "*Shiras HaYam* - the Song by the Sea" (*Shemos* 15:1-22).

This song has made such an impact, that the Shabbos upon which it is read, is called "*Shabbos Shirah* - the Sabbath of Song." To give this song recognition and honor, we will address it this week.

We are instructed to say this song every single day with a loud voice. Our hearts should be filled with tremendous happiness when we say it, just as when it was uttered for the first time.

At the very moment we say this song, we are to imagine and feel that we are standing on dry land, surrounded by water and are being taken out of Egypt. When we do this, we are guaranteed that we are forgiven for all of our sins.

(See the *Shevilei Pinchas* citing the *Sh'lah HaKadosh* on *Yoma*, *Derech Chaim*, # 46, citing the *Sefer Chareidim*, chap. 73, the opening words *Segulah Sh'lishis.* Also see the *Midrash Shocher Tov* on *Tehillim*, #18, and *Shemos* 15:1. Also see the *Chidah* in *Avodas HaKodesh*, *Tziporen Shamir*, chap. 2, # 24.)

I have always found this difficult to understand. How are we supposed to envision ourselves as having gone through these miracles, if we did not? Even if we were there in a previous incarnation, we have no recollection of it. Are we supposed to fool ourselves into feeling something that simply is not there? What could be gained from this?

The Ramban, shares with us a fundamental principal that applies to us practically in our daily lives. He says that the purpose of supernatural miracles is to help us recognize the great miracles that are hidden within nature.

Only after it has been established, in a paranormal way, that God performs overt miracles, are we then supposed to seek those miracles within our natural surroundings.

Through the obvious miracles, we are expected to recognize, admit, and thank God for the miracles that are not so apparent.

This, says the Ramban, is the purpose of Creation and the foundation of the entire Torah. So much so, that a person does not have a real part in the Torah until he or she believes that everything that happens in our lives is miraculous.

In other words, there is no such thing as "nature"; rather, there are just "obvious miracles" and "less obvious miracles."

The *Noam Elimelech* (*Likutei Shoshanah*), drives this point home beautifully when he expounds on the verse that says, "*U'bnei Yisrael halchu bayabashah b'soch hayam* - and the Jewish people traveled on the dry land in the midst of the ocean" (*Shemos* 14:29).

He suggests that this verse is conveying to us that there are righteous people (Yisrael), who even while walking upon dry land (*bayabashah*), which is not considered miraculous, feel as though they are walking in the midst of water (*b'soch hayam*), which is considered miraculous. In other words, they feel that it is just as big a miracle to live in air, as it would be to live in water.

These righteous people are always connected to God and they always see God's greatness wherever they go, even if waters are not literally parting in front of them. Even in day to day life events, they see wonders that astonish them.

However, as we mentioned before, first there is a need for noticeable miracles to impress upon us that God does indeed perform wonders. Once this has been confirmed, then it is our job to be aware of God's constant miracles within nature.

Perhaps we could add an oft-quoted hint that supports this idea. The Hebrew word *HaTeva* (The Nature) has the numerical value of eighty-six, the same numerical value as one of the Hebrew Names of God, *Elokim*. This teaches us that "God" is operating behind every "natural" occurrence.

This is the purpose of saying the "Song by the Sea" every single day, and especially on the "Shabbos of Song." That is, through the overt and undeniable miracle of the waters parting, we are meant to awaken within ourselves the belief that everything is a miracle.

Every breath we take, every moment of eyesight, and every beat of the heart are all miracles. That a people small in number, with a tiny piece of land can survive and even excel, in spite of being enclosed by their enemies - like a sheep surrounded by seventy hungry wolves - is nothing short of a miracle.

This is how we can live up to God's expectation of seeing ourselves as if we went through the miracle of the "Splitting of the Sea," even though we were not there (or do not remember being there). The answer is that we are going through a "Splitting of the Sea" in our own lives, which is just as great a miracle as the famous one. When we begin to realize this, we will burst forth with song to God thanking Him for all the marvels that He implements for us.

When we sing that song with these emotions of gratitude, happiness, and joy, we have fulfilled the purpose of Creation. It is no longer surprising that such a person gets forgiven for all of his sins.

So, let's try to spend a few more seconds on the "*Az yashir*" every day and feel how this song is relevant in our lives.

May we all be blessed with an appreciation of the miracles that God does for us every moment of our lives which will enable us to "whistle while we work" and, thus, deserve to sing this song once again with Moshe Rabbeinu himself, celebrating the wonders that will happen soon in our days.

Yisro

Laugh It Off

Laughter has a way of putting things into perspective. With it, one can diffuse tension; and it can provide us with the resolve to keep on going even in difficult circumstances.

This week's portion, *Yisro*, is preceded in *Parshas Beshalach* by a description of Amalek's attack against the Jewish people after *Krias Yam Suf*, the Splitting of the Red Sea (see *Shemos* 17:8-16).

How could Amalek even think about waging war against Israel after all the miracles that God performed for the Jews? It would seem from the account of *Shiras HaYam*, the Song at the Sea, that all the nations, including Edom - from which Amalek stems (see *Bereishis* 36:16), were filled with fear and awe after hearing about *Krias Yam Suf*.

As it says: "Nations heard; they trembled; terror gripped the inhabitants of Pilishtim. Then the chieftains of Edom were confounded; trembling gripped the mighty of Moav; all the dwellers of Canaan melted" (*Shemos* 15:14-15).

Moreover, according to *Rashi* (citing *Mechilta* on *Beshalach* 14:21), the miracle of *Krias Yam Suf* extended to all bodies of water throughout the world simultaneously - so that Amalek not only heard about *Krias Yam Suf*, but also experienced it themselves! Thus, our original question intensifies: How could Amalek, who witnessed this overt miracle from God, even consider attacking Israel?

The *Emunas Itecha* suggests that Amalek represents the negative trait of *leitzanus*, mockery, and proposes that it was this undesirable quality that led them to wage war against Israel. When a person laughs at someone's words scornfully, he automatically derides what has been said, even if a negation of those words is completely illogical and unreasonable.

In other words, *leitzanus* can cause one to deny a truth. This is why the *Emunas Itecha* equates the trait of *leitzanus* with Amalek. The only way Amalek was able to defy an obvious truth - i.e. the power of God and His relationship with Israel - was by ridiculing and thus playing down reality, even if doing so was absurd and irrational.

In contrast to *tzchok d'leitzanus*, scornful laughter, which is associated with Amalek, we learn about a different type of laughter from *Parshas Yisro* - *tzchok d'kedushah*, holy laughter. *Tzchok d'kedushah* is defined as either laughter that stems from the joy of Torah study or the performance of *mitzvos*, or laughter that is utilized to help bring a person to serve God through happiness. Furthermore, a holy type of laughter has the capacity to outweigh the negativity of *tzchok d'leitzanus*.

In *Shemos* (19:16), we are told that the Torah was given to the nation of Israel amidst the sound of the *shofar*. Why was it necessary to blow the *shofar* at this time? What is the message of the *shofar*?

The *Yalkut Me'am Lo'ez* says that the *shofar* which God blew was the horn from the very same ram that Avraham slaughtered in place of his son, Yitzchak - who, of course, symbolizes laughter. (The root of the name "Yitzchak" is *tzchok* (spelled *tzadi*, *ches*, *kuf*), meaning laughter.) When Sarah was told about the impending birth of a new son in her old age, the Torah says that she laughed, "*Vatitzchak Sarah b'kirbah*" (*Bereishis* 18:12). When God informed Avraham, he also laughed, "*Vayitzchak*" (*Bereishis* 17:17).

Based on the translation of *Onkelos*, however, we learn that these two laughs were of contrasting natures. *Onkelos* translates Sarah's laugh *Vachayechas*, implying a mocking laugh, whereas Avraham's laughter translated as *Vachadi*, suggesting laughter from joy and happiness. Thus, the inconsistency of *Onkelos'* translation of the same Hebrew word teaches us about these two types of *tzchok*, and also demonstrates how *tzchok d'kedushah* can nullify *tzchok leitzanus*, as we mentioned earlier. Avraham's "holy" laugh cancelled out Sarah's scornful laugh, as we find that she was not even punished for her reaction.

So, the *shofar* mentioned in *Parshas Yisro* is connected with the ram, and thus is also connected to Yitzchak himself, who represents two kinds of laughter. He represents the laughter that can be used in a negative way to mock, scorn, and ridicule the truth; or it can be harnessed in a positive and holy way, either by acting as a catalyst for *avodas Hashem* out of happiness, or as a reaction to the joy of serving God. The power of "holy" laughter is so great that the *Me'or Einayim* advises us to use *tzchok d'kedushah* during the low points in our lives to help us overcome difficult situations and raise us to higher places.

All too often, we experience low points or slumps in our journey through life. There is one suggestion I'd like to offer to help us rise from those difficult times. Stand in front of a mirror, look at yourself and just force a smile on your face, even if you don't feel like smiling. Then, just start laughing out loud. Although this will feel awkward, it has the power to break the ice of sadness, so that we can pick ourselves up, get out there and be productive.

May we be blessed with holy happiness that stems from Torah and *mitzvos*, and with the eradication of mockery, enabling us to serve God even during the tough times.

Yisro

Get the Goose Bumps

People may forget what they have studied, but stories are forever. A well-told story makes an impression that is everlasting.

This week's portion begins with the words, "And Yisro heard..." (*Shemos* 18:1). Based on the Talmud (*Zevachim* 116a), *Rashi* says that Yisro was inspired to join the Jewish people in the desert when he heard about the Splitting of the Sea and the war against Amalek.

Question 1: This statement is difficult to understand in light of another *Rashi* later in the same verse, citing the *Mechilta,* that says the Exodus itself was greater than all the miracles put together, including the falling of the Manna, the water miraculously coming out of a rock, and the war against Amalek. If indeed the actual Exodus was greater than them all, why didn't the Exodus alone inspire Yisro to join the Jews in the desert?

Later in the portion it says, "Moshe told Yisro about all the travail that had come upon the Jews by the way and how God delivered them" (*Shemos* 18:8). The next verse goes on to say that Yisro rejoiced about all the good that God did in delivering him out of the hands of Egypt (*Shemos* 18:9).

Question 2: Why does verse 8 speak in the plural, whereas verse 9 speaks in the singular?

In 18:9, it says *Vayichad Yisro*, which *Rashi* says means that Yisro rejoiced. However, *Rashi* then goes on to cite a *Midrash Aggadah* that says the word *Vayichad* is related to another word *chiddudin*, which means prickles, or chills, or goose bumps. *Rashi* states that this means that Yisro got goose bumps on his skin because he grieved at the destruction of the Egyptians (*Sanhedrin* 94a).

Question 3: How can the *drash* be diametrically opposed to the *pshat*? Was Yisro happy or distressed by what happened to the Egyptians?

Question 4: Why did Yisro's skin suddenly become so prickly when Moshe told him the story? It already says in the first verse of the portion that Yisro heard about everything that God did. What did Moshe add in his telling of the story that was new information to Yisro and sent chills up and down Yisro's spine?

There are four ideas that need to be shared before addressing the answer to the aforementioned questions.

Idea 1: The *Chasam Sofer* says that all the salvations of the Jewish people throughout the generations stem from the Jewish people's primary salvation, which was the Exodus from Egypt. He goes on to say that there is an incredible *segulah* (charm) that one can use when one finds oneself in a difficult situation, and that is to say the words "*Yetzias Mitzrayim* - the Exodus from Egypt." By mentioning the Exodus we draw its power upon ourselves, and can thus be delivered from our current tragic situations. This *segulah* helps for both physical and spiritual challenges (see *Devarim* 7:17-18, from where the *Chasam Sofer* derives this).

Idea 2: When one doesn't merely mention the Exodus, but goes further by telling the entire story, it surely works as a charm to tap into the power of the Exodus. However, the degree of how much energy we draw to ourselves depends on the storyteller. If he is just a mediocre type of person, then he can only draw a small measure of the power of the Exodus. Yet, if he is a great and holy person, then he can draw a great measure of the Exodus' power. Not only will the storyteller be impacted by this, but the listener, too, will be affected; so much so, that the salvation of the listener depends on the greatness of the storyteller, whether we are talking about physical or spiritual redemption.

Idea 3: The *Noam Elimelech* (*Shemos* 5:22-23) says that a sure sign that a rebuke to your friend was done for the sake of Heaven, and therefore made the proper impact, is if the person you rebuked gets angry at you for rebuking him, because the truth hurts. (Obviously this only applies when the rebuke is given sincerely, coming from a place of love. The *Noam Elimelech* is not talking about being obnoxious which could, of course, tick anybody off.)

Idea 4: The *Ohr HaMeir* says that whenever a Jew attempts to climb the spiritual ladder of success, the side of evil will rise up against him and try to tear him down. In other words, when a person striving for greatness confronts challenges, it is the greatest sign that he is growing in the right way (see *Tehillim* 27:3).

The *Emunas Itecha* uses these four points to develop the following approach, which will ultimately address the answers to the questions above. He says that Yisro was a spiritual seeker. When he found God, he forsook all of his idolatrous paths, even at the expense of endangering his life and the lives of his daughters from the local Midianites, who weren't thrilled with his choice, to say the least.

When Yisro heard about the Exodus, he wanted to convert to Judaism and serve God from his hometown Midian. However, when afterwards, he heard about the Splitting of the Sea and the war against Amalek, Yisro delved deep to get to the root of all these salvations. He came to understand that all the salvations of the Jewish people stemmed from their primary salvation - the Exodus (as we discussed in Idea 1).

Yisro recognized that the various miracles, such as the water coming out of a rock and the Manna falling down from the Heavens, all stemmed from the Exodus. Yisro also knew that the key to physical and spiritual salvation is by speaking about the Exodus from Egypt (also part of the first idea), and that the salvation can certainly come from telling the entire story (as we said in the second idea).

In addition, Yisro knew that the strength of the Exodus' power that can be drawn to us depends on the greatness of the storyteller. It was then that Yisro decided not to stay in his hometown, but rather to go to the desert to hear the story from the greatest and holiest man of the generation, Moshe. This enabled Yisro to get redeemed spiritually by removing any impurities left inside him from Pharaoh and the Egyptians. The answers to the questions are now beginning to become apparent.

Answer 1: We saw that when Yisro heard about the Splitting of the Sea and the war against Amalek, he was inspired to join the Jews; yet we also saw that the actual Exodus was greater than all the other miracles. So why didn't the actual Exodus inspire him to join the Jews? The answer is that there is no contradiction, because all the salvations and miracles stem from the Exodus itself (as we saw in the first idea). So, it was the Exodus that inspired him to join the Jews, because all those other miraculous salvations stemmed from the Exodus itself.

Answer 4: Now we also understand why Yisro suddenly got goose bumps when Moshe told him the story, even though he had already heard the entire story previously. Yisro got goose bumps because he went to Moshe to hear the story of the Exodus, in order to remove from within himself any impure residue left over by Pharaoh and the Egyptians (as we saw in the second idea).

As soon as Moshe told the Exodus story to Yisro, Yisro's flesh became prickly. Yet Yisro did not have that reaction when he heard that news back in Midian. This reaction only happened to Yisro now because the storyteller was Moshe. It made a bigger impression on Yisro (as discussed in the second idea), and the story that Moshe told was able to rebuke, or beat out, any trace of evil that still remained inside of Yisro.

The evil inside of Yisro got excited and tried to oppose what was happening (as we mentioned in the third idea). This is one reason for the goose bumps.

But also, since Yisro was climbing the spiritual ladder of success, the global forces of evil were awakened and tried to tear him down (as we mentioned in the fourth idea). This battle raging inside Yisro is another explanation as to why his skin became prickly.

Answer 3: The response to the third question is becoming clear: How could the *drash* be diametrically opposed to the *pshat* - i.e. was Yisro distressed or happy at the Egyptian's destruction. Once Yisro saw the goose bumps on his skin, it was the greatest sign to him that he was climbing the spiritual ladder of success, because it meant the evil inside was putting up a fight (as we saw in ideas three and four). It is precisely because Yisro saw the goose bumps that he was so happy, because then he knew that although the process of purification was distressful, he was indeed on the path of purification.

Answer 2: Here we also find the answer to Question 2, as to why the narrative switches from the plural to the singular. Although Moshe told the story about their salvation (about the Jews, in plural); nevertheless, Yisro felt from Moshe's story that he himself was experiencing redemption (as was mentioned in the second idea), which is why it goes on to say how Yisro was happy that he was saved, in the singular. The singular refers to Yisro himself.

One lesson we learn from all this is never to be complacent - getting comfortable with the levels we have already obtained - but to keep striving for higher horizons, just as Yisro did. As we are climbing higher, we should never be discouraged by the challenges that confront us on this path, because it is the greatest sign that we are doing the right thing.

One practical way to keep on the path of constant growth is to utilize the *segulah* of the *Chasam Sofer*. This means to say that whenever we find ourselves in a difficult situation, we should say the words "*Yetzias Mitzrayim*" out loud. Afterwards, think for a moment how God saved our ancestors by performing so many miracles. Then say to ourselves: God can also perform miracles and save me from this issue that is making me suffer. This exercise will help us to constantly grow stronger in *emunah*.

May we all be blessed to keep coming out of our *Mitzrayims* by continually growing spiritually, and never being satisfied with what we have achieved. We should never be discouraged by these challenges, in order for us to become the next generation of *tzaddikim*, impacting our children by telling them our story. Thus, may we merit to witness the eradication of Amalek and evil, sending a chill throughout the world, and deserve to see with our very own eyes the return of the Manna and the Holy Waters.

Yisro

All in the Family

It is in the conceivable realm of possibility that siblings may fight from time to time. When my children were growing up, I would tell them to remember that as they would travel through the journey of life, the only people that they would have to turn to would be each other (besides, of course, their parents and other close relatives). We should never underestimate the importance of family.

At the beginning of this week's portion, *Yisro*, the Torah tells us that Yisro took Moshe's wife, Tzipporah, and her two sons, Gershom and Eliezer, and brought them to Moshe in the desert (*Shemos* 18:2-5).

An obvious question arises: Why didn't Moshe himself make the journey to Midian to retrieve his family?

We could suggest that the very fact that Yisro had to travel to Midian to bring Moshe's wife and children was, in itself, a rebuke directed at Moshe. Yisro was reproaching Moshe for being involved with the needs of the community to such a degree that he forsook his own family.

Rashi (on *Shemos* 18:6) cites a *Mechilta* that demonstrates just how difficult it was for Moshe to break away from the people in order to attend to his family's needs. Once Yisro, Tzipporah, and her two sons arrived at *Har HaElokim*, Yisro sent a message to Moshe saying, "If you cannot leave [the Jewish people] in order to greet me [your father-in-law], then at least come for the sake of your wife; and if not for your wife, then for the sake of your children!"

Yisro was pointing out to Moshe that his preoccupation with the community's needs, to be "*mekarev rechokim* - bringing close the distant Jews" was, in effect, causing him to neglect his own family, and thus be "*merachek kerovim* - distancing those close to him." (The Hebrew word for relatives is *kerovim*, which also means "close ones.")

Yisro maintained that family takes precedence over everything else. We find that this principle is the basis of a *halachah* mentioned (*Bava Metzia* 71a). In a situation where we have the opportunity to give charity either to the poor of our own neighborhood or to the poor of another town, we are obligated to first provide for the needy of our own community. As the saying goes: charity begins at home. The Torah is conveying a message to us through this *halachah*: we have a greater responsibility for people closer to us than for those outside of our circle of influence. What greater duty, then, could there be than to care for and be responsible toward our own family?

It is essential that we give at least as much attention to our family as we offer to others. We must respect and be patient with family members to the same extent as we are with outsiders. (This principle applies, at least, to all immediate family members including parents, siblings, spouses, and children.) After all, family is the foundation upon which the Jewish nation stands.

Therefore, we must strive to balance time spent in the workplace with time spent at home. This challenge not only pertains to Rabbis, who understandably have hectic schedules, but also to other professionals and, in fact, to anyone in a demanding occupation! Although earning a livelihood is ultimately for the sake of the family - to provide for their day-to-day needs - there is one other thing besides money that our family needs, and that is: us!

Our family needs our love, care, attention, and advice. Our family wants our shoulders to lean on and our listening ears. We must do all we can to allow ourselves the necessary time and strength so that we spend quality time with our family. We find a hint to this idea in this week's portion. When Yisro sees that Moshe is working from morning to night judging the people (see *Shemos*18:13), he warns Moshe (in 18:18), "*Navol tibol* - You will surely become worn out [if you continue to carry the burden of the nation single-handedly]."

We could suggest that Yisro intended to convey to Moshe that if he persists in this way, he will have no remaining energy for his family. In assuming responsibility for the nation, Moshe, to some extent, overlooked his obligation towards his own family.

This idea is alluded to by the location of the rebuke within the text. Yisro reprimanded Moshe in chapter 18, verse 18. The number eighteen, doubled, in Hebrew is made up of the letters *yud, ches, yud, ches*. When read backwards, this spells the words "*Chai, Chai* - Life, Life." Yisro was hinting at the importance of balancing the dual life that a person leads - that is, our private life within the home and our public life outside the home. We must take care not to neglect one "life" at the expense of the other, and especially not to disregard our family life on account of the workplace.

It is important to clarify at this point that our intention is not, God forbid, to place criticism or apportion blame on Moshe for failing to balance the needs of his family and the community. Moshe did not choose to be the leader of the Jewish people - God thrust him into this tremendously overwhelming role. Moshe's situation is an extreme example - he had the burdens of an entire nation on his shoulders alone!

God placed him in this almost impossible position to teach us a crucial and powerful lesson - that we must work extremely hard to create a balance between our public and private lives and prioritize our time accordingly.

A third and final hint to the fundamental importance of maintaining good family relationships is found in this week's portion, by the *Asseres HaDibros* (the Ten Commandments). In 20:12, we read about the *mitzvah* of honoring our parents. We may ask why this commandment is included in the *Asseres HaDibros* over another very important *mitzvah* (*Vayikra* 19:18), "Love your neighbor as yourself." Regarding the latter commandment, Rebbi Akiva (cited by *Toras Kohanim* on *Vayikra* 19:18) says, "This is a great principle in the Torah." If it is such a significant *mitzvah*, why is it not part of the Ten Commandments?

We could suggest that the *mitzvah* of honoring our fathers and mothers carries the greater obligation of caring for and respecting our family, while the obligation to love our neighbor incorporates the responsibility that we have to people outside of the home. The fact that the *mitzvah* concerning our relationship with immediate family members is contained in the *Asseres HaDibros* - as opposed to the law concerning our neighbors or friends - ties in with the theme of this week's portion, which is the paramount importance of family.

Furthermore, we find that the Ten Commandments are divided into two parts: (1) *mitzvos* relating to Man and God, and (2) laws concerning interpersonal relationships.

Of the latter type, honoring our parents is mentioned first. This *mitzvah* appears before the prohibitions of murder, adultery, kidnapping, giving false testimony and coveting (20:13-14). The fact that this law - which concerns our relationship with immediate family - precedes the commandments that apply to the public, highlights, yet again, the extent of our duty and responsibility toward our family over the community.

Practically speaking, we could take one step in this direction by setting up family time once a week (besides Shabbos), where we do an activity together either at home or out of the house. The benefits of such a practice are immeasurable.

May we be blessed to appreciate our families. They are the only families we have. May we strive to balance the needs of others with family needs, so that we give our own flesh and blood the time, patience, love, concern and advice they deserve. May we educate our children properly, each one according to his unique strengths and personality, to perpetuate the Torah; and then, we will deserve to witness the day when the greater Jewish family will be reunited in the Land of Israel, serving Hashem in the *Beis HaMikdash*.

Yisro

Praying to Make Shabbos

Life has taught us that we make the bed we sleep in. Who would have thought that the same holds true with Shabbos? We create the type of Shabbos that we rest on.

This week's story deals with one of the greatest events in Jewish history, the giving of the Ten Commandments on Mount Sinai (*Shemos* 20:2-15). The fourth commandment is to remember the Shabbos day and sanctify it (*Shemos* 20:8).

Rashi (*Shemos* 20:8; citing the *Mechiltah*, the opinion of *Elazar ben Chananyah ben Chizkiah ben Chananyah ben Garon*) says that the way we fulfill this commandment is by saving for Shabbos any beautiful items that we find during the week.

However, the Ramban (*Shemos* 20:8; citing the *Mechiltah*, the opinion of Rebbi Yitzchak) says that the way we fulfill this commandment is by remembering, every day, that this world has a Creator who created it.

How do we remind ourselves every day that the world has a Creator? Well, in the story of Creation, it says that God created the world in six days and rested on the seventh (*Bereishis* Ch. 1 & Ch. 2:1-3).

When we remember that God rested on the seventh day, Shabbos, we are testifying that God must have created the world during the previous six days. Otherwise, from what did God rest?

By counting each day of the week and naming it after Shabbos, we remember what Shabbos represents; namely, that God created the world in six days and rested on the seventh. So, we do not give each day of the week a different name like the nations do (i.e. Sunday, Monday, Tuesday, etc.); rather, we name each day according to its relationship to Shabbos.

For example, "Today is the first day of Shabbos; today is the second day of Shabbos; today is the third day of Shabbos, etc." Therefore, one should keep in mind to fulfill this positive Torah commandment every day when we say the "Song of the Day" at the end of the morning service (*Ramban*).

The Arizal (*Sha'ar Hakavanos*, 61:2) adds that naming the weekdays after Shabbos comes to teach us that all the days of the week are dependent and tied to the Shabbos day. In other words, the spiritual light that we can experience each day stems from Shabbos. In fact, the only way we can draw the spiritual energy from Shabbos into the weekdays is by mentioning Shabbos each and every day. (This idea is supported by the *Zohar* in *Parshas Yisro*, pg. 88a. By the way, some have the custom to say this passage from the *Zohar* every Friday night right before the meal.)

Thus far, we have the *Ramban,* who taught us that by mentioning Shabbos every day, we remember that the world has a Creator. We also saw the *Arizal* who said that the only way we can draw blessing and holiness from Shabbos into the weekdays is by mentioning Shabbos every day.

The *Shevilei Pinchas* suggests that these two ideas complement each other. Meaning, that in the merit of mentioning Shabbos and remembering that the world has a Creator, we draw an overabundant flow of sanctity and purity from Shabbos into each and every day.

Parenthetically, this shows us the importance of staying until the very end of the morning service in order to say the "Song of the Day," as opposed to rushing out and running the risk of skipping it, which would cause us to miss out on the spiritual benefits it affords us.

However, there is one question we could ask: If all the days of the week receive blessing from the Shabbos day, then why did God create the world by beginning with the weekdays and ending with the Shabbos day? It would seem that God should have begun with Shabbos and ended with the weekdays, to show that Shabbos impacts the week.

At this point we need to take things to the next dimension. The following idea is found in the *Sh'eiris Yisrael* (*Sha'ar Hazemanim*, *Sukkos*, the 2nd *Ma'amar*, the paragraph that begins with the word *V'lakachta*, who quotes a *Sefer Kadmon*). He says that actually, Shabbos is created by the moments of service to God that we sanctify during the week. In other words, we know that there are six days in a week. So, when we spend four hours each day in the service of God, that equals twenty-four hours of Divine service. It is those twenty-four hours of Divine service that create our Shabbos that week!

The *Sh'eiris Yisrael's* Rebbi, Reb Mordechai of Chernobyl, explains where those four hours a day come from. He says that they come from the three prayers that we pray daily. The Mishnah (*Berachos*, chap. 5, *Ein Omdin*, Mishnah 1, pg. 30b in the Talmud) mentions that the former pious ones would spend an hour on each service.

So far, that makes three hours a day. The fourth hour comes from the *Shema* we recite prior to retiring at night. Since that recitation is supposed to be filled with repentance on that day's sins, it is meant to take an additional hour. This is based on the Mishnah (*Avos* 4:17) which discusses repentance as taking an hour.

It is through these four hours of daily prayer that we create our own *Shabbosos*. The *Shevilei Pinchas* explains the connection between the prayers and Shabbos. He points to the *Zohar* (*Bereishis*, pg. 23b; and the *Tikkunei Zohar*, *Tikkun* 21, pg. 55b) that says that the Hebrew word "Shabbos" carries within it the essence of the day.

"Shabbos" is spelled with three letters: *shin, beis, saf.* The shape of the first letter, *shin,* is such that it has three branches, representing the three

Patriarchs. The next two letters spell the word *bas* (daughter) representing the Jewish people who are considered to be God's daughter, so to speak.

Together this teaches us that when the *bas* (the Jewish people) engages in the three prayers that were instituted by the *shin* (the three Patriarchs) then we create "Shabbos," (see *Berachos*, chap. 4, *Tefillas HaShachar*, pg. 26b, Rebbi Yosi in the name of Rebbi Chaninah).

Now we can understand how the time we invest in the three daily prayers creates our own Shabbos. Both the prayers and Shabbos are connected to the Patriarchs. The time that we devote to prayer produces the Shabbos day.

The recitation of the bedtime *Shema* is the necessary component which enables our prayers to create our Shabbos. This is because, Kabbalistically speaking, the sins we commit during the day create damaging spiritual forces that prevent our prayers from going up to Heaven, and thereby prevent them from having their desired effect.

However, the recitation of the *Shema* prior to retiring at night, with the repentance that accompanies it, actually kills those damaging spiritual forces, enabling the prayers to be accepted, which in turn creates the Shabbos day (*Arizal, Sha'ar Hakavanos, Derushei Halayla, Derush* 7, pg. 56, section 3).

I am aware that this sounds like a tall order. Who has the time to spend four hours a day praying? On the average, men spend about an hour and a half a day praying, (one hour for *Shacharis*, fifteen minutes for *Minchah*, and fifteen minutes for *Maariv*. We could add another five to ten minutes for the nighttime *Shema*, bringing the total to an hour and forty minutes.) Many women, with families to tend to, have even less time than that to pray formally.

Fortunately, our commentaries say that the few moments we do have to dedicate to each service are considered as if we spent an entire hour on that service (see *Shulchan Aruch*, Ch. 93, and the *Mishnah Berurah* Sub. 1, citing the *Talmidei Rabbeinu Yonah* and the *Perisha*).

How fortunate we are to have the opportunity to pray each and every day and, in so doing, have the capacity to craft our *Shabbosos* into the most spiritual experiences ever.

May we all be blessed with the willingness to communicate with God each and every day, building our very own *Shabbosos,* and thus merit greeting the *Moshiach* who will usher in an era that will have the constant spiritual energy of Shabbos.

Mishpatim

Unlimited Nachas

Imagine how proud we make our parents when we grow properly and do the right and prudent thing. God is also a Parent, and He also *kvells* when His children behave. So let's try to give Him unlimited *nachas.*

In this week's portion, *Mishpatim*, God instructs us: "*Va'avadetem es Hashem Elokeichem u'veirach es lachmecha ve'es meimecha v'hasirosi machalah mikirbecha* - And you shall serve the Lord your God, and He shall bless your bread and your water; and I will remove sickness from amongst you" (*Shemos* 23:25).

A few questions arise in connection with this verse:

1. Firstly, we find a technical difficulty based on the language of the text. God commands us in the plural form to serve Him: "*Va'avadetem es Hashem Elokeichem* - you (plural) shall serve the Lord your (plural) God." But then the verse continues to describe the consequences of our adherence to His word in the singular form: "*U'veirach es lachmecha ve'es meimecha...* - and He shall bless your (singular) bread and your (singular) water..."

How can we explain this apparent lack of grammatical consistency? Why does the verse begin in the plural and conclude in the singular?

2. Generally, when the Torah tells us to "serve God," we find that *Chazal* connect the specific instruction to a particular *mitzvah*. For example, we are commanded (*Devarim* 11:13) "*Le'ovdo bechol l'vavechem* - to serve God with all our hearts." The Sages comment (*Ta'anis* 2a) that this "service of God" refers to the *mitzvah* of prayer. However, in this week's *parshah*, *Chazal* do not associate the instruction "*Va'avadetem es Hashem Elokeichem*" with any specific *mitzvah*. Why?

3. Finally, we may ask a question regarding *avodas* Hashem (service of God) in general. It is understandable that a person can serve, or give to, another human being; but how is it possible to serve, or bestow anything upon, God? What can mere mortals give to an all-powerful, omnipotent God?

The *Ohev Yisrael* provides a beautiful insight that will help to answer our questions. Hashem delights in granting His children an overabundance of goodness, but His pleasure in doing so is truly complete only when we (the children) really deserve to receive His rewards. This principle is evident in the relationships we build with our own children. When our children behave well and listen to us (the parents), we are very happy and eager to reward them - after all, they truly earned it!

However, when children misbehave, although we, nevertheless, provide them with food and shelter etc., we simultaneously feel pain and concern, as we think to ourselves, "I am giving to this child even though he doesn't really deserve it. Is this the right thing to do? I am worried that I may be ruining him by continuing to give to him. Will he become spoiled? Will the child ever learn?" Thus, the gladness that we experience in providing for them is deficient.

Similarly, Hashem loves to give to us all that we need and desire; but as the Parent of all humankind, Hashem experiences true delight in rewarding us only when we genuinely deserve it.

The Apter Rebbe applies this notion to explain the purpose of our *avodas* Hashem, and in doing so, answers our third question. When we use all our energy and efforts to serve God, by carrying out His Will, then we will merit His blessings and, thereby, give something to God in the form of *nachas* (translated as satisfaction, enjoyment, or pleasure). God experiences true *nachas*, as it were, when He gives His children reward that they really deserve.

Throughout our lives we should always be cognizant of God's Will and constantly ask ourselves what would bring Him "pleasure," so to speak. If we persistently question whether our thoughts, speech, and behavior will bring *nachas* to Hashem, then we will help prevent ourselves deviating from His Will. If we continually ask ourselves, "How can I give more *nachas* to God?" our performance of the *mitzvos* will improve, as we will be conscious of the true reason for, and purpose of, the commandments. Thus, sincere *avodas* Hashem is equated with giving *nachas* to God because when we execute His Will and live according to the Torah, we are rewarded as deserving children, subsequently bringing God great *nachas.*

Now we can answer the first question regarding the seeming grammatical discrepancy in *Shemos* (23:25). The beginning of the verse is written in plural form because the Torah is referring to the multiplicity of approaches that one may take in his service of God. The Apter Rebbe explains that Hashem is commanding us all: "*Va'avadetem es Hashem Elokeichem* - You (plural) [i.e. all of you] shall serve the Lord your (plural) God [i.e. each of you shall serve Him in your own unique way, based on the distinctive way in which you perceive God's Will] ."

The Torah switches to singular form when describing the reward because the aim of avodas *Hashem* is singular. Regardless of the array of approaches we may assume in our service of God, the purpose of our *avodas* Hashem is to give God *nachas.* If we serve God in a sincere way, then, as the Torah says, we will be rewarded with water, bread, and health, etc. Subsequently, when God bestows His blessings on deserving recipients, it causes Him great delight and happiness.

The Slonimer Rebbe, in his monumental *Nesivos Shalom*, states that the command to serve God in this week's portion is not connected to a specific *mitzvah*; but rather, it is classified as an "umbrella *mitzvah*," a general principle that applies to all the commandments (thus answering the second question). In the instruction to serve God in *Parshas Mishpatim*, the Torah is imparting an important and unique message: "Serve God in a wholesome and sincere way so that we merit an overabundance of Divine blessings, which God will then bestow on us, consequently bringing Him the greatest *nachas* - the only possible thing that we can actually 'give' to God."

Practically speaking, we can keep focused on the whole point of *avodas* Hashem by starting our day by saying, "All my Torah learning and *mitzvah* performance today is in order to give God, my Creator, *nachas*." (See the *Tzetel Katan* #4 by the *Rebbi* Reb Elimelech of Lizensk.) This mere utterance puts a whole new take on our service to God.

May each and every one of us be blessed to give God *nachas* in our own unique way, by directing our service towards the purpose of delighting God, so that He brings down to us the ultimate blessing that will come with the Messianic era.

Mishpatim

Reach Out and Touch Someone

Life flies by in a dash. That dash is represented on a tombstone between the date of birth and the date of death. We are in that dash right now. The question is how can we fill these moments with the meaningful, the eternal, which is also the spiritual.

After a lengthy list of laws, a verse towards the end of this week's portion states a Divine guarantee to the Jewish people. It says, "*Es mispar yamecha amalei* - I will fill the number of your days" (*Shemos* 23:26).

The *Ba'al HaTurim* there points out that in Jewish tradition, the word *amalei* (I will fill) appears two other times in scriptural verse. They are: "*V'otzroseihem amalei* - And I will fill their storehouses" (*Mishlei* 8:21); and, "*Ufi amalei tochachos* - I will fill my mouth with rebuke" (*Iyov* 23:4).

Whenever there is a repetition of a word like this throughout the *Tenach* (*Torah, Neviim, and Kesuvim* - the 24 Books of the Written Law), it always comes to hint at a coded message for us. What is God trying to communicate with us here?

The *Pri Tzaddik* (#3) shares with us a concept that many of us have heard before or that some of us feel instinctively. And that is that Man was created to live on Earth for a short span of time.

The purpose of Man's existence is to fill his days with the service of God. Each and every day has its own unique mission that we are meant to carry out. After 120 years of life, please God, we are supposed to bring all of our days before God.

This presentation is supposed to show how we have taken advantage of

God's most precious gift: time. It is then that we are to display all that we accomplished here on Earth and, thereby, show how we lived up to God's expectations.

One paradigm example of somebody who utilized every moment of life in an industrious way was Avraham. The Torah testifies that he used all of his days to the maximum. The verse says, "*V'Avraham zaken ba bayamim* - And Avraham was old, coming in days" (*Bereishis* 24:1). This indicates that Avraham was able to bring all of his days with him when he got old and show them to God, proving that he had dedicated each and every one of them completely to Divine service.

However, it is very hard for many of us to constantly be productive. As people, we tend to slack off from time to time. In the process, opportunities slip through our fingers. Time is lost and the spiritual benefits we were supposed to gain are ruined. What are we to do with the moments that we have wasted? How can we ever make them up?

Says the *Pri Tzaddik*, that this is precisely what God is promising us in this week's portion when it says, "*Es mispar yamecha amalei* - I will fill the number of your days." In other words, God is telling us that even if we have "killed time" in the past; still, as long as from now on we try our best to serve God properly, He will fill in the gaps of our lives.

We could suggest that since this message is brought to us in a portion called *Mishpatim* (laws), it teaches us that when we decide to fulfill the will of God, which is expressed through His laws, then He will fill in the empty pockets of our lives.

Filling in the emptiness is considered to be a special *chessed* (kindness) that God performs for us. There is even a hint within our verse that this "filling in" of time is a "kindness."

The highlighted word in our verse is "*amalei* - I will fill." This word is spelled with four Hebrew letters: *aleph*, *mem*, *lamed*, *aleph*. Together they have the numerical value of seventy-two, the same numerical value as the word *chessed*, kindness.

This teaches us that when God "fills in" the empty pockets of our life, it is nothing short of a "kindness."

The *Lekach V'Halibuv*, shares with us a practical way through which we can make up for lost time. He says that when we bring Jews closer to God, strengthening them in their observance, then we also benefit from the time they spend in Divine service.

Our generation provides us with this incredible opportunity. So many people are starving for meaning in their lives, and every one of us could nourish these thirsting souls with the satisfying waters of spirituality. It could be a neighbor or co-worker. We could have such a profound impact on them.

The *Lekach V'Halibuv* says that this explains the *Ba'al HaTurim* who connected three verses that share the same word, "*amalei* - I will fill." The first verse said, "*Es mispar yamecha amalei* - I will fill the number of your days." This is the guarantee that God promised; namely, that He would fill in the empty gaps of our days here on Earth. As we suggested earlier, this will only happen once we decide to fulfill God's *mishpatim*, laws.

Once the Earthly days have been filled in below, then the storehouses of reward can be filled above, in Heaven. This accounts for the second verse, "*V'otzroseihem amalei* - I will fill their storehouses," referring to the "full" reward awaiting us in the next world.

However, how can we procure for ourselves this guarantee to have our days filled below and our reward filled above? The answer is found in the third verse, "*Ufi amalei tochachos* - I will fill my mouth with rebuke."

Meaning, when we encourage others to live a more committed life to God by observing the precepts of the Torah, then we also gain from the time that they invest in Divine service.

By the way, *tochachah,* rebuke, does not mean to lambaste, attack, criticize or condemn another person. Rather, it means to fill the other person on the inside with our heartfelt concern and love for him.

We can see this from the root of the word *tochachah* which is *toch* (inside). This comes to teach us that all we have to do is share the warmth in our hearts with other people so that they feel it "inside" their hearts. This is the way to bring people back to authentic Torah Judaism and closeness to God.

How fortunate are we to be living in a generation with so many opportunities to bring our brothers and sisters closer to God, and more in touch with the Divine spark that we carry around on the inside.

Inviting people over for Shabbos or setting up a time to learn with them are practical ways of having a positive impact on others.

May we all be blessed to use all of our resources to help our extended family, the Jewish people, to believe in God and His Torah, and strengthen all the broken hearts, and thus merit to be filled below and above with sweetness.

Mishpatim - Shekalim

Connecting the Dots

When people are fed up, they ask, "What's the point?" One answer could be that the "point" is something so precious buried inside of us.

This week's portion, *Mishpatim*, often falls together with another portion which is read at this time of year, called *Shekalim*. The portion of *Shekalim* is the first of four special portions (namely, *Shekalim*, *Zachor*, *Parah*, and *Chodesh*) that are read during this time period.

We read this *parshah* to remember and commemorate the half-shekel that each Jew was expected to donate on the first of *Adar*, so that on the first of *Nissan*, the animals that would serve as the daily offerings for the rest of the year could be purchased. Today, since we don't have this *mitzvah*, we read its portion (*Shemos* 30:11-16) so that it is considered as if we did the *mitzvah* through the utterances of our lips (*Hoshea* 14:3, *Megillah* 29a, *Shulchan Aruch, Orach Chaim* 685:1 and *Mishnah Berurah* 1 & 2).

The *Pri Tzaddik* says that these special four portions are actually incredible lights that are beyond our grasp. He goes on to say that these four portions correspond to the four letters in God's Tetragrammaton Name. The first portion, *Shekalim,* is connected to the first letter of that name, which is the *yud*. The letter *yud* represents that inner point inside every one of us that is so holy it is beyond any impurity or ruination that results from sin.

We could add that not only do we see this by the fact that *Shekalim* is connected to the letter *yud*, which appears to be a dot on the parchment, but also through the *mitzvah* of giving *shekalim*. The half-shekel is a coin shaped like a dot. The dot shape is similar to the dot that makes up the letter *yud*. This dot represents this inner point that we all share in common.

To demonstrate this inner point, the *haftarah* (which is taken from *Melachim II* 12:1-17), tells the story of Yeho'ash. Yeho'ash was a Jewish King who strengthened the Jewish people's observance regarding this *mitzvah* of *shekalim*. Yet we find (*Divrei Hayamim II* Ch. 22-24) that he turned evil later in life, and even claimed that he was a god.

The *Emunas Itecha* suggests that it is specifically Yeho'ash who was chosen to be the personality that would teach us about the importance of *shekalim*. This was so that we may derive a most important lesson: even if a person goes way off the deep end, like Yeho'ash did, there is still a point deep inside every one of us that is so holy that it cannot be affected by the ruination of sin. This should encourage us to strive for spirituality, no matter what has happened in the past.

Perhaps every time we give a coin to charity, we should look at it just for a moment, let it remind us that we have a dot on the inside, too. And just like the coin has value, so does my spark on the inside. This will help build our self-confidence.

May we all be blessed with the realization that deep down there is a point so holy that nothing can damage it. Thus, we should be encouraged to build from that place, constantly calling out to God, and subsequently to deserve the coming of *Moshiach* and the re-institution of the half-shekel *mitzvah* this *Rosh Chodesh Adar* so that we can offer up the sacrifices once again.

Mishpatim - Shovevim

Freedom at Last

Many of us enjoy our freedom so much that we are even willing to fight for it. But what does freedom really mean?

This week's portion, *Mishpatim*, concludes a very special section of time on the Jewish calendar. According to the Arizal, the six-week stretch from the reading of *Parshas Shemos* until the reading of *Parshas Mishpatim*, is a propitious time for obtaining personal purity.

These six weeks are nicknamed "*Shovevim.*" This is because the six letters in the word *Shovevim* (*shin*, *vav*, *beis*, *beis*, *yud*, and *mem*) serve as the acronym for the six Torah portions read at this time of year: *Shemos, Va'eira, Bo, Beshalach, Yisro,* and *Mishpatim.*

The reason that these six weeks are conducive to repairing personal impurity is because the first portion, *Shemos*, discusses Jewish bondage in Egypt. According to the Kabbalists, one of the reasons for the Egyptian exile was in order to rectify Adam HaRishon's sin of spilling seed (see *Eruvin* chap.2, *Osin Pasim,* pg. 18b).

The Jews at that time were the spiritual children of those lost drops, and had to undergo the fiery furnace of Egyptian slavery in order to purge themselves from the spiritual impurity of those wasted drops.

So, when we read from the portion of *Shemos* publicly, which talks about the Egyptian slavery, it re-awakens that energy. As we read about the Jews going through their purification, we are invited to join in and take the necessary steps to try to improve our own shortcomings in this area.

This is why some have the custom to say additional prayers at this time of year, coupled with fasting.

Incidentally, according to the *Ba'al Shem Tov*, one should not fast more than the official fast days already established in the Jewish calendar. This is because when one fasts, one cannot learn, pray and carry out acts of kindness properly. Instead, one should immerse himself in a *mikveh*, because on a day that a person immerses himself in a *mikveh*, God credits him as if he fasted that day (see *Ba'al Shem Tov Al HaTorah*, *Parshas Yisro*, paragraph 14, *Mekor Mayim Chaim* #18, citing *Likutim Yekarim* page15, column 3 and see *Kesser Shem Tov* pg. 21b).

This process of *teshuvah* continues from the reading of *Shemos* until the reading of *Mishpatim*, this week's portion.

The reason that this mending concludes with *Parshas Mishpatim* is because the opening subject of the *parshah* is the *eved ivri,* the Jewish slave.

On a deeper level, this topic alludes to those Jews who are, unfortunately, slaves to their lustful passions. Yet, it says about the Jewish slave, "If he shall arrive by himself, he shall leave by himself" (*Shemos* 21:3). This verse hints at the Jewish slave who is liberated from his lustful passions and is by "himself" after letting go of his pockets of darkness.

When we read in *shul* about the Jewish slaves going free, we connect to this energy and free ourselves from the shackles of the *yetzer hara* (see the *Be'er Heitev*, by Rabbi Yehudah Ashkenazi, *Orach Chaim* chap. 685:2, in the laws of *Megillah* citing the *Arizal* on his commentary to the Torah).

This is why towards the end of *Parshas Mishpatim* it says, "There will not be women who lose their young or infertile women in your land, the number of your days I will fill" (*Shemos* 23:26).

Meaning, when we follow the *Mishpatim*, the laws or ordinances (namely, preserving personal purity), only then are we blessed with holy children who will fill the number of our days with happiness and joy.

One practical application of this teaching could be as follows. Sometime over the Shabbos upon which we read this portion *Mishpatim*, let us take two minutes to sit privately in a quiet room alone and contemplate one small way that we can free ourselves of the *yetzer hara*'s shackles. When we think of an idea, let us implement it immediately, thereby concretizing this lesson so that we walk away from the *Shovevim* experience a changed person.

May we all be blessed at the conclusion of *Shovevim* to receive all the blessings from Hashem by clinging to the *Mishpatim*, which means leading a life of sanctity and purity, physically and spiritually.

Terumah

It All Comes Together

The concept of "the whole is greater than the sum of its parts" definitely comes into play in this week's subject matter.

According to the Midrash (*Shemos Rabbah* 33:1), the second verse of this week's *parshah*, "Take for Me a donation [to build the Sanctuary]" (*Shemos* 25:2), clarifies the verse in *Mishlei*, "For I have given you a good possession, do not forsake my Torah" (*Mishlei* 4:2). The Midrash continues by explaining that Hashem told the Jewish people, "Do not forsake the possession [Torah] that I gave you."

Sometimes, when people purchase precious items, a particular item will contain gold, but no silver, or silver, but no gold. But the possession that I gave you contains not only silver - as it says, "The words of Hashem are pure words, like purified silver" (*Tehillim* 12:7), but also gold - as it says, "They [words of Torah] are more desirable than gold and greater than the finest gold" (*Tehillim* 19:11).

We might wonder how the Midrash can compare the holiness of the Torah to mere silver and gold, which, after all, are only material items. Doesn't the sanctity of Torah far exceed the value of even the most precious physical objects?

The *Ohr Gedalyahu* explains that Torah is all-inclusive. When an object is made up of many parts, we don't view the object as merely a compilation of many components and details; rather, the whole object becomes its own entity that is much greater than the sum of its parts. For example, a beam of light is made up of many different colors. These different colors can be individually distinguished when light is focused through a prism. But light is not merely a combination of different colors; it is something much greater than that. The general qualities of light cannot be understood from its component colors alone.

This example will help us to understand why the Midrash refers to the Torah as "silver and gold" as opposed to just "silver" or just "gold." We can learn from this phrasing that Torah includes every possible detail. It contains everything. Moreover, on a deeper level, the *Zohar* (*Terumah* 161b) teaches that "Hashem looked into the Torah and from there created the world." In other words, every physical manifestation in the world stems from a spiritual source in Torah. Just as Torah contains silver and gold, so does it contain the essence of every other attribute and object in the physical world.

This idea, on a concrete level, means that the silver we are familiar with in the material world is in fact a physical expression of "spiritual silver." This spiritual silver is love of God. We see a hint to this in the Torah when Lavan confronts Yaakov and says, "You have left because you yearned greatly (*nichsof nichsafta*) for your father's home" (*Bereishis* 31:30). The root of both these words is contained in the word ***kessef***, which means "silver." The sense of yearning and longing for a beloved person or place is the spiritual side of silver. In essence, our desire to possess physical silver stems from a deep desire to have a loving relationship with Hashem.

Gold, as well, has a spiritual counterpart. Spiritual gold is fear and awe of God. The verse teaches, "Gold comes from the north" (*Iyov* 37:22). "North" can refer to the uppermost part of the body: the head. Inside the head is where wisdom resides, and the verse tells us, "The beginning of wisdom is the awe of God" (*Tehillim* 111:12). We can learn from this chain of correlations (gold comes from the north, north refers to the mind, the mind is the place of wisdom, wisdom is called awe) that gold is associated with awe of God. Again, our desire to possess physical gold stems from a deep spiritual desire to develop fear and awe of Hashem.

The example of the beam of light that the *Ohr Gedalyahu* mentioned above is a particularly appropriate description of Torah. The *Ba'al HaTurim* notes

(*Shemos* 25:10) that the letters of the Hebrew word for Ark, ***Aron***, can be rearranged to spell the word ***Oran***, meaning "their light." This is not merely a play on words; the Ark houses the Torah, hinting to us that the Torah itself can be considered light. Furthermore, the letters of ***Aron*** can also be rearranged to spell the word ***Nora***, meaning "awesome." The all-inclusiveness of Torah is awe-inspiring, and through its light, we can come to serve God in totality and completion.

Torah is not the only vehicle for achieving completion in Divine service. The *Mishkan* (Sanctuary) that this week's *parshah* discusses in minute detail is also greater than the sum of its parts, and can inspire us to serve God in totality.

The *Zohar* and *Midrash Ne'elam* both state that the 613 parts of the *Mishkan* directly correlate to the 613 parts of the human body. For example, the *Menorah* corresponds to the eyes; the Table that held the showbreads corresponds to the mouth; the incense Altar corresponds to the nose, and so on. Often, in *divrei Torah*, we focus on improving one particular part of ourselves: our thoughts, our heart, or our powers of hearing or speech. This week, we would do well to learn the message of the *Mishkan* and join all 613 parts of ourselves together in order to serve Hashem in totality. Although it is critical to pay attention to guarding our speech, or seeing only good in others, we must not get so absorbed in the details of self-growth that we lose sight of the big picture.

This is why the Midrash connects the donation to build the *Mishkan* and the verse in *Mishlei*, "Do not forsake My Torah." Both the *Mishkan* and the Torah are composed of many details, yet both are far more than the sum of their parts. The goal is integration. When all the disparate elements of ourselves join together and form a complete unit, we can serve Hashem in totality.

May every single one of us be blessed with fullness and completion, so that we may shine like the greatest light, and subsequently deserve to see the building of the Third *Mikdash*, with the awesome *Aron* at its center.

Terumah

Do It for the Loved One in Your Life

The words "Mirror, mirror on the wall" may have been embedded into some of our minds. However, a more pertinent expression would be "Mirror, mirror in the sky."

This week's portion, *Terumah*, discusses the contributions that the Jews made toward the construction of the Sanctuary, its vessels, and the priestly garments. God instructs Moshe (*Shemos* 25:2) to tell *Bnei Yisrael*, "*V'yikchu li terumah me'es kol ish asher yidvenu libo* - Take for Me a portion, from every man whose heart is willing."

The *Chasam Sofer* questions - how is it possible to donate anything to God? We are told (*Tehillim* 24:1), "The Earth and its fullness...is Hashem's." Furthermore, it says (*Chaggai* 2:8), "*Li hakessef v'li hazahav* - [God says] Mine is the silver and Mine is the gold." If everything is owned by God, can we really give anything to Him?

The *Chasam Sofer* explains that the only thing we can actually give to Hashem is our hearts. It follows, then, that if a person contributes resources to the Sanctuary with a reluctant heart, he hasn't really donated anything at all. Thus, continues the *Chasam Sofer*, we can read the second verse in this week's portion as follows: "*V'yikchu li terumah me'es kol ish* - Let them take for Me a portion, from every man; *asher yidvenu libo* - who [figuratively] donates his heart."

Based on the *Chasam Sofer*, we could suggest taking this idea to the next level. And that is that even giving of our hearts to God is not really an act of giving - because the actual beneficiary of a good, wholesome heart is ourselves. *Avodas* Hashem (service of God) is, in essence, *avodas atzmeinu* (serving ourselves), i.e. it is for our own benefit.

This is because every one of us is the author of our own novel - with ourselves as the central character. We create the personality of the main character and develop our own story with every decision that we make. God's vision for each one of us is that we strive to achieve our potential and fulfill our objective in this world, becoming all that we can become. At 120 years, when we meet our Maker, we will see whether the picture that we created of ourselves in this world matches the picture that God envisioned for us.

This idea is hinted at in the Torah when God calls to our forefathers, "*Avraham, Avraham*" (*Bereishis* 22:11); "*Yaakov, Yaakov*" (*Bereishis* 46:12); and to Moshe, "*Moshe, Moshe*" (*Shemos* 3:4). Why did God, in each of these cases, repeat their names? Wouldn't once have sufficed?

Rashi comments by all of these instances that God called their names twice to convey His love for them. We could suggest an additional explanation. Hashem, by repeating their names, was alluding to the two Avrahams, Yaakovs and Moshes that exist - the Avraham, Yaakov and Moshe "*d'l'tatah* - below, i.e. on Earth"; and the Avraham, Yaakov and Moshe "*d'l'eila* - above, in the Divine vision." By calling their names twice, God was indicating that the Avraham, Yaakov, and Moshe living on Earth, matched the Avraham, Yaakov, and Moshe in Heaven - meaning that they had fulfilled God's expectations of them.

For example, in the case of Avraham, Hashem called his name twice just after the *Akeidah* - when Avraham passed his ultimate test. How fitting that exactly at this point, the "Avraham *d'l'tatah*" matched the "Avraham *d'l'eila*."

Avraham, Yaakov, and Moshe each reached their potential through their sincere and dedicated *Avodas* Hashem. Ultimately, their service of God enabled them to reach great heights. Similarly, when we do the will of God, and think, speak, and behave accordingly, we are the greatest benefactors. If we choose to go against God's Will, we are the only ones who lose out. God does not need our service - we do.

So, before we engage in any activity, speech, or thought, let us ask ourselves the following question, "Am I going to benefit from this activity or will I lose out because of it?" This simple question will help us gain clarity in making decisions for the rest of our lives.

May we be blessed with the awareness that as we give our hearts to God, we are really improving ourselves - and, thus, take advantage of the opportunity to sculpt ourselves so that our lower selves match our higher selves. May we subsequently deserve that God matches the higher *Mikdash* in Heaven by building the lower *Mikdash* on Earth.

Terumah

Thinking About the Box

Boxing has never really been a Jewish sport; but in light of *tefillin,* boxing takes on a whole new meaning.

This week's portion discusses the command to build a Sanctuary and make vessels to be used in the service of God (*Shemos* 25:8). This is one of the 248 positive commandments in the Torah (see *Rambam*, *Sefer HaMitzvos* # 20).

Today, in exile, how can we fulfill this charge? One approach may be to build synagogues and study halls in which to pray and learn Torah. They could serve as a form of a Sanctuary.

Another method might be to create a spiritual environment in our homes. Then they can be considered as miniature sanctuaries.

However, the *Zohar* and the *Sh'lah* suggest another manner in which to fulfill this *mitzvah*. They say that the *tefillin* (phylacteries) serve as a substitute for the Sanctuary, (see *Shevilei Pinchas* citing *Midrash Ne'elam*, *Parshas Chayei Sarah*, pg. 129a, and see the *Sh'lah*, Tractate *Chullin*, *Perek "Torah Ohr,"* #6, and the *Sh'lah* in *Sefer Mitzvas Tefillin* chap. 1, #4).

They say that in the merit of the *tefillin*, God rests His Divine presence on the Jewish people, just as He did when we had the Temple. This is why one should say the *Korbanos* (offerings) with *tefillin* on. When we say the *Korbanos*, we are credited as if we actually brought those offerings. Therefore, we should have our *tefillin* on at that time so that we are credited as if we are bringing the offerings in the Sanctuary itself.

The whole purpose of building a Sanctuary is so that the Divine presence rests on the Jewish people, like the verse says, *"V'asu li Mikdash v'shachanti b'socham* - And make for Me a Sanctuary and I will dwell amongst them" (*Shemos* 25:8). By donning *tefillin*, the Divine presence also rests on us. Therefore, by dressing ourselves with the *tefillin*, we are, in a way, fulfilling the *mitzvah* of building the Sanctuary.

Wearing *tefillin* is tantamount to building the Sanctuary to such an extent that there are those who have the custom to recite this verse right after donning *tefillin* (*Siddur Arizal*, *Kol Yaakov*, and the *Siddur Tefillah Yesharah*).

There is even a hint in this Scriptural verse that the *mitzvah* of building a Sanctuary can be accomplished through wearing *tefillin*. Our verse had said, "And make for Me a Sanctuary and I will dwell, *b'socham*, amongst them." When you separate the last *mem* of the word *b'socham*, it reads as two words: *b'soch mem* (inside the letter *mem*).

Since the shape of a final m*em* is square, it hints at the boxes of *tefillin* which also have to be square (*Megaleh Amukos*, *Parshas Kedoshim*, and *Menachos* 35a).

Now the verse reads as saying, "I will dwell *b'socham*, *b'soch mem*, amongst the *tefillin* that are shaped like a *mem*."

However, the point is not so much that the Divine presence should rest on the *tefillin*; rather, the idea is that the Divine presence should rest on the Jewish people. This can be seen from our verse which concludes, "*v'shachanti b'socham* - and I will dwell amongst them."

Since the simplistic theme of the verse is talking about the Sanctuary, the verse should have ended in the singular form, with the words "*v'shachanti b'socho* - and I will dwell in it [the Sanctuary]." This would have been grammatically correct. Why, then, did the Torah write "*v'shachanti b'socham* - and I will dwell in them," in the plural, the seemingly incorrect form?

The wording here comes to teach us that ultimately the goal is to dwell "*b'socham*," amongst them - the Jewish people (see *Alshich* in *Toras Moshe*,

Shemos 26:10).

In other words, we are supposed to become so holy that we can be considered as walking, talking sanctuaries. Then, the Divine presence will rest upon each and every one of us. This is God's vision for the Jewish people.

The question is, how can we make such a profound transformation? What does it take to sculpt ourselves into living, breathing sanctuaries?

Herein lies the secret behind *tefillin*. The two boxes are placed on the arm and on the head. They correspond to the heart and the brain. It is when we infuse these two organs with holiness that we become a thinking, feeling Sanctuary.

What does it mean to imbue the heart and mind with purity? Well, part of what it means is to straighten out our *hashkafos* (view-points/outlooks) intellectually, and iron out our *middos* (personalities/character traits) emotionally.

When we direct our minds and hearts towards a commitment to God and the Jewish people, then we are well on the way to spiritual refinement; so much so, that we will be deemed worthy of God's Divine presence resting upon each and every one of us.

Tefillin serve as a reminder to constantly work towards this goal. Any person who lives by this standard is considered to be a "*tefillin* donner." We could suggest that even if the *tefillin* are not physically on our bodies, when we live up to this expectation, it is as though we have the *tefillin* on; or better yet, it is as if we carry the *tefillin* around with us on the inside.

Perhaps we could bring a proof to support this idea. The Talmud says that Rebbi Zeira lived a long life because he never went four cubits without his *tefillin* on (see Tractate *Megillah*, chap. 4, *Bnei Ha'ir*, pg. 28a). How could this be true? There are certain days and certain places when it is forbidden to wear *tefillin* (for example, on Shabbos and in restrooms). Did Rebbi Zeira violate Shabbos by wearing *tefillin* on that day or by entering a bathroom with *tefillin* on?

Of course he did not. Rather, we could propose that Rebbi Zeira worked on himself so much, taking the message of the *tefillin* to heart (and to mind), that even when he was not actually wearing them on his body, he still carried them around with him on the inside. With such *tefillin*, one may walk around with them on Shabbos and enter a washroom.

Possibly, this explains his longevity. Since Rebbi Zeira transformed himself into a living Sanctuary, God's Divine presence rested upon him. Since God is eternal, this quality manifested itself on the Sage (at least partially), causing him to live an unnaturally long life.

We are so fortunate to have the tools which help us align our minds and hearts to carry out God's Divine Will. In so doing, we receive the gift of God's Divine presence residing within us.

Wearing *tefillin*, looking at them, or looking at a picture of them will all help remind us to let God into our thoughts and feelings.

May we all be blessed to constantly carry a pair of *tefillin* with us on the inside by cleansing our minds and refining our hearts, thereby turning ourselves into individual sanctuaries of God. May we merit to witness the day when all of our homes, synagogues and study halls fly back to *Eretz Yisrael*, where we will celebrate with each other and with God, around our permanent Sanctuary: the Temple in our holy city, Jerusalem.

Terumah

Get a Little Closer

Some people believe that deodorant lets us get a little closer, but observant Jews know that something entirely different allows us to really get close.

This week's portion, *Terumah*, discusses the building of the Sanctuary and its vessels. One of the vessels in particular is of striking interest. I am referring to the Ark cover with its two *keruvim* (baby faced, winged, angelic-looking statues) standing on top of it.

The Slonimer Rebbe suggests that one of the statues represents God, while the other represents the Jewish people. But what brings them together is what is found between the two statues: the Torah contained inside of the Ark. This explains the deeper meaning of the *Zohar* (volume 3, page 73a) that states, "God, Torah and Israel are one," meaning that God and Israel become one through Torah.

We could add to this idea by pointing to what the *Ba'al HaTurim* says about the following words in this week's portion (25:2): "*V'yikchu li terumah* - and take for me an offering." He says that another way to read this verse is, "*V'yikchu li* - you all can take Me." How? The answer is found in the next word: *terumah*, which has the same letters as "Torah," plus a *mem*. So, we can acquire God through the Torah that was given in *mem* (numerically 40) days.

Although every vessel in the Sanctuary represented a different approach in the service of God, the commonality between them is that a Jew should reach *d'veikus* (clinging or attaching oneself) to Hashem. As it says, "And make for Me a Sanctuary that I may dwell among them" (*Shemos* 25:8).

The greatest way to attach ourselves to God is through Torah study. This is because it is hard for a person of flesh and blood to cleave to God, who is depicted as an all-consuming fire (*Devarim* 4:24 and 9:3). However, the study of Torah has the power to purify a Jew to such a degree that their materialistic side becomes spiritual and their bodies are transformed into souls.

Sometimes, during our Torah learning, we tend to forget that all the study is about getting closer to God. Sometimes, we get caught up in the details and lose sight of the big picture. To stop this trend, I think it would be a good practice to announce, right before studying Torah, "I am now going to learn Torah in order to come closer to God." With this small proclamation alone, our entire Torah study will take on a whole new dimension, and have much more meaning.

May we all be blessed to get closer and closer to God through Torah study, transforming our bodies into souls, in order for us to deserve to witness the return of our *keruvim* with the building of the Mega *Mishkan*, which is called the *Beis HaMikdash*.

Tetzaveh

How to Take the Torah "Light-ly"

You are rushing to get everything ready before Shabbos when suddenly there is a blackout. Even worse would be a blackout on Friday night itself. How much more we appreciate the lights when they are turned back on. Similarly, we are living in a world of darkness; how much we would appreciate it if the lights were turned on. All we have to do is find out where the switch is.

This week's portion begins by discussing the commandment of lighting the *Menorah* in the Sanctuary. One verse reads, "Aharon and his sons must arrange it from evening until morning before God, an eternal decree *l'dorosam*, for their generations" (*Shemos* 27:21). The word *l'dorosam* is missing two *vavs*: one *vav* after the *daled*, and one *vav* after the *reish*. Why?

Perhaps we could suggest that the letter *vav* represents the *Menorah* itself. This is because, numerically, *vav* is six, signifying the six branches of the *Menorah* (*Shemos* 25:32). Additionally, the shape of the letter *vav* symbolizes the central stem of the *Menorah*.

Based on this, the two *vavs* signify the two *Menorahs* that existed throughout Jewish history. One of them stood in the first Temple (that was taken from the *Mishkan*), and the other one stood in the second Temple. Since both Temples were destroyed, both *Menorahs* disappeared as well. That is why specifically the word *l'dorosam* is missing two *vavs*. Plus, the very word "*l'dorosam*," which tells us about the obligation to light the *Menorah* "in all generations," is missing two *vavs* to prophetically teach us that the two *Menorahs* (represented by the two *vavs*) will be missing in our two exiles (Babylonian and Roman), and we will not be able to fulfill this *mitzvah* during those times.

However, perhaps we could go on to propose that there is a way of keeping the flame of the *Menorah* burning even during our long exile. We are told to "take pure olive oil to kindle the *Menorah* continually" (*Shemos* 27:20). The concept of having the *Menorah* lit constantly is applicable even today, once we become privy as to what the *Menorah's* light characterized.

The *Menorah's* light represents Torah wisdom and the scholars who study it. One source which provides support that the *Menorah's* light represents Torah wisdom is the Talmud, which states that if a person wants to become wise, he should face the south when he prays (see Rebbi Yitzchak in *Bava Basra*, chap. 2, *Lo Yachpor*, pg. 25b).

Parenthetically, my Rebbe, Rabbi Chaim Pinchas Scheinberg, *zt"l*, commented on this passage. He said that, of course, one should pray in the required *halachic* direction, facing Israel, Jerusalem, and the Temple Mount (see *Berachos*, Ch. 4, *Tefillas HaShachar*, pg. 30a; see *Shulchan Aruch*, *Orach Chaim*, Ch. 94:1 & 2). However, at some point during the prayer, one can sway from side to side, facing the south for a moment, and connect with the energy of wisdom that comes from the south.

In any case, the connection between the south and wisdom is made by the *Menorah* which was situated on the southern side of the holy room it was in. Since the *Menorah* was placed on the southern side, wisdom is generated from the south. Thus, we deduce a connection between the *Menorah* and wisdom.

A source which provides support to the fact that the *Menorah* represents Torah scholars is found in the Talmud, which states that if a person wants to have children who will become Torah scholars, one thing they should do is regularly light candles (see *Rav Huna*, *Shabbos*, Ch. 2, *Bameh Madlikin,* pg. 23b). *Rashi* there explains that the *Chanukah* candles are one of the types of candles a person should be careful to light regularly. *Chanukah* candles today are an extension of the *Menorah's* lights in the Temple (see

Rashi Bamidbar 8:2 citing *Tanchumah* #5, see also *Ramban Bamidbar* 8:2).

Rashi goes on to cite a verse that teaches us that through the lighting of the candles, one will merit benefiting from the Torah's light. That verse says, "*Ki ner mitzvah v'Torah ohr* - For a commandment is a lamp and the Torah is light" (*Mishlei* 6:23). This means to say that one can access the light of Torah through lighting the candles of *Chanukah*.

According to this, we can all fulfill the *mitzvah* of lighting the *Menorah* every single day. When we study Torah, we are drawing wisdom from the *Menorah's* light, and we are involved in the process of becoming Torah scholars. In this way, we keep its candles burning brightly.

After establishing that the *Menorah* is connected to Torah scholars and to Torah wisdom, we can begin to understand the meaning behind the *Menorah* being lit constantly. This means to say that if we truly want to become Torah scholars and benefit from the Torah's wisdom, then we have to be diligent in our Torah study constantly.

Those who have the privilege of spending their entire days immersed in Torah study (and actually do so) are certainly called *masmidim*, diligent, and have fulfilled keeping the *Menorah's* light burning constantly. However, even those who must spend considerable time providing for their families can be labeled *masmidim* by keeping the *Menorah's* light burning constantly.

This can be achieved by spending some time each day in Torah study. We see this from *Rashi*'s comments about the *Menorah* being lit *tamid*, constantly (*Shemos* 27:20). He says that just by lighting it every day, it is considered *tamid* even though it does not stay lit all day long. (see *Sifsei Chachamim* #7). Similarly, one who studies every day can be called a *masmid,* even though he cannot study throughout the entire day.

This idea can certainly improve our daily Jewish living. All we have to do is make a commitment to study as much Torah as we can each and every day.

Then we stand the greatest chance of becoming true Torah scholars who will shine and brighten this world of ours.

May we all be blessed with the appreciation of Torah study, and with the strength to commit ourselves to constant Torah study, and subsequently benefit from its light; not just us, but our children as well.

Tetzaveh - Purim

Taking the Hit

Imagine walking down the street where you see somebody fall into a filthy puddle of mud. As much as he tries, the poor fellow cannot extricate himself from his predicament. Naturally, you want to help, but you realize that doing so would not only make your hands dirty, but it would soil your freshly laundered clothing. Do we have the stuff that it takes to help another person even if it results in a loss to us?

The thematic idea of this week's portion deals with the commandment to make the priestly garb (*Shemos* 28:2). The *Kohen Gadol* (High Priest) wore eight different garments, whereas the *Kohen Hedyot* (the "average" priest) wore four garments (Mishnah *Yoma*, chap. 7, *Bah Lo Kohen Gadol,* pg. 71b).

The four garments of the *Kohen Hedyot* were all white. The *Kohen Gadol* also wore those white garments, but in addition to them he wore four other garments that had gold in them (ibid).

These uniforms were known to atone for a variety of sins (see *Zevachim*, Ch. 9, *HaMizbe'ach Mekadesh*, pg. 88b, the opinion of Rebbi Aynini Bar Sasson). Although today, in our exile, we have lost this attire with its benefits, we can achieve atonement as well by engaging in its study (see *Menachos*, Ch. 13, *Harei Uhlai Isaron*, pg. 110a, the opinion of *Reish Lakish*).

The Talmud (*Sanhedrin*, Ch. 4, *Echad Dinei Mammanos*, pg. 39a) shares a fascinating dialog between a certain heretic and Rabbi Avahu. The heretic said to Rabbi Avahu that the Jewish God is a *Kohen*. Proof of this is the opening verse of *Parshas Terumah* which states that God commands the Jewish people to give Hashem a *terumah,* contribution (*Shemos* 25:2). Since a *terumah* is traditionally given to a *Kohen*, we can conclude that God must be a *Kohen*.

We also know, continued the heretic, that God himself buried Moshe (*Devarim* 34:6). Now, a dead body exudes impurity; however, a *Kohen* must maintain a high level of purity. So, what did God immerse Himself in to achieve that level of purity after burying Moshe?

Rabbi Avahu responded that God immersed Himself in fire. In support of this, Rabbi Avahu cited a verse that says "For behold, God will come in a fire" (*Yeshaya* 66:15).

The Tosafist (beginning with the word "*Bimai*") asks why the heretic was only bothered by the means with which God purified Himself. There is by far a much greater question that he should have posed. Since God is a *Kohen*, how could He have made Himself impure to begin with?

The Tosafist's answer that there was never a difficulty regarding Hashem's becoming impure to bury Moshe since the Jewish people are considered to be God's children (*Devarim* 14:1), and we know that a Kohen is allowed to become impure for his child.

Rebbi Shimshon Mi'astrapoli (cited in the *Shevilei Pinchas*) is shocked by the Tosafist's answer. Rebbi Shimon points out that only a *Kohen Hedyot* is allowed to become impure for his child; however, a *Kohen Gadol* may not become impure even for his child.

Obviously, God would have the status of a *Kohen Gadol*. If so, how could He become impure even for Moshe, His precious child?

Rebbi Shimshon says that a very deep secret lies beneath this passage. He cites the *Zohar* and Kabbalists in many places that say that God lowers Himself to the level of a *Kohen Hedyot* just out of the great love that He has for His children, Israel.

God does this in order to be able to descend to the places of impurity to which His children have fallen. It is in those very places that God purifies them.

The Arizal adds that in order to do this, God clothes Himself, so to speak, only with the four white garments of a *Kohen Hedyot*.

Perhaps we could suggest that it is for this very reason that the *Kohen Gadol* only dresses himself in the four white garments of a *Kohen Hedyot* on *Yom Kippur* when he enters the Holy of Holies.

After all, the job of a *Kohen* is to atone for his people. The one *Kohen* who carries this responsibility more than any other is the *Kohen Gadol*. Therefore, the *Kohen Gadol* must be prepared to stoop to the lowest of places in order to rescue those who have fallen to the bottom of spiritual filth.

The *Kohen Gadol* demonstrates the willingness to do whatever it takes to save his people by wearing just the white priestly garb on *Yom Kippur*. In other words, he is making a statement that he is prepared to get his hands dirty, as it were, just so that he can help others rise out of the mud.

We could add that it is no coincidence that this week's portion falls out right before the holiday of *Purim*. The parallel might be that this is precisely what Mordechai and Esther did for their people.

The Jews had fallen to a very low spiritual place by partaking of Achashverosh's decadent meal, and by bowing down to Haman and the idol that was worn around his neck.

Like true leaders, Mordechai and Esther helped set their people straight. Esther called for the Jews to fast (*Esther* 4:16), as this would purge them from the food they ate at the corrupt party. Mordechai was their role model by not bowing down to Haman (*Esther* 3:2); thus, fixing the sin of idolatry (see the *Vilna Gaon*'s commentary on the book of *Esther*).

Perhaps, this could be why, at the end of the story, when Mordechai exits the palace and stands before the Jewish people, it describes the clothing that he wore (*Esther* 8:15). When you count the number of garments correctly, there are eight in all.

We could suggest that the eight pieces of attire that Mordechai wore correspond to the eight garments worn by the *Kohen Gadol.* This shows that Mordechai achieved what a High Priest was meant to do - to fix and mend the people by bringing them to atonement.

However, Mordechai wore the eight pieces of clothing only after he brought the Jews to repentance. We could infer from this that earlier in the story, Mordechai only wore four garments of white when he was involved in moving his people to *teshuvah* (see *Esther* 4:1, where specifically four words are used to describe what Mordechai wore, hinting at the four garments).

This illustrates that Mordechai was willing to go the distance to save the Jewish people and do whatever it took to rescue them. Mordechai was willing to lower himself in order to help his fellow brothers and sisters.

Indeed, that is precisely what happened. The end of *Megillas Esther* reports that the *Sanhedrin* (the Jewish Supreme Court) put Mordechai on a lower level of stature than where he had previously been prior to the onset of the whole story (10:3; See *Megillah*, chap. 1, *Megillah Nikreis,* pg. 16b).

This piece of information has always been upsetting to me. It seems unfair. Here is a man who was willing to sacrifice himself for his people, and what thanks does he get? He is put on a lower status by the *Sanhedrin.* It just doesn't seem right.

However, I was thinking that the lower status which was accorded to Mordechai, in and of itself, shows his greatness. The *Sanhedrin* actually praised Mordechai by putting him on a lower standing.

In other words, the *Sanhedrin* was saying, "Look at this man's greatness. He was willing to stoop to lower levels just to help his fellow people." In order to make it authentic, they had to demote Mordechai. This is something Mordechai himself wanted.

Mordechai and the *Sanhedrin* wanted to teach the Jewish people a powerful lesson. That is: that sometimes in life we have to be willing to take a hit just in order to help somebody else. This commitment is the stuff that makes people great!

In today's day and age, even though it is unfortunate to be surrounded by so many people in need, it presents us with opportunities for our spiritual growth, especially when we lose out a little bit in the process of assisting them.

This could be why we have a custom to dress up in costumes on *Purim*. Sometimes, we even look foolish parading around in these get-ups. When we deliver gifts to the poor and to our friends in these outfits, the message is clear. We are declaring that we are willing to lower ourselves, even to appear silly in the world's eyes, if that is what it takes to reach out and help another person.

After all, the *Ba'al Shem Tov* (see *Ba'al Shem Tov Al HaTorah, Parshas Acharei Mos* #2, *Parshas Lech Lecha* #6 and *Parshas Vayikra* #10) used to say, "If we want to help a person get out of the mud, we have to be willing to get our hands dirty."

Let's try to find one person in need and go out of our way to help him even when it hurts. The more we all behave like this, the closer we will be to our redemption.

May we, the "Kingdom of priests" (*Shemos* 19:6), be blessed to live up to our name and find the inner strength to sacrifice for others even when it hurts. In that merit, may we deserve to be rescued by the ultimate Priest of Priests, the Holy One Blessed be He, who will descend all the way down to us and wipe away all of our sins on this *Yom HaPurim*!

Tetzaveh

Soul Food

How important it is to exercise and eat right. However, it is not only our bodies that need to be kept in shape, it's our souls as well.

In this week's portion, *Tetzaveh* (30:1), God commands the Jewish people to build the *mizbe'ach p'nimi,* inner Altar, and cover it in gold.

We may wonder why they were required to construct this altar in view of the fact that they had already been told to build the *mizbe'ach chitzoni,* the outer, Copper Altar, in last week's portion (*Shemos* 27:1-8). We do not find God commanding Israel to build a second Ark or Candelabra. What, then, was different about the *mizbe'ach*? Why was it necessary to have two altars when, seemingly, the sacrificial service could have been done on just one altar?

The *Kli Yakar* (*Tetzaveh* 30:1) lays down a principle which will help us answer this question.

The function of the Altar was to atone for the transgressions of the Jewish people. When a person makes a mistake, it is inevitable that both the body and soul are involved in executing the wrongdoing. A sin cannot be committed by the body alone or by the soul alone. It is the combination of both body and soul that forms a person; and therefore, it takes the contribution of both to transgress.

Based on this concept, we can understand why it was essential to build two altars. The purpose of the *mizbe'ach chitzoni* was to atone for the body's participation in the sin, while the *mizbe'ach p'nimi* atoned for the soul's involvement in the negative action. This is alluded to by the distinct offerings that were brought upon the altars, and also by the respective dimensions of the altars.

On the *mizbe'ach chitzoni* (which atoned for the body), an animal was sacrificed. When the person who had transgressed offered up the animal, he was to imagine himself in its place. Really, his body should have been destroyed on account of his misdeed, but instead, the animal (representing the sinner's physical, animalistic component) was sacrificed. Thus, the outside Altar atoned for the participation of the physical body in the sin.

Furthermore, we are told (Shemos 27:1) that the *mizbe'ach chitzoni* was three cubits tall. The Kli Yakar points out that this is also the height of the average human being's body (1 cubit = 1.5 - 2 feet), further supporting his view that the outside Altar atoned for the body's involvement in the transgression, specifically.

Concerning the *mizbea'ch p'nimi,* however, incense was offered on it, suggesting its function as atoning for the soul of the transgressor. We could suggest a support for this idea from the Talmud in *Berachos* 43b, where a connection is made between the neshamah and *rei'ach*, scent. The Talmud questions the origin of the obligation to recite a blessing on a pleasant aroma, and resolves its query by citing *Tehillim* (150:6): "*Kol haneshamash tehallel Y-ah* - All souls shall praise God." The Talmud states that the one thing from which the soul alone receives pleasure (and from which the body does not) is *rei'ach.*

The fact that the Talmud derives the *mitzvah* to bless God for pleasurable fragrances from the word *neshamah* confirms the association between the soul and *rei'ach.* This, in turn, supports the *Kli Yakar*'s opinion that the purpose of the *mizbe'ach p'nimi* was to atone for the soul of the transgressor.

The Kli Yakar finds another allusion to the unique function of the inside altar by observing its measurements, which were one cubit in length by one cubit in width (see Shemos 30:2). The number "one" alludes to the *neshamah* which is also referred to as *yechidah*, one, further supporting his opinion that the *mizbe'ach p'nimi* atoned for the soul of the person who sinned. (In fact, there are five parts to the soul, with *yechidah* as the highest aspect. In ascending order, the soul is composed of: *Nefesh*, *Ru'ach*, *Neshamah*, *Chayah* and *Yechidah*.)

Thus, *Bnei Yisrael* were commanded to build two altars in order to fully atone for their transgressions, which involved both the body and soul.

In today's day and age, with the absence of the Altar, the table upon which we eat our meals substitutes for the Altar (*Rabbi Yochanan* and *Reish Lakish* in *Chagigah* 27a). As such, our meals have the power to atone for us as well. But, as we mentioned, both body and soul require atonement. How can we obtain forgiveness during our meals? Here are two ideas, one for the body and one for the soul.

Based on the Talmud in *Chagigah*, it would follow that the food we eat is in place of the offerings, and we are in place of the *Kohanim* (see *Shemos 19*:6). Therefore, it is imperative that we have the right thoughts when we eat, so as to not to ruin the offering.

One possible thought would be to visualize the Hebrew word *ma'achal* (food), spelled *mem, aleph, chaf, lamed*. The numerical value of *ma'achal* is ninety-one, which shares the same numerical value as the sum of two of God's names: *Havayah* (twenty-six), and *Adni* (sixty-five). (See *Tzetel Katan* by the Rebbe Reb Elimelech of Lizensk, paragraph 15.) This reminds us that our food, *ma'achal*, is meant to be directed towards serving God (*Havayah-Adni*).We accomplish this when we make up our minds to use the strength we get from our food to serve God better.

This atones for our bodies. How do we atone for our souls?

Not only does the body have food, but so does the soul. Soul "foods" are the words of the Torah itself. So let us share a Torah thought at our tables during our meals, so it will atone for our souls.

Tetzaveh - Purim

Follow Your Nose

There is a reason that certain fragrances can send us back to the time when we were children and first experienced that sense. There is a reason that we would love to stop and smell the roses. Something profoundly deep is going on, and it's right under our noses.

In this week's portion, *Tetzaveh,* we are commanded to build the Altar of Incense (30:1-7). It is very fitting to discuss the incense at this time of year, in the month of *Adar,* before the holiday of *Purim.*

The *Bnei Yissaschar* (*Adar* 1:9), cites the *Arizal* (in *Likutei Torah, Ta'amei Hamitzvos* on *Parshas Bo*), who says that out of all our five senses, the sense of smell is the highest.

This is because at the time of the first sin with the Tree of Knowledge, all of Eve's senses are mentioned as having participated in the sin (see *Bereishis* 6:6-8), with the exception of the sense of smell. This teaches us that the sense of smell did not partake of the sin.

As such, the sense of smell was never stained by sin, and therefore transcends sin, making it the highest of the senses. This is very much connected to *Adar* and *Purim.*

The *Arizal* taught that all the Jewish months correspond to the different organs on a person's head. Some months correspond to the eyes, and others correspond to the ears, and so on. The month of *Adar*, however, is connected to the nose.

So, if the sense of smell is the highest sense, then the nose is the highest organ, which makes *Adar* the highest month. This means that *Purim*, which is the highlight of *Adar*, is the highest holiday.

This is why there are specifically two heroes in the *Purim* story, Mordechai and Esther. They represent the two nostrils of the nose. This also explains why their names are so connected to spices and the sense of smell.

The name Mordechai comes from the verse *Morr Dror* (*Shemos* 30:23), which were the names of some of the spices brought on the Altar of incense. *Onkelos* there translates those spices into the Aramaic with the words *Meira Dachya*. These two words sound like Mordechai when they are put together. Thus, Mordechai's name comes from the spices and the sense of smell (see *Chullin*, chap.12, *Shiluach Haken*, pg.139b). How appropriate this is because Mordechai is connected to one of the nostrils of the nose.

Esther, on the other hand, had a second name, Hadassah (see *Megillas Esther* 2:7). This name represents the *hadassim*, or myrtles, used for spices to smell at the *havdalah* ceremony (see *Shulchan Aruch*, *Orach Chaim* 297:4, and the *Mishnah Berurah* there subchapter 8). How fitting this is because Esther is connected to the other nostril.

Since *Purim* is the highest holiday, even *Yom Kippur* takes a back seat to it. This is because we come into *Yom Kippur* with sin, and then the day atones for the sin. This means that we are forgiven for our sins and won't be punished, but the stain of sin is still there.

However, on *Purim*, we come into the day with sin, and then the day uproots the sin retroactively, to the point that there was no sin to begin with.

This is because on *Yom Kippur* our *teshuvah* (repentance), comes from a place of fear. We are petrified on *Yom Kippur* because our lives hang in the balance. When *teshuvah* is done from fear, then our intentional sins are transformed into accidental sins (see *Yoma*, Ch. 8, *Yom Hakippurim*, pg. 86b). Although we may not be punished for accidental sins, because they were accidents; nevertheless, the taint of sin still remains.

However, on *Purim*, our *teshuvah* comes from a place of love, happiness and joy. When *teshuvah* is done from love, then our intentional sins are transformed into merits (*Yoma* Ch. 8, *Yom Hakippurim*, 86b). This means that not only has there been atonement, but the stain of sin has been completely removed.

This is why the Torah calls the Day of Atonement, "*Yom Kippurim*" (*Vayikra* 23:28). This hints to us that that day is a "*Yom K'Purim,*" meaning a day "like *Purim*." When we compare *Yom Kippur* to *Purim*, it shows that as great as *Yom Kippur* is, *Purim* is even greater. Just like we always compare people who are "less than" to people who are "more than"; so too, we compare a lesser holiday to a greater holiday.

This is why *Parshas Tetzaveh* is read on the Shabbos prior to *Purim*. This is because *Tetzaveh* and *Purim* share a commonality. *Purim* is connected to *Adar*, which is connected to the nose, representing the sense of smell. *Parshas Tetzaveh* also talks about this, because it discusses the Altar of Incense, which is connected to the nose and the sense of smell.

Both *Tetzaveh,* with its incense, and *Purim* are the highest of the high. Meaning, we can reach the greatest heights in *Adar* and on *Purim*. Unlike on *Yom Kippur*, on *Purim* there is a lot of eating and drinking. Additionally, in our day, *Purim* can never really fall out on Shabbos.

This teaches us that the power of *Purim's* light reaches even the most mundane. *Purim* touches even those who have fallen to the lowest, furthest and darkest of places. Even Jewish transgressors represented by the *chelbena*, galbanum, one of the spices brought on the Altar of Incense that had a foul odor (see *Shemos* 30:34), are included in the service of the *ketores*, incense, reaching the highest of levels (see tractate *Krisus*, chap. 1, *Shloshim v'shesh*, pg. 6b).

Perhaps on every Motzei Shabbos in *Adar* we should take a few moments to slowly and deeply breathe in the fragrance of the spices that we smell at the *havdalah* ceremony, and think of the spiritual opportunities that we have at this time of year.

May every one of us be touched by the Divine light this *Adar*, and especially on *Purim* itself, by following our nose - "It Always Knows"...to return to Hashem from a place of love, so we can be forgiven and cleansed from any trace of sin, and obtain complete closeness with our Parent in Heaven.

Ki Sisa

In the Blink of an Eye

Ask the fellow who won the million-dollar lottery - he will tell you how everything can change in just one moment. The truth of the matter is that this holds true for every single one of us.

This week's *parshah*, *Ki Sisa*, discusses the copper basin that the priests used to wash their hands and feet before performing the daily Temple service (*Shemos* 30:17-21). We might wonder why the basin is first introduced in this *parshah*, when last week's *parshah* discussed all of the other vessels and utensils used in the Temple. Why is the basin mentioned separately?

One of the themes of *Parshas Ki Sisa* is that "Hashem's salvation comes in the blink of an eye" (based on *Yalkut Shimoni*, *Nitzavim*, #960). This lesson is seen in the primary story of the *parshah*, the sin of the Golden Calf. After the sin, Hashem is so angry at the Jewish people that He actually says "I will annihilate them" (*Shemos* 32:10). Yet, a mere four verses later, the Torah tells us, "Hashem was appeased regarding the evil He said He would do to His Nation" (*Shemos* 32:14). Even when the Jewish people participated in blatant idolatry, Hashem was willing to spare them from destruction!

We see from this extreme example that, no matter how far we've fallen or how impure we feel we've become, there is always another chance. Hashem can save people at a moment's notice. Thus, we have no reason, ever, to despair or be distraught, since salvation is right around the corner.

The two components of the copper basin suggest this lesson as well. The inside of the basin contained water. The Slonimer Rebbe compares water to *teshuvah*, based on the verse "I will sprinkle upon them purifying waters" (*Yechezkel* 36:25). Water is often associated with purity, and the ability to be cleansed from past mistakes.

The *Noam Elimelech* discusses the second element of the basin: the copper exterior (*Shemos* 30:18). The Hebrew word for copper, *nechoshes*, shares a linguistic root with the *nachash*, meaning "snake." The snake is often compared to the *yetzer hara* (evil inclination), since the snake in the Garden of Eden was the original embodiment of evil. The two contrasting elements of the basin suggest an important message.

A person approaching the basin first touches the copper (*nechoshes*), recalling impurity and evil. But right behind that copper wall is a source of clean, purifying water, ready to wash away past mistakes! In other words, even if a person has been bitten (*nashach*) by the *nachash* (*yetzer hara*), and has succumbed to the temptations of negativity, "Hashem's salvation comes in the blink of an eye."

Perhaps this is one reason that the basin is discussed separately from all the other Temple vessels. This *parshah*, which discusses Hashem's instantaneous salvation of the Jewish people after the sin of the Golden Calf, is a fitting place to mention the basin. Its two components, water and copper, show us that the source of purity and healing is right behind the negativity, and can cleanse us from darkness at a moment's notice.

At times, we find ourselves in situations that almost seem unbearable. Perhaps we could suggest one exercise. When going through a hard circumstance, blink both eyes intentionally and quickly. This will remind us that Hashem's rescue can happen in the bat of an eyelash (by the way, people often blink their eyes at others as a sign that everything will be okay). When we connect to God with this thought, it may bring about the salvation that we so much seek.

May we all be blessed with the awareness of this lesson, so that even if we have weakened and behaved like a snake, we do not allow ourselves to slip into despair or depression. Instead, may we remember that salvation can come at the blink of an eye. In this merit, may we soon deserve to see the building of the Temple and the reinstitution of the basin, so that we may be cleansed and lifted to the highest of levels.

Ki Sisa

It Smells So Clean

There are two things that people are universally attracted to. One of them is water, and the other is fragrant smells. We would be hard-pressed to find somebody who dislikes these two items. It is for no small reason that these two ingredients were found in the *Beis HaMikdash.*

In the beginning of this week's portion, *Ki Sisa,* we continue reading about the vessels and the service in the *Mishkan* (Sanctuary).

In *Shemos* (30:17-21), God commands Moshe to make a basin (*kiyor*) of copper. Aharon, the High Priest, and his sons would wash their hands and feet in the basin before entering the tent of meeting.

God instructs Moshe in the following verses (22-38) regarding the details of *ketores,* the incense that was burnt as offerings to God on the *mizbe'ach p'nimi* (Inner Altar) which was overlaid with gold (see *Shemos* 30:3).

Based on the *Noam Elimelech,* we could suggest that these two aspects of the service in the Sanctuary represent the two main components of our *avodas* Hashem, service of God.

As we mentioned above, the basin was made of copper (*Shemos* 30:18). The Hebrew word for copper is *nechoshes* (spelled *nun, ches, shin, taf*), which stems from the word *nachash* (spelled *nun, ches, shin*) meaning "snake." (See *Rashi* on *Bamidbar* 21:9 and *Bereishis Rabbah* 31:8 for further insight into the connection between these two words, and also see the previous essay "*In the Blink of an Eye.*") The *Noam Elimelech* explains that, on a symbolic level, the copper (*nechoshes*) basin represented the snake (*nachash*) in the Garden of Eden, which, ultimately, caused severance in the relationship between man and God. The water in the *kiyor,* which washed away impurities, served as a *tikkun* (rectification) for the sin caused by the *nachash* by removing the barriers - i.e. layers of impurity - that stood between the Jewish people and God.

The inside altar, on which the *ketores* was offered, was, as we said earlier, covered in gold. A precious and expensive metal, gold represents haughtiness and arrogance, traits that obstruct interpersonal relationships, causing division and dispute among people.

Although the Golden Altar hints at these negative characteristics, it also symbolizes their *tikkun*. The *Noam Elimelech* explains that if we analyze the Hebrew word for gold (*zahav*), we find that the *gematria* (numerical value) of the letters decreases. The first letter, *zayin*, has a numerical value of seven. The next letter, *hey*, is numerically five; and the final letter, *beis*, has a *gematria* of two. This diminution in number alludes to the trait of humility. A humble person does not have a false sense of pride, and is, therefore, able to create harmonious relationships, thereby fostering unity between people, the ultimate rectification for arrogance and conceit.

The incense offerings that were brought on the Golden Altar also allude to this *tikkun* of unity, since both pleasant and foul-smelling spices were brought as offerings to God. In *Shemos* (30:34), Moshe is instructed to offer up *chelbena* (galbanum) together with the other fragrant spices. The Sages derive from here that sinners (represented by the *chelbena*) must be included with the community (represented by all the other spices) in prayer (see *Krisus* 6b). Thus, the incense expresses the concept of Jewish unity because it demonstrates that transgressors also have a share in *avodas* Hashem.

Once we imbibe into ourselves the messages of the *kiyor* and *ketores*, we will be able to rectify the sins that resulted in the destruction of both the First and Second Temples.

We learn in the Talmud (*Yoma* 9b) that the First Temple was destroyed on account of the three cardinal sins. Those crimes could be considered as rebelling against God. Although murder is listed amongst them, and would really seem to be a crime committed against one's fellow man, it could still be considered as a rebellion against God.

This is based on the *Kli Yakar* (*Shemos* 20:13) who points out that the Ten Commandments were not written on one tablet. Rather, five were on one tablet and the other five paralleled the first set on the second tablet. Therefore, there is a connection between the two sets. This means to say that there is a connection between the first commandment and the sixth, between the second and the seventh, between the third and the eighth, etc.

The *Kli Yakar* says that the connection between the first commandment (I am Hashem your God; *Shemos* 20:2) and the sixth (You may not murder; *Shemos* 20:13) is to teach us that anybody who spills the blood of another person is actually diminishing the likeness of God from this world. This is because man was created in the likeness of God. (See *Bereishis* 9:6 where it says "Whoever sheds the blood of man, by man shall his blood be shed; for in the image of God He made man.")

Based on this we could suggest that in the first Temple era, when people murdered, it was with the intention of removing God's Presence from Earth. This was therefore considered as an affront against God. The second Temple, however, was destroyed as a result of crimes committed against our fellow man. The remedies for both these aspects of *avodas* Hashem are expressed in this week's portion by the *kiyor* and *ketores.*

The water in the basin rectified our relationship with God, as it removed the impurities that obstructed the connection between God and the Jewish people. Let us learn to "wash away" our impurities by constantly working on ourselves to improve our service of God.

The incense offerings, on the other hand, emphasized the importance of our relationships with others by reminding us to humbly accept, and relate well with others, regardless of their weaknesses or negative actions.

Although today we do not have the *kiyor* nor the *ketores*, we can still do something to connect to these ideas. In substitution of the *kiyor*, we have a *mitzvah* called *negel vasser* (literally, fingernail water-the water with which we wash our hands when we wake up in the morning). Let's make sure to have a cup, basin and towel to do this *mitzvah* properly.

When pouring the water over our hands, think of how we are like the *Kohanim* (see *Shemos* 19:6) who are attempting to wash away any impurities that may cause a barrier between ourselves and God.

In substitution for the *ketores*, we could take myrtle, for example, and recite a blessing over them prior to smelling them. While inhaling the fragrance, we should close our eyes and decide to take in (or accept) all types of people. In this way we can improve in both areas of *Bein Adam Lamakom* and *Bein Adam Lachaveiro*.

May we be blessed to remove all barriers that separate us from God and each other, and subsequently deserve to witness the building of the Temple, when we will celebrate the reinstitution of *avodas hakiyor* and *avodas haketores*, ushering an era of true peace into the world.

Ki Sisa - Parshas Parah

Holy Cow

You were just hired or promoted to a new position. Shortly thereafter, you made a terrible mistake which cost the company thousands, or millions of dollars. You feel sick to your stomach. How can you face the manager? You realize that you blew it big time. Wouldn't you be relieved to discover that your boss is willing to give you a second chance? What if you knew that your boss also gives other chances, even after repeated mistakes? How comfortable would that make you feel, and how loyal would you be to him? Well, our Boss's policy is just that; always willing to give us more chances.

Although this portion discusses a variety of topics, the highlight of the *parshah* is undisputedly the incident of the Golden Calf (*Shemos* Ch. 32). The only rivalry to its fame is its disturbing nature.

Here is a nation that witnessed so many miracles including the Ten Plagues, the Splitting of the Sea, manna falling from the sky daily, water gushing out of a rock, Clouds of Glory, and pillars of fire and cloud, and yet, they opted to serve an idol instead of God.

Not only that, but they had the audacity to say about the Golden Calf that it was the "god" that took them out of Egypt (*Shemos* 32:4). However, these are the same people that were able to point at God after the waters parted and say, "This is my God and I will glorify Him" (*Shemos* 15:2; *Rashi* citing *Mechilta*).

You can bet your bottom dollar that the "God" they envisioned at the Splitting of the Sea was not a Golden Calf, because God stresses over and over, in the Torah, that He has no image (*Devarim* 4:12).

Klal Yisrael's turning to the Golden Calf baffles the mind. How could they have been so foolish as to worship a four-legged, sluggish, and unintelligent creature?

It is here that we need to open our hearts in the deepest of ways. Rebbi Yehoshua Ben Levi teaches that the Jews only worshipped the Calf in order to encourage future sinners to repent (*Avodah Zarah*, Ch. 1, *Lifnei Eideihen*, pg. 4b).

Rashi elucidates and clarifies this statement so that we do not mistakenly dismiss the importance of what Rebbi Yehoshua Ben Levi wants to convey. *Rashi* says that the Jews at that time were spiritually powerful and they were in complete control of their inclinations.

As a matter of fact, says *Rashi*, they were so strong spiritually, that they should never have been able to have been beaten by their evil impulses.

Rather, *Rashi* explains, it was a Divine decree that the evil inclination should rule over them. Why? In order to encourage future sinners to repent. How so?

Well, should a sinner say, "I will not repent because I am so bad that God is disgusted with me and will not accept me"; then we say to him, "Go and learn from the Golden Calf, where the Jews denied God's existence, thereby becoming heretics, and yet they were accepted in repentance."

The Jews, at that time, were on a higher spiritual level than us. They witnessed more miracles in one day than we could ever dream of glimpsing in a lifetime. Yet, they fell to one of the lowest of crimes, idolatry.

If they, who were expected to achieve so much more, could make a comeback from the lowest of places, than we, who are not expected to achieve so much, and who have not drifted as far, can surely do so.

In other words, God removed the Jews' free will for a few moments and forced them to sin with the Golden Calf and to say what they said, just in order to make a point: it is never too late to return to God.

Paranthetically, this Gemara could raise a difficulty. If the Jews were indeed forced to commit the sin of the Golden Calf, why were they punished afterwards? The following are two brief approaches to explain this difficulty.

The first approach is that the Jews who were punished enjoyed the sin even though they were forced into it. Although they were forced to sin, nobody said that they had to enjoy it. They were then punished for the enjoyment that they got out of it.

The second approach is that even if the Jews did not enjoy the sin, they were nevertheless punished in order to teach us another lesson. When it comes to helping somebody else, we have to be willing to pay a price for it. God wants us to have the willingness to help others even at personal loss. An elaboration on these two approaches, as well as other approaches, are beyond the scope of this work (See Chukas, "*The Needs of the Many Outway the Needs of the Few*").

God's message was that no matter what we do, say, or think, we are never beyond the point of return.

We could add that it is for this reason that *Parshas Ki Sisa* is often read together with *Parshas Parah*. *Parshas Parah* deals with the Red Heifer whose ashes were used to purify people who were spiritually unclean (*Bamidbar* 19:2-22).

According to Rebbi Moshe HaDarshan (cited in *Rashi*), the Red Heifer atones for the sin of the Golden Calf. This shows us that it is possible to repent and purify spiritual filth, even for the worst wrongdoings.

The Slonimer Rebbe says many times throughout his *Nesivos Shalom* that if a Jew thinks that he or she can do, say, or think something so bad that they are beyond the point of return, then that Jew does not know the ABC's of

Judaism and has not crossed its threshold.

This lesson is so crucial for today's day and age. Sometimes our evil inclination whispers a message of despair into our ears. Some of us may be able to recall that inner voice that declares with such certainty that we are finished, washed-up, with no hope of improving our standing.

It is precisely for a generation that is plagued by despondency that the episode of the Golden Calf transpired. We must remind ourselves that we are important; we are special; and that God loves us eternally, no matter what.

Then we will have the self-confidence to pick ourselves up after we fall and climb to the greatest of heights.

Perhaps each morning we should make the following declaration: "I will try my best not to succumb to temptation today. However, in case I do fall, I believe in God, who believes in me. I always have another chance to fix things and get closer once again." This declaration has the power to set the tone of the day so that it will be a successful one.

May we all be blessed with the strength to fight off temptation to begin with. However, in the eventuality that we do stumble, may we be blessed with the knowledge that there is always another chance, and thereby commit ourselves with an unbreakable resolve to return to our eternal loving Parent in Heaven.

Ki Sisa

Shaking Off the Heavy Hitters

Imagine that a person you know scratches you, head-butts you, and spits on you. How would you feel about that person? ...Oh! By the way, that person is an infant. That changes everything, doesn't it? We must realize that every time God looks at us, He sees that innocent baby. How different our lives would be if we could see each other that way.

The main focus of this week's portion discusses the sin of the Golden Calf. We are taught that every generation has to pay the price for this iniquity (*Shemos* 32:34; *Sanhedrin*, Ch. 11, *Cheilek*, pg. 102a). It comes as no surprise to find a source which indicates that the Jews wanted God to forget about the entire incident.

The Talmud reports that the Jews said to Hashem that since there is no concept of forgetting by the Throne of Glory, perhaps God will never forget the episode of the Golden Calf. To that, Hashem replied that He is prepared to forget about it. Then the Jews claimed that if the concept of forgetting does exist by the Throne of Glory, then maybe God will forget about how the Jews accepted the Torah at Sinai. To that Hashem responded that He would never forget about that (see *Berachos*, chap. 5, *Ein Omdin*, pg. 32b; *Yeshaya* 49:14-15).

One question on this passage is how the Jews could have said that the concept of forgetting exists by the Throne of Glory, implying that they thought that God could actually forget. Even though God said that He was prepared to "forget" about the sin, it does not mean that He was going to actually forget. Forgetting is a weakness that does not apply to God. Rather, it means that Hashem was willing to "forgive, overlook, and turn the other way" with regard to the sin. So, what were the Jewish people thinking?

The *Shevilei Pinchas* explains that the Jews were concerned that the crime of the Golden Calf would never be forgotten because one of the angels that carries God's Throne of Glory has a face in the shape of an ox (*Yechezkel* 1:10). Since an ox is in the same family as the Calf, this angel's very presence by the Throne would serve as a constant reminder of the Golden Calf, causing constant prosecution against the Jewish people for stooping so low with this idolatry.

However, God told them that He would forget the incident. When the Jewish people heard that, they thought that the way in which Hashem would "forget" about the ox's prosecution would be for God to no longer sit on the Throne. They thought that God would have the Throne "stored in the attic," so to speak, and in this way God would not have to hear the constant prosecution coming from the angel whose face is in the shape of an ox.

In other words, the Jews never thought that God would actually forget about the sin because God never forgets anything. Rather, they thought that He would not sit on the Throne anymore so as not to listen to the ox's prosecution. However, this too caused the Jews to be concerned.

You see, the very existence of the Throne of Glory is a constant advocate for the Jews because it testifies that they made Hashem into a King by accepting the Torah upon themselves. After all, there can be no King without a people pledging allegiance to Him (*Rabbeinu Bachya*, *Bereishis* 38:30). But, if Hashem no longer sits on His Throne, then God would no longer hear of the Jewish people's acceptance of the Torah.

God responded by saying that He did not have to refrain from sitting on the Throne in order to avoid listening to the ox's prosecution. God said that He could sit on the Throne and still not hear any prosecution. This is because God has many ways of dealing with things. In this case, God transformed the ox into a baby face (*Reish Lakish*, *Chaggigah*, Ch. 2 *Ein Dorshin*, pg. 13b).

In fact, Yechezkel the Prophet prayed to God that He remove the face of the ox and substitute it with the face of a baby. This would demonstrate that even after sinning with a mega crime, like the Golden Calf, one can repent and return to the innocence of a newborn baby, whose slate is completely clean (*Shevilei Pinchas*; *Yalkut Shimoni*, *Tehillim* 102:19; also see *Rashbi*, *Avodah Zarah*, Ch. 1, *Lifnei Eideihen*, pg. 4b).

In this way, when God sits on the Throne, He will hear the Throne's constant testimony that the Jewish people accepted the Torah and in doing so made God into a King. Simultaneously, God will hear the constant defense of the angel with the baby face who testifies that the Jews have repented and returned to their original sweetness.

This whole episode teaches us a most valuable lesson. We see from the Golden Calf that we can rectify even our worst mistakes. Therefore, a good exercise over this Shabbos would be to think about one major sin we know we are guilty of. This sin should be the one that we think is the most severe, our darkest secret. Let's try to fix it.

We should think about how damaging it is, and regret the past. We should try to think about how beneficial it would be to stop, and resolve to change in the future. We should admit our mistakes to God and ask Him for assistance in overcoming the challenge of this sin.

Even if we do not completely rid ourselves of it, we can, nevertheless, make a dent. This would be a huge accomplishment and a great beginning to eventually breaking those proclivities. In this way, we make the episode of the Golden Calf meaningful.

May we all be blessed with the realization and self-confidence that we can atone and fix anything we have broken. May we understand that God is willing to ignore the negative and focus on the positive. This will lift us up and take us soaring all the way to the Throne of Glory where we will dance around the Divine presence with all the holy angels.

Vayakhel-Pekudei

Light Your Fire

You are walking down the sidewalk in a busy city, when you notice a whole crowd of people standing, clustered together, looking up, and pointing to something above with sheer excitement on their faces. You just have to look; you've got to see what the fuss is about. This is the type of excitement that we are supposed to have in our practice of Judaism. When other people see the excitement on our faces, they will just have to explore, to check it out for themselves.

This week's double portion discusses the actual building of the Sanctuary and the designing of the priestly garb. However, before the Jews begin to engage in this construction, they are cautioned to observe Shabbos.

This warning brings a clear message. Even though they are erecting a House of God, they must, nevertheless, protect the sanctity of Shabbos by not producing anything on it. Rather, they must rest on the seventh day by disengaging from any creative activity.

The verse which cautions the Jews to guard Shabbos says, "These are the things that God commanded you to do; six days you shall do work, and on the seventh day it will be for you holy, a day of solemn rest to God; anybody that does work on it will be put to death; do not light a fire in any of your dwelling places on the Shabbos day" (*Shemos* 35:1).

It seems a bit strange that out of the thirty-nine different types of creative activity that could have been mentioned in Scriptural verse, only kindling a fire was stated (see *Mishnah Shabbos*, pg. 73a). Why was burning a fire chosen from all the other Shabbos prohibitions? (See *Rashi* citing the Talmud in *Shabbos* on pg. 70a, and see the *Rashbam* for different approaches in resolving this question.)

The *Chasam Sofer* (pg. 151b, the paragraph starting with the words "*Lo seva'aru*") teaches a deeper dimension to the Torah's choice of the prohibition of lighting a fire on the Shabbos. He says that the verse is telling us that preferably a Jew's heart should be on fire with the love of God, prayer, and the study of Torah the entire week.

This means that a Jew should work at being so ablaze with fiery passion to serve God the whole week, that by the time Shabbos comes, the spiritual fire burns on its own.

In other words, regarding the prohibition of starting a flame on Shabbos, the Torah is trying to say, "Do not begin to kindle the spiritual flame on Shabbos; rather, that process should start from the beginning of the week, so that by the time it is Shabbos the person is already 'on fire.'"

The *Shevilei Pinchas* suggests that this approach of the *Chasam Sofer* broadens the meaning behind the commandment to remember the Shabbos every single day (*Shemos* 20:8; see *Ramban* citing *Mechiltah*).

He says that this commandment is meant to remind us to work at developing a sizzling desire in service to God every day of the week. Only then will the spiritual candle "burn brightly" on the Shabbos day.

After all, it says, "One who toils on the eve of Shabbos, he will eat on Shabbos; however, one who does not toil on the eve of Shabbos, what will he eat on Shabbos?" (*Avodah Zarah*, pg. 3a).

There is one particular vessel in the Sanctuary which personifies this relationship between the weekdays and Shabbos. That vessel is the *Menorah* (Candelabra).

We are told that the lighting of the *Menorah* must be done in such a way that the flame goes up by itself (see *Rashi* in *Bamidbar* 8:1 expounding on the word "*Beha'alosecha.*") Isn't it obvious that the *Kohen* must hold the lighter to the candles of the *Menorah* until they can stay lit on their own? If the *Kohen* pulls the lighter away from the wicks before they catch fire, it is evident that he has not fulfilled the commandment. Why then was it necessary to specify that the lighting of the *Menorah* must be done until the flame goes up by itself?

The *Shem MiShmuel* (*Parshas Beha'alosecha*, pg. 188) explains what's going on based on the *Yalkut Shimoni*, which says that the seven branches of the *Menorah* correspond to the seven days of the week. The central post of the *Menorah* (which is attached to the base) represents Shabbos.

The six branches which stem out of the central post (three on each side) represent the six days of the week. We also know that the wicks at the top of the six branches leaned toward the central post (*Rashi* on *Bamidbar* 8:1).

All this comes to enlighten us! The six branches facing the center post teach us that the six days serve the seventh. Just as the brightness in the center post is assisted by the other six branches, so does the spiritual light of the Shabbos burn bright when assisted by the other six days.

This lesson is empowering as much as it is demanding. We all have active and busy lives. There are so many projects that demand our attention. Although we should attend to these matters, we must never lose sight of the spiritual opportunities that surround us. By doing so, we actually build our own Shabbos, which is tantamount to building a Sanctuary.

One example would be to say the *berachah* of *Asher Yatzar* with real passion. I chose to begin with this *berachah* because we can all relate to the importance of health. Since saying this *berachah* also serves as a *segulah* for good health, we may find it easier to say it slower with more meaning. Once we begin to say this *berachah* more passionately, then other things can follow.

May we be blessed to sow the seeds of passion, excitement, and fun into our hearts as we glowingly learn Torah, pray, and do *mitzvos* during the week, thus creating our own blazing "Sanctuary of Time." In that merit, may we deserve to light the *Menorah* in our permanent House of God speedily in our days.

Pekudei

How "Two" Lead the People

So, you want to go for a degree; that's great. You'll just have to find the best professor for you. If you are clueless about the subject, then the teacher who is most qualified in introducing the material is preferable. But, if you are already well-versed on the topic, then a professor who teaches at a more advanced level is better for you. The same formula applies to those who seek a mentor in life. At first we may need to receive from one person, but later on we may need somebody else.

This week's portion, *Pekudei*, details the contributions made to the *Mishkan* (Sanctuary) and describes how these donations were utilized. In the beginning of the *parshah*, the Torah mentions the two individuals - Betzalel and Oholiav - who were appointed to oversee the construction of the *Mishkan*. Betzalel is introduced (38:22) as, "Betzalel, son of Uri, son of Chur, of the tribe of Yehudah." The Torah introduces Oholiav (38:23) as, "Oholiav, son of Achisamach, of the tribe of Dan."

Why was it necessary to have two people in charge of the building of the Mishkan? Wouldn't it make more sense to have one leader?

We could suggest that Betzalel and Oholiav personified two different types of leaders who were specifically chosen to guide the diverse Jewish nation. Betzalel helped the people who were already connected to God and who observed His commandments. Oholiav, on the other hand, guided individuals who felt distant from God and who were lacking in the realm of observance. We see these differing leadership roles hinted at in their names and lineage.

Let us examine Betzalel first.

1. Betzalel is spelled *beis, tzadi, lamed, aleph, lamed.* Therefore, the name "Betzalel" can be divided to form the phrase, "*BeTzel Kel,*" meaning "in the shadow of God." Thus, Betzalel was the type of leader who guided and encouraged people who were already in God's shadow, i.e. close to Him. (This idea is based on a Talmud in *Berachos* (55a) which says that Betzalel was *BeTzel Kel.* Here, we are applying this concept to the people whom Betzalel led.)

2. Betzalel was the son of "Uri," which means "my light," or which could be interpreted "*Or Yud,*" (light of God - the letter *Yud* representing Hashem). The name of his father, thus, hints at the type of people whom he led - those who were already basking in the Divine light, through their observance of Torah and *mitzvos.*

3. Betzalel's grandfather was called "Chur," translated as "hole," representing the Jewish people whose connection to God was deeply engrained within them.

4. Finally, Betzalel was from the tribe of Yehudah (spelled *yud, hey, vav, daled, hey*). The name "Yehudah" contains the Tetragrammaton name of God, symbolizing the people whom he guided - those already strongly attached to Him. (Moreover, the letters that form the name of God (*yud and hey, vav and hey*) can be arranged in several different ways. The highest combination is the order in which they appear in the actual name of God - which is the same order as we find in the name "Yehudah," alluding to the most spiritually-elevated individuals!)

Thus, we see that Betzalel's role involved helping those who were already connected to God, strengthening and encouraging them to improve, ensuring that their *avodas* Hashem never became habitual, and subsequently enabling them to achieve even greater spiritual heights.

However, Oholiav is spelled *aleph, hey, lamed, yud, aleph, beis.* This indicates a whole different type of leader.

1) His role is hinted at in his name, which forms the words, *Oholei Av*, (father's tents). The Jews who felt distant from God needed a father figure who would guide them into the "tent of God" and make them feel safe and protected.

2) Oholiav was the son of "Achisamach" (spelled *aleph, ches, yud, samech, mem, chaf*). Achisamach can be divided into two words: *achi*, which means "my brother," and *samach*, which is translated as "rely upon." The Jews who felt far from Hashem required a "big brother," so to speak, upon whom they could rely to draw them closer to God.

3) Finally, Oholiav was from the tribe of Dan, which symbolizes the people who are furthest from God. In *Devarim* (25:18) we read about Amalek's attack on the Jewish nation. *Rashi* (citing *Midrash Tanchuma*) expounds that these specific Jews, who were vulnerable to Amalek, lacked strength on account of their sins, which subsequently caused the Clouds of Glory to expel them, leaving them unprotected from external dangers. The *Mussaf Rashi* (commentary gathered from *Rashi*) identifies these particular people as the tribe of Dan. (The *Mussaf Rashi* cites a verse from *Yechezkel* (16:15) where Israel is rebuked for "lavishing her fornications," and where *Rashi*, citing a *Psikta*, comments that this is a reference to the tribe of Dan who practiced idolatry - which in essence is adultery against God.)

So, Dan represents the Jews who were repelled by God because of their transgressions and who required a leader to redirect them to the right path, thus bringing them closer to Him. Oholiav characterized this exact type of leader.

Thus, we see that God purposely appointed two different individuals to oversee the construction of the Sanctuary in order to successfully guide the different types of Jews in their *avodas* Hashem.

May we all be blessed to find the right *Rebbe* (leader) who will bring us back to the correct path, and who will help us improve our *avodas* Hashem.

Vayakhel-Pekudei

Just Keep On Trying

"Whaddaya mean pay you for the new kitchen cabinets you installed? They all fell apart the moment after you hung them on the wall." "But sir, I worked for days on this project; you owe me. I have to feed my family." Which litigant do you think would win in a court of law? Who would God favor in such a case?

This week's double portion, *Vayakhel-Pekudei*, discusses the construction of the Sanctuary, its vessels and the priestly garments. (This *parshah*, which details the actual building of the *Mishkan*, follows two similar *parshiyos* - *Terumah* and *Tetzaveh* - where God commands Moshe regarding the specifications of the Sanctuary.)

The *Midrash Tanchuma* (in *Pekudei*, #11) comments on the verse (*Shemos* 39:33), "They brought the Tabernacle to Moses...." Although the Jewish people constructed the Tabernacle, utensils and priestly garments, they were unable to erect the Sanctuary because the components, particularly the beams, were too heavy to lift. Therefore, they approached Moshe with their dilemma. Moshe thought to himself, "If the people as a group cannot assemble the parts, how can I, an individual, succeed?" Moshe called out to God, "I cannot do this!"

Hashem responded; "Busy your hands [i.e. try to pick it up], and it will appear to everyone as though you are lifting it, when in reality, the beams will lift themselves [i.e. I, God, will do it]. Nevertheless, in My Torah, you [Moshe] will be credited for setting up the Mishkan."

Indeed, we find that the Torah tells us (*Shemos* 40:17) "*Hukam HaMishkan* - the Tabernacle was erected," which seems to imply that the Mishkan erected itself or was assembled by God. However, as the Midrash points out, Moshe is credited for setting up the Sanctuary, as we find the verse states explicitly (in 40:18), "*Vayakem Moshe es HaMishkan* - Moshe set up the Mishkan."

We learn from here the importance of trying. God expects us to do our utmost to serve Him as best as we can. The outcome of our attempts, however, is in God's hands, not ours. Nonetheless, if we exert sincere effort in *avodas* Hashem, God will reward us for the result as if we achieved it on our own.

This idea is reminiscent of a prayer that is said on a daily basis. The *Mishnah* in *Berachos* (28b) says that Rabbi Nechunya ben HaKoneh would recite a short prayer upon entering and leaving the Torah study hall. The Talmud cites a section of the prayer: "I toil [in Torah], and they toil [in the mundane world]. I toil and get rewarded [i.e. paid], whereas they toil [and do not get paid]." (See *Shulchan Aruch*, *Orach Chaim* 110:8.)

This prayer seems to suggest that people in the working world do not receive payment, when we know, of course, that workers do earn salaries. Moreover, the more time and effort one puts into a job - for example, building a house - the more money the laborer will receive. What, then, is this prayer really implying?

The *Chofetz Chaim*, famed for his succinct answers, explains: In the secular world there is no concept of paying a person for his toil, in absence of a final product. This point can be illustrated by the following story.

Jim, the local craftsman made a beautiful mahogany table. One day, however, the table suddenly collapsed. A customer walked in to Jim's store, wanting to buy a mahogany table. Jim directed him to the collapsed piece of furniture and told him the price - $500. The customer, aghast, exclaimed that a pile of wood is worth nothing, never mind $500! Jim, feeling very upset and humiliated, responded, "But I spent three whole months working tirelessly on this table!" Naturally, the customer was not interested, and walked out of the store. After all, no product, no pay!

Yes, in the working world a person's pay is often associated with the amount of time and energy the worker applies, but only in context of an existing product or outcome.

In the Torah world, however, a person is rewarded for his efforts alone, regardless of whether or not an outcome was attained. Any effort we spend learning Torah or trying to do a *mitzvah* is recognized - regardless of whether we understood the piece of Torah, or accomplished the *mitzvah*. God expects us to try our hardest; the end result is in His hands.

This concept helps us to understand why Betzalel was appointed Chief Supervisor of the Sanctuary's construction. In *Shemos* (35:30), Moshe says, "See, Hashem has proclaimed by name, Betzalel, son of Uri, son of Chur, of the tribe of Yehudah." What was unique about Betzalel that he was selected for this role?

We could propose, based on the ideas discussed thus far, that Betzalel was a person who was always willing to try his best. We find several allusions to this attribute in Betzalel's name.

1) Firstly, we could suggest that the letters in the name "Betzalel" (spelled *beis, tzadi, lamed, aleph, lamed*) form an acronym for the following phrase: "*Tzarich l'nasos bekocho lekayem achrayoso* - A person must try with all his strength to fulfill his responsibility." What is our responsibility? Our duty is to put in maximum effort in the service of God. This is the trait that Betzalel exemplified.

2) Secondly, the letters in the name Betzalel, in *gematria katan* (a system of numerical values where all the zeros are dropped), add up to the number 18 (*beis* = 2, *tzadi* = 9, *lamed* = 3, *aleph* = 1, *lamed* = 3; totaling 18).

Eighteen is also the *gematria katan* of the infinitive *lenasos* (spelled without a *vav: lamed* = 3, *nun* = 5, *samech* = 6, *taf* = 4; totaling 18), which means "to try."

Betzalel's name hints at his essence - he was a person who always tried his best. This quality is essential for life, hinted at by the *gematria* of the word *chai,* life, which also equals 18.

3) Thirdly, the Talmud (Berachos 55a) expounds on Betzalel's name as follows: As mentioned in the previous essay, "*How 'Two' Lead the People,*" the name "Betzalel," when divided into two, produces the phrase "*betzel Kel* - in the shadow of God." Betzalel recognized that he lived in God's shadow, reminding us of the verse in *Bereishis* (1:27) which states that Man was created "*B'Tzelem Elokim.*" Although often translated, "in the image of God" (which seems to go against the tenets of our faith, since God has no image), the word *tzelem*, derived from the root word *tzel* (shadow), can be more accurately translated, "in the shadow of God." What does it mean to live in God's shadow?

We could propose the following approach: shadows can achieve nothing on their own. The actions of a shadow are completely dependent on the one casting the shadow. In a similar way Betzalel recognized that he, a shadow of God, does not have the power to achieve perfection and completion - only God is perfect and complete. In other words, Betzalel recognized his limitations and understood that the only thing he can do is try his best, with the hope that the "Master Caster," God, will complete the job.

We, as shadows of God, can only try our hardest to fulfill our role in this world, but ultimately the one casting the shadow is in charge - the result of our labor is in God's hands.

This idea is highlighted in *Shemos* (35:30) where Bezalel's lineage is described: "Betzalel, son of Uri, son of Chur, of the tribe of Yehudah." When we analyze the lives of Chur and Nachshon ben Aminadav, who was the leader of the tribe of Yehudah, we see that both individuals gave of themselves fully in the service of God.

The *Midrash Shocher Tov* (#76) says that Nachshon ben Aminadav did everything possible to cause the *Yam Suf* to split. He jumped into the sea first and advanced into the water until it reached his nostrils, at which point the sea split. Thus, Nachshon, the leader of Yehudah, put in all of his effort to do God's Will and experienced a final result.

Chur, explains the *Midrash Tanchuma* on *Ki Sisa* (#20), attempted to prevent the *Eirev Rav* from making the Golden Calf, but was not successful - the *Eirev Rav* murdered Chur and proceeded to commit the crime of idolatry. Thus Chur, Betzalel's grandfather, also tried his best to do God's Will, but did not experience success in his mission.

From the Torah's perspective however, both Nachshon and Chur were equally successful in their life's task. Why? Because God does not measure success by results. Rather, success is measured by the sincere effort and motivation that are exerted in the process of reaching our goals. Whether the objectives are realized or not is irrelevant, because we are not in control of the outcome.

Betzalel learned this vital lesson from his ancestors - both equally righteous people. Once we understand this message and strive to do the utmost in our *avodas* Hashem, we will bring light into this world - hinted at in the name of Betzalel's father, Uri. When divided into two parts, the word Uri (spelled *aleph, vav, reish, yud*) forms the words "*Ohr Yud* - light of God" (*yud* is the first letter of the Tetragrammaton name of God).

Finally, the fact that God commanded us in building the *Mishkan*, knowing that we would be unable to assemble it, teaches us one of life's most powerful and important lessons: God is concerned about our efforts and not about the results. This explains why Betzalel was chosen as supervisor of the construction - he embodied this all-important attribute. It is the effort that counts.

May we all be blessed to be willing to try our best every single day, realizing the importance of the process and not the destination, so that when Hashem builds the Third Temple, we will be credited for it, as well as the purity that it will bring to the entire world - all because we tried our best.

Vayakhel-Pekudei - Parshas HaChodesh

New and Improved

Looking for the best time to start that diet again? Waiting anxiously to start reading that new novel? Yearning to begin that new exercise regimen you have been planning to start for some time now? This just might be the best time of year to launch your project, especially if it's to complete that *mesechta* you always wanted to learn or begin that new *chessed* campaign you've been itching to start.

This week's *parshah* (or *parshiyos*) is *Vayakhel-Pekudei.* However, sometimes, the portions of *Vayakhel-Pekudei* are read together with another portion called *Parshas HaChodesh*, which is the fourth and last of the special portions read at this time of year (*Shekalim*, *Zachor*, *Parah*, and *Chodesh*).

Parshas HaChodesh is read on the Shabbos before *Rosh Chodesh Nissan* in order to sanctify the month of *Nissan*. However, this is not the primary way to sanctify the month. Back in the days when we had a *Sanhedrin*, witnesses who saw the new moon would testify in front of the judges and they would sanctify the month of *Nissan* officially. So, the mere reading of *Parshas HaChodesh* is only a Rabbinic way of sanctifying the month of *Nissan* (see *Mishnah Megillah* 29a and *Shulchan Aruch, Orach Chaim* 685:4 and the *Mishnah Berurah* subchapter 1). *Parshas HaChodesh* is taken from *Shemos*, otherwise known as *Parshas Bo* (12:1-20).

The Slonimer Rebbe in his *Nesivos Shalom*, tells us that during the year there are many times in which a Jew can renew himself or herself and become like a new creation, like on Shabbos or *Yom Tov*, for example. But, the month of *Nissan* is the most propitious time - more than any other - for renewal and rejuvenation.

One proof of this is a teaching in the Talmud that says, "in the month of *Nissan*, we were redeemed and in the month of *Nissan*, we will be redeemed" (*Rosh HaShanah* 11a, opinion of *Rebbi Yehoshua*). We see from that statement that *Nissan* is a time of redemption, which means, by definition, renewal and starting all over again. This is what it means when it says, "*HaChodesh hazeh lachem, rosh chadashim* - this month will be for you, the head of the months" (*Shemos* 12-2).

A deeper message hinted to in this verse is as follows: "This month [*Nissan*] is at the head of *hischadshus* - renewal" (a play on the Hebrew word for month - *chodesh*, which can also be pronounced *chadash*, meaning "new"). This means that in the month of *Nissan*, a Jew has the greatest advantage in changing himself and renewing himself, even in the most difficult areas for him to overcome, even in those areas where he has not yet succeeded during the rest of the year.

As a matter of fact, the first twelve days of *Nissan* were when the princes of each of the twelve Jewish tribes brought their offerings in dedication of the new Sanctuary that was built, and in order to inaugurate the new Altar (see *Bamidbar* 7:83 and *Rashi* 7:1).

Reb Menachem Mendel of Rimnov, and the *Agra DeKallah* in the name of his *Rebbe*, the *Chozeh MiLublin*, say that those first twelve days of *Nissan* correspond to the twelve months of the year, each day being connected to a different month. Those twelve days at the beginning of *Nissan* give the strength and power of renewal to all twelve *Roshei Chadashim,* and to all the twelve months, because the princes brought new offerings, each one giving them the strength to get close to God in ways that were never done before.

It is for this reason, the *Megaleh Amukos* explains, that the month of *Nissan* is given another name, which is *Aviv* (see *Shemos* 13:4). Although *aviv* usually translates as "springtime," he suggests that the Hebrew word *aviv* (spelled *aleph, beis, yud, beis*) forms the words *Av Yud-Beis*, which means "the father of the twelve," indicating that *Nissan* is the father of the twelve months. This is because the first twelve days of *Nissan* give birth to and enlighten the twelve months of the year.

All this shows us just how precious *Nissan* is for tapping into the energy of renewal. This fits in so nicely with the portions of *Vayakhel* and *Pekudei*, which discuss the building of a new Sanctuary and the making of new priestly garb, representing the building of holy things from scratch.

We could suggest a practical way of starting all over again with renewed strength, vim and vigor. On each of the first twelve days of *Chodesh Nissan*, let us recite the prince of that day with his offering that was brought to inaugurate the Sanctuary (this can be found in the back of most *siddurim*). With the recitation of each prince, let us think of how we can refresh ourselves in an area that that tribe represents.

For example, when reading about Yissachar, let's think of new ways to improve our Torah study, for which Yissachar was famous. When reading about Zevulun, let's think of new ways to improve giving *tzedakah*, an area where Zevulun excelled, etc. This will set the pace for a year of rejuvenation.

May we all be blessed this *chodesh* to change ourselves for the better and maintain this pace all twelve months of the year, in order that we will deserve to witness God creating for us a new Temple with its priestly garb this *Nissan*.

GLOSSARY

The following glossary provides a partial explanation of some of the Hebrew, Aramaic and Yiddish words and phrases used in this book. The spellings and explanations reflect the way the specific word is used herein. Often there are alternate spellings and meanings for the words.

ACHDUS – unity.

ADAM – man; also, the name of the first person.

ADAR – name of the twelfth and final Jewish month (lunar cycle).

ADMOR – acronym for Adoneinu Moreinu V'Rabbeinu – our master, our teacher, and our Rabbi. Usually used as an honorable introductory title for a Chassidic Rabbi.

AKEIDAH – lit. binding; refers to the binding of Yitzchak.

AKEIDAS YITZCHAK – the binding of Yitzchak.

ALEPH – the name of the first Hebrew letter.

AL HANISSIM – lit. for the miracles; a prayer inserted into the liturgy on Chanukah and Purim, thanking God for the miracles that occurred.

ALIYAH – to go up; a term used in reference to being called up to the Torah; also refers to one who immigrates to the land of Israel.

AM YISRAEL – the nation of Israel.

AMIDAH – the silent prayer, composed of eighteen (now nineteen) benedictions, and recited quietly while standing.

AMOS – cubits.

ANEINU – lit. answer us; a prayer inserted into the liturgy on fast days.

ANSHEI K'NESSES HAGEDOLAH – the Men of the Great Assembly .

ARAVOS – willows; traditionally used for worship on the holiday of Sukkos.

ARICHAS YAMIM – longevity.

ARON – ark; can refer to the Ark of the covenant or to the structure in which a Torah scroll is kept.

ASSERES HADIBROS – the Ten Commandments.

ASSERES YEMEI TESHUVAH – the ten days of Repentance from Rosh HaShanah until Yom Kippur.

AV – name of the fifth Jewish month (lunar cycle).

AV BEIS DIN – the head of the Jewish Supreme Court.

AVAK LASHON HARA – lit. the dust of gossip; refers to any gesture of slander.

AVEIRAH – sin.

AVINU – our father.

AVODAH – worship; work.

AVODAS HASHEM – worship; service of God.

AVOS – lit. fathers, often referring to our Patriarchs.

AYIN – the name of the sixteenth Hebrew letter.

AZ YASHIR – lit. then they sang; a reference to the song sung by the Jews after experiencing the Splitting of the Sea.

BNEI YISRAEL – the Children of Israel.

BA'AL TESHUVAH (BA'ALEI TESHUVAH) – repentant(s), or one who has decided to lead a religious life.

BARUCH SHEM – lit. blessed is the Name; refers to the sentence recited right after the Shema.

BEIN ADAM LACHAVEIRO – commandments between man and man.

BEIN ADAM LAMAKOM – commandments between man and God.

BEIN HAMETZARIM – lit. between the straits; refers to the three weeks of mourning between the seventeenth of Tammuz and the ninth of Av.

BEIS – the name of the second Hebrew letter.

BEIS HAMIDRASH (BATEI MIDRASHOS) – study hall(s) of Torah.

BERACHAH – blessing.

B'EZRAS HASHEM – with the aid of God.

BIKKURIM – first fruits brought to the temple where a ceremony is performed with them.

BIMAH – stage, podium. Commonly refers to the area where the Torah is read from in the synagogue.

BIRCHAS HATORAH – blessings recited prior to the study of Torah.

BISHUL AKUM – lit. food cooked by a non–Jew. Refers to a Rabbinic prohibition that such food may carry.

BITACHON – trust (in God).

BRAISAH – it. outside one; a section of Oral Law that was not committed to writing, l- for it was not part of the Mishna compilation of Rabbi Yehudah Hanasi.

BRIS HAGUF – a covenant made with the body.

BRIS HANESHAMAH – a covenant made with the soul.

BRIS MILAH – the covenant of circumcision; usually refers to Jewish circumcision itself.

B'TZELEM ELOKIM – in the image, likeness or shadow of God.

CHACHAM – a wise person. May refer to the Sages who led/lead the commuity.

CHAF – the name of the eleventh Hebrew letter.

CHAG – holiday, festival.

CHALAV YISRAEL – lit. Jewish milk; milk that was extracted from a kosher animal under Jewish supervision.

CHALLAH (CHALLOS) – the special loaf/loaves of bread eaten on Shabbos or *Yom Tov*; an amount of dough separated from the bread as a tithe.

CHANUKAH – an eight–day holiday which commemorates the miracle of oil lasting eight days. This occurred after the Hasmoneans defeated the Greeks, and is celebrated by lighting the menorah.

CHANUKIA – menorah or candelabra.

CHASSAN – groom.

CHASSIDIM – the different branches of observant Jews who follow the teachings of the Ba'al Shem Tov.

CHASSIDUS – the teachings of the Ba'al Shem Tov and other Chassidic masters.

CHATAS – a sin–offering.

CHAVIVUS – belovedness.

CHAVRUSAH – study partner.

CHAYAV – obligated or liable.

CHAYAV MISAH – one who is liable to the death penalty.

CHAZAL – an acronym for Chachameinu Zichronam Livrachah – our wise men of blessed memory; a title given to the Sages who lived in Talmudic times.

CHEDER – lit. a room; refers to a school dedicated to teaching Torah to little boys.

CHEDVAH – a form of happiness.

CHEISHEK – desire, motivation.

CHELBENAH – galbanum; one of the spices used for the incense offering.

CHES – the name of the eighth Hebrew letter.

CHESHVAN – name of the eighth Jewish month (lunar cycle).

CHESSED – kindness, acts of kindness.

CHODESH – month.

CHUMASH – the five books of Moses, or one of them.

CHURBAN – lit. destruction; typically referring to the destruction of the Temples.

CHUTZ LA'ARETZ – outside the Land of Israel.

DA'AS – knowledge.

DALED – the name of the fourth Hebrew letter.

DAVEN / DAVENING – pray / the act of praying.

DERECH – way; can also refer to a particular approach to serving God.

DIN – the law; strict justice.

DIVREI TORAH – words of Torah.

DOR HAFLAGAH – the generation that was dispersed after having built a tower from which to wage war against God.

DOR HAMABUL – the generation that was destroyed by the Great Flood.

DRASH – an advanced level of discourse on Torah.

EIGEL – lit. calf; usually a reference to the Golden Calf that the Jews sinned with in the wilderness.

EIREV RAV – the mixed multitude of Egyptian converts who joined the Jewish people in the Wilderness.

EIS RATZON – a favorable heavenly moment during which it is propitious for us to ask God our requests.

EITZOS – pieces of advice.

ELIYAHU HANAVI – Elijah the prophet.

ELOKIM – one of the names of God, usually used in the context of strict justice. Also: judge.

ELUL – name of the sixth Jewish month (lunar cycle).

EMES – truth.

EMUNAH – faith; faithfulness.

ERETZ YISRAEL – the Land of Israel.

ESROG – citron; a citrus fruit traditionally used for worship on the holiday of Sukkos.

GALUS – exile. May be used to refer to the time prior to the redemption of the Messiah.

GAN EDEN – Garden of Eden. Can refer to a paradise above in heaven, or to paradise on earth.

GEDOLIM – the Torah leaders of the generation.

GEHINNOM – Purgatory.

GEMARA / GEMAROS – the Talmud / various pieces of the Tamud.

GEMATRIA – numerical value of Hebrew letters and words.

GEMATRIA KATAN – a system of numerical value where all the zeros are dropped.

GEULAH – redemption.

GILGUL – reincarnation.

GIMMEL – the name of the third Hebrew letter.

GLATT – lit. smooth; a high standard of kashrus or a phrase which implies doing something 100% right.

HADASSIM – myrtle branches; traditionally used for worship on the holiday of Sukkos.

HAFTARAH – the section of the Prophets read in conjunction with the weekly Torah portion.

HAGADDAH – the text used at the Seder table on Passover.

HAKHEL – lit. gather; the *mitzvah* for all Jews to gather at the Temple once every seven years to hear the king read from the book of Deuteronomy.

HALACHAH (HALACHOS) – Jewish law(s).

HASHEM – lit. the Name; a reference to God.

HASHKAFOS – outlooks, worldviews or viewpoints.

HAVDALAH – lit. separation; the ceremony on Saturday night which makes a distinction between Shabbos and the weekdays.

HESTER PANIM – lit. concealment of the face; referring to the times that God hides Himself from us.

HEY – the name of the fifth Hebrew letter.

HOSHANAH RABBAH – lit. the great Hoshana; the last day of Sukkos where a special ceremony is perfomed with Aravos.

IKVESA D'MESHICHA – lit. the footsteps of the Messiah, referring to the End of Days.

IMAHOS – lit. mothers; usually referring to the Matriarchs.

IMEINU – our mother; usually in conjunction with a Matriarch.

IYAR – name of the second Jewish month (lunar cycle).

KABALLAH – Jewish mysticism. Also, acceptance of a certain practice or stringency. Also, a piece of knowledge transmitted orally, personally.

KADESH, URCHATZ – lit. making Kiddush and washing the hands; referring to a passage in the preface to the Passover Seder listing its fifteen stages.

KADOSH – holy. Also, removed from physicality.

KAF – the name of the eleventh Hebrew letter.

KALLAH – bride.

KAPPAROS – the atoning ceremony performed prior to Yom Kippur, traditionally using a chicken.

KASHRUS – Jewish dietary laws. Or the Kosher status of an animal or ritual object.

KAVOD – honor.

KAVOD HATORAH – honor of the Torah.

KEILIM – vessels.

KESHER – knot, connection.

KESHER SHEL KAYAMAH – a lasting knot or a lasting connection.

KETORES – incense.

KIBBUD AV V'EM – respecting a father and mother.

KIDDUSH – a ceremony performed at the onset and morning of Shabbos or *Yom Tov* over a cup of wine.

KIDDUSH HASHEM – sanctification of God's name; giving people a positive impression of God's Torah and the Jewish people.

KIRUV – outreach.

KISHKES – intestines. Often used to mean "inner workings."

KISLEV – name of the ninth Jewish month (lunar cycle).

KIYOR – sink, washbasin; usually referring to a specific vessel in the Temple with that function.

KODESH – holy.

KODESH KODOSHIM – the Holy of Holies.

KOHEN (KOHANIM) – priest(s).

KOHEN GADOL – the High Priest.

KOHEN HEDYOT – regular priest (not the High Priest).

KORBAN PESACH – Pascal lamb or kid.

KORBANOS – ritual offerings, usually sacrificed upon the Temple Altar.

KOSHER – description of food that conforms to Jewish dietary laws.

KRIAS HATORAH – the reading of the Torah.

KRIAS YAM SUF – the Splitting of the Sea.

KUF – the name of the nineteenth Hebrew letter.

KVELL – (coll. yid.) to receive tremendous pleasure and pride, usually from a child.

LAG BAOMER – the thirty–third day of the Omer celebrating the revelation of the Zohar.

LAMED – the name of the twelfth Hebrew letter.

LASHON HAKODESH – the holy tounge; biblical Hebrew.

LASHON HARA – lit. evil tongue; refers to derogatory speech about others.

LECHEM HAPANIM – the showbread; the 12 breads exhibited on the Shulchan in the Temple all week.

LEITZANUS – mockery, making fun.

LEVI (LEVIIM) – Levite (Levites).

LIMUD HATORAH – the study of Torah.

LULAV – palm branch traditionally used in worship on Sukkos.

MA'ARIV – the evening service.

MACHLOKES – argumentativeness; fighting.

MACHZOR – prayer book for the holidays.

MAGGID – preacher.

MAKOM – place. Hashem is sometimes referred to as HaMakom - the Place.

MALACH – angel. Rarely, a messenger.

MALCHUS – sovereignty; kingship; kingly.

MANHIGIM – leaders.

MAOZ TZUR – the song traditionally sung after kindling the Chanukah lights.

MASMID (MASMIDIM) – diligent student(s) of Torah.

MATAN TORAH – the giving of the Torah.

MATZAH (MATZOS) – round or square-shaped unleavened bread(s) eaten on Passover.

MAZAL (MAZALOS) – lit. fortune(s), or zodiac sign(s).

MELACH – salt.

MELAVEH MALKAH – lit. escorting the queen; refers to traditional meal after the Sabbath, on Saturday night.

MEM – the name of the thirteenth Hebrew letter.

MENORAH – candelabra; either refers to the one in the Sanctuary or Temple, or the one we light in our homes on Chanukah.

MENTCH – decent person endowed with refined interpersonal qualities such as respect, appreciation, kindness and friendliness.

MESECHTA – tractate of Talmud.

MESORAH – the/a tradition; the transmission of our teachings throughout the generations.

METZORA – a (spiritually-caused) type of leper.

MEZUZAH – a parchment containing two sections of Shema from the Torah, affixed to the doorposts of Jewish homes and businesses.

MIDDOS – traits and qualities with regard to ones personality. Also, measures or measurements.

MIDRASH – teachings from the Tannaic and Amoraic Sages on the Tanach.

MIKVEH – a pool used as a ritual bath for purification.

MILAH – circumcision. See Bris Milah.

MILCHEMES HAYETZER – the conflict with our evil inclination.

MINCHAH – the afternoon service. Also, a meal offering. Also, a gift.

MINHAG – custom.

MINYAN – a quorum of ten Jewish men above the age of thirteen, required for the daily services.

MISHKAN – the Tabernacle, Sanctuary.

MISHNAH – the first body of Oral Law that was committed to writing.

MISONENIM – the complainers; refers to the group of Jews in the wilderness who complained about how weary they had become on the journey.

MITZVAH (MITZVOS) – commandment(s).

MIZBEACH – altar.

MODEH ANI – lit. I thank you; the prayer said upon rising in the morning.

MOHEL – circumciser.

MOSHIACH – lit. the anointed one; usually refers to the Messiah. It may also refer to an anointed king.

NAARISHKEIT – silliness.

NACHAS – pleasure, satisfaction; refers to the pleasure a parent gets from a child, or that God receives from His children.

NACHASH – snake.

NASI – prince; a title usually reserved for the Chief Rabbi in Tannaic times who descended from the Davidic dynasty.

NAZIR – nazarite; one who vows to be a nazir, whose laws include refraining from wine, haircuts, and entering a cemetery.

NEFESH – soul, person; can refer to a specific part of the soul.

NEGEL VASSER – lit. fingernail waters; refers to ritual washing of hands upon arising from sleep.

NEILAH – lit. the locking; refers to last service of Yom Kippur where we still have a chance to repent before the gates of heaven are closed and locked.

NESHAMAH – soul; can also refer to a specific part of the soul.

NISSAN – name of the first Jewish month (lunar cycle).

NUN – name of the fourteenth Hebrew letter.

NUSACH – text; refers to a certain version of liturgical or Talmudic text.

OHR GANUZ – hidden light that God stashed away for the righteous in the future.

OLAH – burnt offering.

OLAM HABA – the World to Come.

OLAM HAZEH – this world.

PARAH ADUMAH – red heifer.

PARNASSAH – livelihood.

PARSHAH (PARSHIYOS) – portion(s), as in the Torah portion of the week.

PARSHAS HACHODESH – one of the four additional portions read prior to Passover, discussing the mitzvah of Rosh Chodesh.

PARSHAS PARAH – one of the four additional portions read prior to Passover, discussing the red heifer.

PARSHAS SHEKALIM – one of the four additional portions read prior to Passover, discussing the mandatory contribution by every person to the temple fund for the purchase of animals needed for communal offerings.

PARSHAS ZACHOR – one of the four additional portions, read prior to Purim, discussing the mitzvah of eradicating Amalek.

PAS YISRAEL – Jewish-made bread.

PASSUL – invalid.

PESACH – Passover.

PEY, PHEY – the name of the seventeenth Hebrew letter.

POSEK / POSKIM – authority / authorities on Jewish law.

PSHAT – the plain understanding of the Torah.

PURIM – holiday celebrating Jewish salvation from Haman's evil decree which called for annihilation of the Jewish people.

RASHA (RESHAIM) – wicked person (people).

RASHB"I – acronym for Rebbi Shimon bar Yochai.

RATZON HASHEM – the will of God.

RAV – a Rabbi; a halachic authority; the Amoraic sage called Rav.

REBBE – Rabbi; usually refers to a Chassidic leader. Also used to refer to a teacher in a Cheder or a personal mentor.

REBBETZIN – wife of a Rabbi.

REISH – the name of the twentieth Hebrew letter.

REMEZ – hint; or the coded level of understanding the Torah.

RISHON – first, or first one. Also used to refer to those authorities living in the Medieval period.

ROSH CHODESH (ROSHEI CHADASHIM) – lit. the head(s) of the month(s); refers to the first day of a month. In a 30 day month it also refers to the last day of the previous month.

ROSH HASHANAH – lit. the head of the year; refers to the High Holiday of judgment which commences the new Jewish year. (Note: the Jewish year consists of many cycles. Rosh HaShanah is the beginning of one of them. For other things, however, the cycle starts elsewhere. The monthly cycle begins at Nissan.)

SAF – the name of the twenty-second and final Hebrew letter.

SAMECH – the name of the fifteenth Hebrew letter.

SANHEDRIN – Jewish supreme court.

SCHLEP – (yid. coll.) to travel or carry in a very tiring and uncomfortable way. Also used to denote anything tiresome.

SCHLEPPING – traveling or carrying things in a very tiring and uncomfortable way.

SEDER – lit. order; a set time for Torah study. Also: the Passover ceremony on the first night, and second night in the diaspora.

SEFER (SEFARIM) – (holy) book(s).

SEFER TORAH – Torah scroll.

SEFIRAH (SEFIROS) – count/countings; the mitzvah of counting the days between Pesach and Shavuos; can be used as a general name for a kabalistic sphere(s) or attribute of Hashem.

SEFIRAS HAOMER – the mitzvah of counting from the second day of Passover (on which the Omer offering was brought) until Shavuos.

SEGULAH – Jewish charm or omen.

SEKILAH – stoning.

SELICHOS – prayers of supplication, begging God for forgiveness for our sins.

SHA'ATNEZ – garment containing a mixture of wool and linen and prohibited to wear.

SHABBOS (SHABBOSOS) – Sabbath(s).

SHABBOS HAGADOL – lit. the Great Sabbath; refers to the Shabbos prior to Passover.

SHABBOS SHIRAH – lit. Sabbath of Song; refers to the Shabbos when we read the song that was sung by the Jews at the sea.

SHACHARIS – morning service. Or morning.

SHALOM – peace.

SHAMASH (SHAMASHIM) – either a helper(s) in the synagogue, or a helper(s) of a great or important person. Also refers to the candle used to kindle the Chanukah candles.

SHAS – acronym for Shishah Sidrei (the six orders); refers to six orders of Oral Law which were committed to writing. May refer to the Talmud.

SHAVUOS – lit. weeks; usually refers to the holiday when Jews celebrate receiving the Torah.

SHECHINAH – the Divine presence.

SHEKEL (SHEKALIM) – monetary currency; in scripture refers to the currency used in Biblical times.

SHEM HAVAYAH – one of God's names that is spelled: yud, hey, vav, hey. It is not read as spelled.

SHEMA – lit. hear; refers to part of the liturgy containing the sentence declaring God's oneness, followed by three other paragraphs, which is recited twice daily.

SHEMINI ATZERES – the eighth day of Sukkos, technically considered a holiday unto itself.

SHEMIRAS EINAYIM – protecting ones eyes from gazing at inappropriate things.

SHEMITTAH – the Sabbatical year in Israel that occurs every seventh year where the land may not be worked. Also refers to the seven-year period as a whole.

SHEMONEH ESREI – lit. eighteen; refers to the silent prayer that has eighteen (now nineteen) benedictions (see Amidah).

SHEVAT – name of the eleventh Jewish month (lunar cycle).

SHEVET – tribe. Also, stick or staff.

SHIDDUCH (SHIDDUCHIM) – match(es) between a man and a woman.

SHILUACH HAKEN – the mitzvah of sending the mother bird away from the nest, and then taking the chicks or eggs.

SHIN – the name of the twenty-first Hebrew letter.

SHIRAS HAYAM – the song sung by the Jews at the Sea of Reeds after the Egyptians were drowned in it. (See Az Yashir).

SHLEIMUS – completion; referring usually to wholeness either in personality or as a people.

SHOFAR – a horn; typically a ram's, blown on Rosh HaShanah.

SHOVEVIM – an acronym that stands for the six Torah portions Shemos, Va'era, Bo, Beshalach, Yisro, Mishpatim. Some have the custom to fast and add additional prayers to ask Hashem for forgiveness in areas of immorality during the weeks that these portions are read.

SHTEI HALECHEM – the two loaves of breads offered on the holiday of Shavuos.

SHTICK – tricks; usually referring to pranks that are meant to be humorous or clever.

SHUL – a synagogue.

SIDDUR (SIDDURIM) – prayerbook(s).

SIMAN (SIMANIM) – sign(s), or chapter(s).

SIMCHAH – happiness; also refers to a Jewish celebration such as a wedding or a Bris.

SIMCHAS BEIS HASHO'EIVAH – the joyous occasion of drawing the water from the Shiloach spring and pouring it as a libation on the outside Altar during Sukkos.

SIMCHAS TORAH – the joyous holiday celebrating the completion of the yearly cycle of Torah reading which is on the same day as Shemini Atzeres in Eretz Yisrael, but in the Diaspora it is celebrated on the day after Shemini Atzeres.

SIN – the name of the twenty–first Hebrew letter.

SIVAN – name of the third Jewish month (lunar cycle).

SUKKAH – booth or hut, that Jews dwell in for the seven or eight days of Sukkos commemorating the booth or Clouds of Glory that protected our ancestors as they wandered in the Wilderness.

SUKKOS – plural of Sukkah, or the name of the holiday.

SULAM – a ladder.

TA'ANIS DIBBUR – a fast of speech, where people accept upon themselves to remain completely silent for a period of time with the exception of prayer and Torah study.

TAF – the name of the twenty–second and final Hebrew letter.

TAFEL – that which is secondary to something. Also, something tasteless.

TALLIS – lit. garment; prayer shawl worn during the morning service.

TAMMUZ – name of the fourth Jewish month (lunar cycle).

TANACH – acronym for Torah, Neviim and Kesuvim, which comprise the body of the Written Law.

TARYAG – an abbreviation whose numerical value is 613, representing the 613 commandments in the Torah.

TASHLICH – lit. to throw; refers to the custom of saying certain prayers near a body of water containing fish on Rosh HaShanah, thus symbolically demonstrating that we want to cast our sins away.

TEFILLAH (TEFILLOS) – prayer(s); also refers specifically to the silent prayer, the Amidah. One of the Tefillin.

TEFILLIN – phylacteries; black boxes containing four Torah portions on parchment, bound to the arm and head with black leather straps, worn by adult Jewish men daily (except for Shabbos and certain holidays). They remind us of the exodus from Egypt and thereby we subjugate our heart and mind to God.

TEFILLIN SHEL ROSH – the box worn on the head.

TEFILLIN SHEL YAD – the box worn on the arm.

TES – the name of the ninth Hebrew letter.

TESHUVAH – return, repentance. Also, a response, commonly as a letter responding to a query.

TEVES – name of the tenth Jewish month (lunar cycle).

TIKKUN – fixing; may refer to a spiritual remedy.

TISHAH B'AV – the ninth day of the Hebrew month of Av, marking the Jewish national day of mourning over the Temples' destruction and other tragedies which occurred on that date over the course of Jewish history.

TISHREI – name of the seventh Jewish month (lunar cycle).

TOCHACHAH – rebuke.

TORAH – the Bible; can either refer to the five books of Moses, or to the entirety of Tanach, or can even include the Oral Law. Can also refer to a specific teaching.

TOV – good.

TZADI – the name of the eighteenth Hebrew letter.

TZADDIK / TZADDIKIM – righteous person / people.

TZARA'AS – a (spiritually generated) form of leprosy which can be found on the walls of a home, on clothing, or on a person's skin or hair.

TZE'AKAH – crying out, usually to Hashem.

TZEDDAKAH – charity. Also, justice.

TZIDKUS – righteousness.

TZITZIS – fringes or strings tied to four–cornered garments, reminding us to fulfill the commandments.

USHPIZIN – lit. guests; refers to seven shepherds of Israel: Avraham, Yitzchak, Yaakov, Moshe, Aharon, Yosef, and David who visit the Jewish people in their Sukkos on the holiday of Sukkos.

VAV – the name of the sixth Hebrew letter.

VIDUI – confession.

YAM HAMELACH – lit. the sea of salt; the Dead Sea.

YAM SUF – the Sea of Reeds, usually associated with the Red Sea.

YAMIM NORAIM – Days of Awe, referring to the High Holidays.

YAYIN NESECH – wine that was poured in idolatrous worship.

YEFAS TOAR – lit. beautiful form; refers to an attractive woman that a Jewish soldier is allowed to take during war as a wife.

YESHIVA – lit. sit; refers to a Torah academy.

YESOD – foundation; one of the kabbalistic spheres, or attributes of Hashem.

YETZER HARA – evil inclination.

YETZER HATOV – positive inclination.

YEZTIAS MITZRAYIM – the Exodus from Egypt.

YIRAS HASHEM – awe or reverence of God.

YIRAS SHAMAYIM – lit. awe of heaven; refers to the awe or reverence of God.

YISRAEL – the Jewish people; or another name for our Patriarch Yaakov.

YISRAELIM – Israelites; members of the general Jewish population, excluding priests and Levites.

YOM KIPPUR – day of atonement.

YOM TOV – lit. good day; refers to a holiday.

YUD – the name of the tenth Hebrew letter.

ZAKEN – elder; old person.

ZAYIN – the name of the seventh Hebrew letter.

ZEMIROS – songs; refers to holy songs sung at the Shabbos or *Yom Tov* meals.

ZERIZUS – alacrity, care and vigilance in carrying out Mitzvos. Alacrity in general.

First Printing: 2015

ISBN: 978-0-9965158-5-6

Ramot Press

Jerusalem, Israel

www.RamotPress.com

First Printing: 2015

ISBN: 978-0-9965158-4-9

Ramot Press

Jerusalem, Israel

www.RamotPress.com

First Printing: 2015

ISBN: 978-0-9965158-3-2

Ramot Press

Jerusalem, Israel

www.RamotPress.com

First Printing: 2015

ISBN: 978-0-9965158-2-5

Ramot Press

Jerusalem, Israel

www.RamotPress.com

First Printing: 2015

ISBN: 978-0-9965158-1-8

Ramot Press

Jerusalem, Israel

www.RamotPress.com

First Printing: 2015

ISBN: 978-0-9965158-0-1

Ramot Press

Jerusalem, Israel

www.RamotPress.com

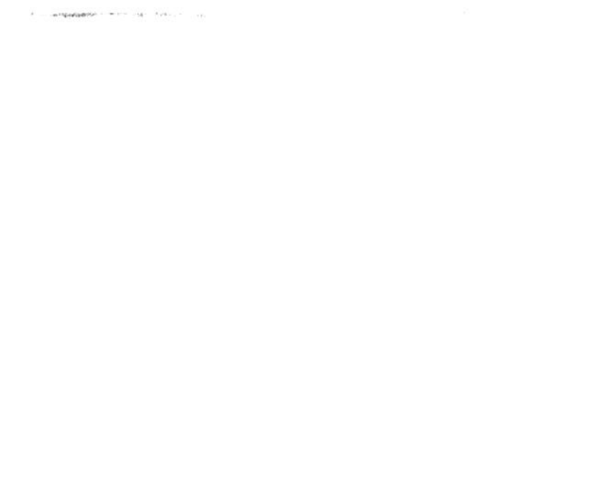

CPSIA information can be obtained
at www.ICGtesting.com
Printed in the USA
LVHW052144180319
611031LV00010B/227/P